National Firearms Act Handbook

As Published by ATF in 2009
with updates through August 1, 2017

Content by RocketFFL Copyright 2017
All other content is the work of the U.S. Government and is in the public domain

All rights reserved.

Published by:

RocketFFL

To learn about how to get your FFL, become an SOT, and stay compliant with the laws, rules, and regulations contained in this book, please visit RocketFFL.com

ISBN 10: 1974163172
ISBN 13: 978-1974163175

Dear Reader,

This book contains the laws, rules, and regulations as published by the ATF in 2014 with updates to include ATF Rulings up to March 1, 2017. This book is provided, for free, to all FFLs who enroll in the RocketFFL.com ATF Compliance Course.

The following content in this book is exactly as it appears from the ATF. RocketFFL makes no claim as to the accuracy nor completeness of the information provided by the ATF. If you are in doubt of the information herein, or you would like more clarification on how to comply with the content within, you should seek legal counsel and/or consider taking an online training course from RocketFFL.com

Every bit of the information that follows in this book is available online for free and is in the public domain. This book was published in an effort to provide FFLs with a resource that they can keep on their desk and make notes/references as appropriate. Electronic documents are handy (especially for searching), however, it is sometimes preferable to have a physical copy to read and reference.

Additionally, this book is available as a download through Kindle. The Kindle format of this book may make it useful for some FFLs depending on how they choose to read and reference electronic documents.

If you have any questions, feel free to reach out to us at info@RocketFFL.com

If you'd like free updates of changes in ATF rules and regulations, firearm industry news, and FFL resources, subscribe to the newsletter on RocketFFL.com

PREFACE

This handbook is primarily for the use of persons in the business of importing, manufacturing, and dealing in firearms defined by the National Firearms Act (NFA) or persons intending to go into an NFA firearms business. It should also be helpful to collectors of NFA firearms and other persons having questions about the application of the NFA.

This publication is not a law book. Rather, it is intended as a "user friendly" reference book enabling the user to quickly find answers to questions concerning the NFA. Nevertheless, it should also be useful to attorneys seeking basic information about the NFA and how the law has been interpreted by ATF. The book's Table of Contents will be helpful to the user in locating needed information.

Although the principal focus of the handbook is the NFA, the book necessarily covers provisions of the Gun Control Act of 1968 and the Arms Export Control Act impacting NFA firearms businesses and collectors.

The book is the product of a joint effort between ATF and the National Firearms Act Trade and Collectors Association. ATF takes this opportunity to express its appreciation to the Association for its assistance in writing and making this publication possible.

TABLE OF CONTENTS

CHAPTER 1. INTRODUCTION

Sec. 1.1	History of the National Firearms Act (NFA)	1
1.1.1	The NFA of 1934	
1.1.2	Title II of the Gun Control Act of 1968	
1.1.3	Firearm Owners' Protection Act	
Sec. 1.2	Meaning of terms	2
1.2.1	"AECA"	
1.2.2	"ATF"	
1.2.3	"ATF Ruling"	
1.2.4	"CFR"	
1.2.5	"DIO"	
1.2.6	"FFL"	
1.2.7	"FTB"	
1.2.8	"GCA"	
1.2.9	"NFA"	
1.2.10	"NFRTR"	
1.2.11	"SOT"	
1.2.12	"U.S.C."	
Sec. 1.3	Administration and enforcement of Federal firearms laws	3
Sec. 1.4	What are regulations and rulings?	3
1.4.1	Regulations	
1.4.2	Rulings	
Sec. 1.5	Other ATF publications	3
1.5.1	ATF's internet website	
1.5.2	ATF P 5300.4	
Sec. 1.6	ATF points of contact	4
Sec. 1.7	ATF Forms	4

CHAPTER 2. WHAT ARE "FIREARMS" UNDER THE NFA?

Sec. 2.1	Types of NFA Firearms	5
2.1.1	Shotgun	
2.1.2	Weapon made from a shotgun	
2.1.3	Rifle	
2.1.4	Weapon made from a rifle	
2.1.5	Any other weapon	
2.1.6	Machinegun	
2.1.7	Silencer	
2.1.8	Destructive device	
2.1.8.1	Explosive devices	
2.1.8.2	Large caliber weapons	

	2.1.9	Unserviceable firearm
Sec. 2.2		Antique firearm 21
Sec. 2.3		Curios or relics 21
Sec. 2.4		Applications to remove firearms from the scope of the NFA as collector's items 22
Sec. 2.5		Removal of firearms from the scope of the NFA by modification/elimination of components 23
	2.5.1	Removal of machineguns and silencers from the scope of the NFA

CHAPTER 3. REGISTRATION OF NFA FIREARMS

Sec. 3.1		The National Firearm Registration and Transfer Record (NFRTR) 24
Sec. 3.2		Who may register NFA firearms 24
	3.2.1	Amnesty registration
	3.2.2	Registration by State and local agencies
	3.2.3	Registration by makers
	3.2.4	Registration by importers
	3.2.5	Registration by manufacturers
	3.2.6	Registration to transferees
	3.2.6.1	Transfers by persons other than FFLs/SOTs to other such persons
	3.2.6.2	Transfers by FFLs/SOTs to persons other than FFLs/SOTs
	3.2.6.3	Transfers by non-FFLs/SOTs to FFLs/SOTs
	3.2.6.4	Transfers by FFLs/SOTs to other FFLs/SOTs
	3.2.6.5	Transfers to State and local government agencies
Sec. 3.3		Status of unregistered firearms 26
Sec. 3.4		ATF disclosure of NFA registration information 26
	3.4.1	Restrictive use of information
	3.4.2	Prohibition on ATF's disclosure of tax returns or tax return information
	3.4.3	Determining the registration status of an NFA firearm
Sec. 3.5		Lost or stolen registration documents 27
Sec. 3.6		Correcting incorrect registration documents 27
Sec. 3.7		Maintaining registration documents 27

CHAPTER 4. TAXES IMPOSED BY THE NFA

Sec. 4.1 Taxes		28
	4.1.1	Making tax
	4.1.2	Transfer tax
	4.1.3	Special (occupational) tax
Sec. 4.2		Exemptions from tax 29
	4.2.1	Making tax
	4.2.2	Transfer tax
	4.2.2.1	Unserviceable firearms
	4.2.3	Special (occupational) tax
	4.2.4	Exportation of firearms

CHAPTER 5. QUALIFYING TO DO BUSINESS IN NFA FIREARMS

Sec. 5.1	Licensing under the GCA 30
5.1.1	Application for GCA license
5.1.1.1	Definition of "person" for GCA purposes
5.1.2	License fees
5.1.2.1	Manufacturers
5.1.2.2	Importers
5.1.2.3	Dealers
5.1.3	Licensing standards under the GCA
5.1.3.1	Age
5.1.3.2	Prohibited persons
5.1.3.3	"Responsible persons"
5.1.3.4	Removing disabilities
5.1.3.5	Prior willful violations
5.1.3.6	False statements
5.1.3.7	Business premises
5.1.3.8	May a license be obtained to do business solely away from the licensed premises at gun shows?
5.1.3.9	Gun storage and safety devices
5.1.4	Multiple business locations
5.1.4.1	Locations solely for storage
5.1.5	Establishing a common expiration date for licenses at multiple locations
5.1.6	Engaging in business as both an importer and a manufacturer
5.1.7	Do importers and manufacturers need a dealer's license to deal in the firearms they import or manufacture?
5.1.8	License renewal
5.1.8.1	Right to operate while renewal application is pending; "letters of continuing operation"
Sec. 5.2	Payment of special (occupational) tax to do business in NFA firearms 33
5.2.1	Every "person" who engages in the business of importing, manufacturing, or dealing in firearms (including pawnbrokers) shall pay a special tax
5.2.1.1	Definition of "person" for NFA purposes
5.2.2	Tax must be paid for each business location
5.2.3	Rate of Tax
5.2.3.1	Importers and manufacturers
5.2.3.2	Dealers
5.2.4	How to pay special tax
5.2.4.1	Employer identification number (EIN)
5.2.4.2	Renewal of special tax
5.2.5	Exemption from special tax
5.2.6	Collectors acquiring NFA firearms for their personal collections by acquiring dealers' licenses and paying NFA special tax
Sec. 5.3	Registration by firearms manufacturers and exporters with the U.S. Department of State (DOS) 34
5.3.1	How manufacturers should register
Sec. 5.4	Registration by firearms importers with ATF 35

	5.4.1	How importers should register	
Sec. 5.5		Filing by facsimile transmission	35

CHAPTER 6. MAKING NFA FIREARMS BY NONLICENSEES

Sec. 6.1		Requirements for making NFA firearms	36
Sec. 6.2		Preparation of Form 1	36
	6.2.1	Description of firearm	
	6.2.2	Photograph of applicant	
	6.2.3	FBI Form FD-258, fingerprint card	
	6.2.4	Law enforcement certification	
	6.2.4.1	What if the proposed maker is unable to find any official in his or her jurisdiction willing to sign the law enforcement certification?	
Sec. 6.3		Submission of Form 1	37
	6.3.1	State permit or license for possession of an NFA weapon	
Sec. 6.4		Approval of Form 1	38
Sec. 6.5		Disapproval of Form 1	38
Sec. 6.6		Reactivation of a registered unserviceable NFA firearm	38
Sec. 6.7		Incorrect description of Firearm	38
Sec. 6.8		Withdrawal or Cancellation of an ATF Form 1 and Refund if Making Tax	39

CHAPTER 7. MANUFACTURING NFA FIREARMS

Sec. 7.1		Qualifying to manufacture NFA firearms	40
	7.1.1	Licensing under the GCA	
	7.1.1.1	Engaging in business at multiple locations	
	7.1.1.2	Engaging in business as both an importer and a manufacturer	
	7.1.1.3	Do importers and manufacturers need a dealer's license to deal in the firearms they import or manufacture?	
	7.1.1.4	Manufacturers of destructive devices	
	7.1.2	Payment of special (occupational) tax to do business in NFA firearms	
	7.1.3	Registration by firearms manufacturers with the U.S. Department of State	
	7.1.3.1	Registration exemption for fabricating articles for "research and development."	
Sec. 7.2		What is a "manufacturer"?; What is "manufacturing"?	41
	7.2.1	"Manufacturer"	
	7.2.2	"Manufacturing"	
	7.2.3	What is the difference between manufacturing and gunsmithing?	
	7.2.4	Do you know how ATF would classify your product?	
	7.2.4.1	ATF classification letters	
Sec. 7.3		Registering the manufacture of NFA firearms	43
	7.3.1	Preparation of ATF Forms 2	
	7.3.2	Filing ATF Forms 2	
	7.3.2.1	Existing firearms modified into NFA firearms or reactivated	
	7.3.3	Reactivation of a registered unserviceable NFA firearm	

	7.3.3.1	Incorrect description of firearm
	7.3.3.2	Reactivation of a registered unserviceable NFA firearm
Sec. 7.4		The identification of firearms 44
	7.4.1	Serial numbers
	7.4.1.1	What is an acceptable serial number?
	7.4.2	Additional information
	7.4.3	Measuring the depth of markings
	7.4.4	Obtaining variances to the marking requirements
	7.4.4.1	Variances in the name and location of the manufacturer
	7.4.4.2	Variances for manufacturers' contractors
	7.4.4.3	Marking destructive devices
	7.4.4.4	Marking parts, other than frames or receivers, defined as NFA firearms
	7.4.5	Marking frames or receivers that are not complete weapons at the time of disposition
	7.4.6	Marking silencer parts
Sec. 7.5		Manufacturing machineguns 47
	7.5.1	Manufacture of machineguns for sale to government agencies or as "sales samples"
	7.5.2	Manufacture of machineguns for exportation
	7.5.3	May machineguns be manufactured for distribution to U.S. Government contractors?
	7.5.4	May machinegun receivers be manufactured and used as replacement parts for machineguns lawfully registered and possessed prior to May 19, 1986?
Sec. 7.6		Manufacture of NFA firearms by contractors 48
	7.6.1	Contractors' manufacture of machineguns
	7.6.2	Manufacture of machineguns solely for purposes of testing
Sec. 7.7		Manufacturing NFA firearms exclusively for the United States 48
Sec. 7.8		Locations 49

CHAPTER 8. IMPORTING NFA FIREARMS

Sec. 8.1		Qualifying to import NFA firearms 50
	8.1.1	Licensing under the GCA
	8.1.1.1	Engaging in business at multiple locations
	8.1.1.2	Engaging in business as both an importer and a manufacturer
	8.1.1.3	Do importers and manufacturers need a dealer's license to deal in the firearms they import or manufacture?
	8.1.1.4	Importers of destructive devices
	8.1.2	Payment of special (occupational) tax to do business in NFA firearms
	8.1.3	Registration by importers of U.S. Munitions Import List articles with ATF
Sec. 8.2		What is an "importer"?; What is "importation"? 51
	8.2.1	"Importer"
	8.2.2	"Importation"
Sec. 8.3		Importation of NFA firearms 51
	8.3.1	Importation of machineguns
	8.3.2	Importation for use of the United States, qualifying political subdivisions, and law enforcement agencies

8.3.3	Importation for use by Nuclear Regulatory Commission (NRC) licensees and authorized contractors	
8.3.4	Importation for authorized scientific or research purposes	
8.3.5	Importation for use as a model by a registered manufacturer	
8.3.6	Importation for use as a "sales sample"	
8.3.7	Importing multiple quantities of the same model firearm as sales samples	
8.3.8	Importation of NFA weapons classified as curios or relics	
8.3.9	Conditional importation	
8.3.10	Temporary importation of NFA firearms	
8.3.11	Re-importation of NFA firearms temporarily exported from the United States by nonlicensees.	
8.3.12	What is the difference between a Customs Bonded Warehouse (CBW) and a Foreign Trade Zone (FTZ)?	
8.3.12.1	Customs Bonded Warehouse	
8.3.12.2	Foreign Trade Zone	
8.3.13	Preparation of ATF Forms 6	
8.3.14	"eForm6"	
8.3.15	Preparation of ATF Forms 6A	
Sec. 8.4	Registering the importation of NFA firearms	56
8.4.1	Preparation of ATF Forms 2	
8.4.2	Filing ATF Forms 2	
Sec. 8.5	The identification of firearms	56
8.5.1	Serial numbers	
8.5.1.1	What is an acceptable serial number?	
8.5.2	Additional information	
8.5.3	Measuring the depth of markings	
8.5.4	Obtaining variances to the marking requirements	
8.5.4.1	Variances in the name and location of the importer	
8.5.4.2	Marking frames or receivers that are not complete weapons at the time of disposition	
8.5.4.3	Marking destructive devices	
8.5.4.4	Marking parts, other than frames or receivers, defined as NFA firearms	
8.5.5	When must markings be applied to imported NFA firearms?	

CHAPTER 9. TRANSFERS OF NFA FIREARMS

Sec. 9.1	Definition of "transfer"	59
Sec. 9.2	Only previously registered firearms may be lawfully transferred	59
Sec. 9.3	Interstate transfers of NFA firearms	59
Sec. 9.4	ATF forms for use in transferring NFA firearms	59
9.4.1	ATF Form 3	
9.4.2	ATF Form 4	
9.4.2.1	Copies of transferees' State or local licenses or permits	
9.4.2.2	Transfers to entities other than individuals that are not FFLs/SOTs	
9.4.3	ATF Form 5	
Sec. 9.5	Conveyances of NFA firearms not treated as "transfers" under the NFA	61

    9.5.1.1   Repair of firearm silencers
    9.5.2   Possession of firearms by employees of FFLs/SOTs for employers' business purposes
    9.5.3   Distribution of estate firearms
    9.5.3.1   Distributions to heirs
    9.5.3.2   Distributions to persons outside the estate
    9.5.3.3   Uncertainty about the registration status of decedents' firearms
    9.5.3.4   Unregistered estate firearms
    9.5.3.5   Distribution of decedents' "sales samples."
Sec. 9.6   Manufacturers' use of contractors to perform work on firearms 63
Sec. 9.7   Transfers of unserviceable NFA firearms 63
Sec. 9.8   Government-owned firearms 63
Sec. 9.9   Law enforcement certifications 63
    9.9.1   Is a law enforcement officer required to sign the certification?
    9.9.2   Is a law enforcement certification acceptable if signed by an official outside the jurisdiction where the transferee resides?
Sec. 9.10   Transfers of imported NFA firearms 64
    9.10.1   Firearms imported for government agencies
    9.10.2   "Sales samples"
    9.10.3   Transferring multiple quantities of the same firearm model as "sales samples"
Sec. 9.11   Transfers of machineguns imported or manufactured on after May 19, 1986 65
    9.11.1   Machinegun prohibition in 18 U.S.C. 922(o)
    9.11.2   May machineguns subject to section 922(o) be transferred to government contractors?
Sec. 9.12   Are FFLs/SOTs required to initiate a background check of the transferee under the Brady Law in connection with the transfer of an NFA firearm? 65
Sec. 9.13   May an FFL/SOT transfer a personally owned destructive device without qualifying to do business in destructive devices? 66
Section 9.14   Transferable Status and the Form 10 66

CHAPTER 10. COLLECTORS OF NFA FIREARMS

Sec 10.1   Curios or relics 67
    10.1.1   Definition of curio or relic
    10.1.2   Curio or relic classification
    10.1.3   NFA firearms classified as curios or relics
    10.1.4   The Firearms Curios or Relics List (ATF P 5300.11)
    10.1.5   DEWATS
    10.1.5.1   Reactivation of DEWATS
Sec. 10.2   Licensed collector 69
    10.2.1 Collector of curios or relics license
    10.2.2 Receipt of NFA curios or relics by a licensed collector
    10.2.3 Transfer of NFA curios or relics by a licensed collector
Sec. 10.3   Recordkeeping requirements 70
    10.3.1   Acquisition and disposition records
    10.3.2   Termination of a collector's license.

CHAPTER 11. EXPORTATION OF NFA FIREARMS

Sec. 11.1 Arms Export Control Act (AECA), 22 U.S.C. 2778 71
    11.1.1 State Department regulations implementing the AECA
    11.1.2 Firearms and firearm component parts subject to the AECA
    11.1.2.1 Category I
    11.1.2.2 Category II
Sec. 11.2 Registration of exporters and manufacturers under the AECA 71
    11.2.1 Submission of registration form, DSP-9
    11.2.2 Transmittal letter must accompany Form DSP-9
    11.2.3 Notification of changes in information furnished by registrants
Sec. 11.3 License requirement for permanent export of a defense article..................................72
Sec. 11.4 License requirement for temporary export of a defense article 72
Sec. 11.5 Prohibited exports and sales to certain countries... 72
Sec. 11.6 ATF requirements relative to the exportation of firearms 72
    11.6.1 Applying for an export permit on ATF Form 9
    11.6.2 Transfers to another person for export
    11.6.3 Proof of exportation

CHAPTER 12. RECORDKEEPING

Sec. 12.1 Maintaining proof of registration...74
    12.1.1 Manner in which registration documents must be kept
    12.1.2 Recordkeeping where registered firearms are kept on premises other than the registered owner's place of business
Sec. 12.2 Verifying the description of firearms on registration documents 74
Sec. 12.3 Correcting an error in the description of a registered firearm 74
Sec. 12.4 Custody of NFA firearms by employees of FFLs/SOTs 75
    12.4.1 Who is an "employee" of an FFL/SOT?
Sec. 12.5 Firearms acquisition and disposition records...75
    12.5.1 Commercial records of firearms received
    12.5.2 Variances in the recordkeeping requirements for the acquisition and disposition of firearms
    12.5.2.1 Computerized records.
Sec. 12.6 Forms 4473 77
    12.6.1 Firearms acquired from an FFL by an organization
    12.6.2 Return of firearms delivered to an FFL for repair or customizing
    12.6.3 Maintaining Forms 4473
Sec. 12.7 Record retention period...78

CHAPTER 13. REQUIRED REPORTS AND NOTIFICATIONS TO ATF

Sec. 13.1	Change of business address	80
13.1.1	GCA requirements	
13.1.1.1	Application for amended license	
13.1.2	NFA requirements	
Sec. 13.2	Change in trade name	80
13.2.1	GCA requirements	
13.2.2	NFA requirements	
Sec. 13.3	Change in control	81
13.3.1	Changes in an FFL's "responsible persons"	
13.3.2	A "change in control" is distinguishable from the sale or transfer of a firearms business to another person or entity	
Sec. 13.4	Reporting firearms transaction information	82
Sec. 13.5	Reporting thefts or losses of firearms	82
13.5.1	GCA requirements	
13.5.2	NFA requirements	
Sec. 13.6	Reporting theft or loss of NFA registration documents	83
Sec. 13.7	Reporting information in response to ATF trace requests	83
Sec. 13.8	Requesting permission to transport certain firearms in interstate or foreign commerce ..	83
13.8.1	A written (letter) request	
13.8.2	Form 5320.20	
13.8.3	One-year approval	

CHAPTER 14. GOING OUT OF BUSINESS

Sec. 14.1	Disposition of GCA records	85
14.1.1	"Records" for purposes of this section	
14.1.2	Transfer of the business to a new owner	
14.1.3	Discontinuance of the business	
Sec. 14.2	Disposition of NFA firearms (other than "post-'86 machineguns")	85
14.2.1	Sole proprietors	
14.2.2	Corporations, partnerships, and associations	
14.2.2.1	Effect of dissolution of a corporation, partnership, or association	
14.2.3	Avoiding NFA transfer tax	
Sec. 14.3	Disposition of "post-'86 machineguns"	86

CHAPTER 15. PENALTIES AND SANCTIONS

Sec. 15.1	NFA	88
15.1.1	Criminal	
15.1.2	Forfeiture	
15.1.3	Assessment of NFA tax	
Sec. 15.2	GCA	88
15.2.1	Criminal	
15.2.2	Forfeiture	
15.2.3	License denial or revocation	
Sec. 15.3	AECA	89
15.3.1	Criminal	
15.3.2	Forfeiture	

APPENDIX A (NFA, 26 U.S.C. Chapter 53) 90

APPENDIX B (ATF Rulings and articles) 141

APPENDIX C (ATF Forms) 179

APPENDIX D (Sample form letters) 207

CHAPTER 1. INTRODUCTION

Section 1.1 History of the National Firearms Act (NFA)

1.1.1 The NFA of 1934. The NFA was originally enacted in 1934.[1] Similar to the current NFA, the original Act imposed a tax on the making and transfer of firearms defined by the Act, as well as a special (occupational) tax on persons and entities engaged in the business of importing, manufacturing, and dealing in NFA firearms. The law also required the registration of all NFA firearms with the Secretary of the Treasury. Firearms subject to the 1934 Act included shotguns and rifles having barrels less than 18 inches in length, certain firearms described as "any other weapons," machineguns, and firearm mufflers and silencers.

While the NFA was enacted by Congress as an exercise of its authority to tax, the NFA had an underlying purpose unrelated to revenue collection. As the legislative history of the law discloses, its underlying purpose was to curtail, if not prohibit, transactions in NFA firearms. Congress found these firearms to pose a significant crime problem because of their frequent use in crime, particularly the gangland crimes of that era such as the St. Valentine's Day Massacre. The $200 making and transfer taxes on most NFA firearms were considered quite severe and adequate to carry out Congress' purpose to discourage or eliminate transactions in these firearms. The $200 tax has not changed since 1934.

As structured in 1934, the NFA imposed a duty on persons transferring NFA firearms, as well as mere possessors of unregistered firearms, to register them with the Secretary of the Treasury. If the possessor of an unregistered firearm applied to register the firearm as required by the NFA, the Treasury Department could supply information to State authorities about the registrant's possession of the firearm. State authorities could then use the information to prosecute the person whose possession violated State laws. For these reasons, the Supreme Court in 1968 held in the *Haynes* case that a person prosecuted for possessing an unregistered NFA firearm had a valid defense to the prosecution - the registration requirement imposed on the possessor of an unregistered firearm violated the possessor's privilege from self-incrimination under the Fifth Amendment of the U.S. Constitution.[2] The *Haynes* decision made the 1934 Act virtually unenforceable.

1.1.2 Title II of the Gun Control Act of 1968. Title II amended the NFA to cure the constitutional flaw pointed out in *Haynes*.[3] First, the requirement for possessors of unregistered firearms to register was removed. Indeed, under the amended law, there is no mechanism for a possessor to register an unregistered NFA firearm already possessed by the person. Second, a provision was added to the law prohibiting the use of any information from an NFA application or registration as evidence against the person in a criminal proceeding with respect to a violation of law occurring prior to or concurrently with the filing of the application or registration.[4] In 1971, the Supreme Court reexamined the NFA in the *Freed* case and found that the 1968 amendments cured the constitutional defect in the original NFA.[5]

---

[1] National Firearms Act, Public Law 474, approved June 26, 1934.
[2] Haynes v. U.S., 390 U.S. 85 (1968).
[3] Gun Control Act of 1968, Public Law 90-618, approved October 22, 1968.
[4] 26 U.S.C. 5848
[5] U.S. v. Freed, 401 U.S. 601 (1971)

Title II also amended the NFA definitions of "firearm" by adding "destructive devices" and expanding the definition of "machinegun."

1.1.3 Firearm Owners' Protection Act. In 1986, this Act amended the NFA definition of "silencer" by adding combinations of parts for silencers and any part intended for use in the assembly or fabrication of a silencer.[6] The Act also amended the GCA to prohibit the transfer or possession of machineguns.[7] Exceptions were made for transfers of machineguns to, or possession of machineguns by, government agencies, and those lawfully possessed before the effective date of the prohibition, May 19, 1986.

Section 1.2 Meaning of terms. Certain terms and abbreviations used in this book are defined as follows:

1.2.1 "AECA" means the Arms Export Control Act, 22 U.S.C. 2778.

1.2.2 "ATF" means the Bureau of Alcohol, Tobacco, Firearms and Explosives, U.S. Department of Justice.

1.2.3 "ATF Ruling" means a formal ruling published by ATF stating its interpretation of the law and regulations as applied to a specific set of facts.

1.2.4 "CFR" means the Code of Federal Regulations in which Federal firearms regulations are published.

1.2.5 "DIO" means an ATF Director of Industry Operations responsible for regulating the firearms industry within an ATF field division.

1.2.6 "FFL" means a Federal firearms licensee, person or entity having a license to import, manufacture, or deal in firearms under the GCA.

1.2.7 "FTB" means ATF's Firearms Technology Branch.

1.2.8 "GCA" means the Gun Control Act of 1968, 18 U.S.C. Chapter 44.

1.2.9 "NFA" means the National Firearms Act, 26 U.S.C. Chapter 53.

1.2.10 "NFRTR" means the National Firearms Registration and Transfer Record containing the registration of NFA firearms.

1.2.11 "SOT" means a special occupational taxpayer, a person or entity qualified to import, manufacture, or deal in NFA firearms by having paid the special (occupational) tax to do so under the NFA.

---

[6] Firearm Owners' Protection Act, Public Law 99-308, approved May 19, 1986.
[7] 18 U.S.C. 922(o)

1.2.12 "U.S.C." means the United States Code in which Federal firearms laws are codified.

Section 1.3 Administration and enforcement of Federal firearms laws

Until January 24, 2003, authority to administer and enforce Federal firearms laws was the responsibility of the Bureau of ATF within the U.S. Department of the Treasury. As a result of enactment of Section 1111 of the Homeland Security Act of 2002, ATF and its firearms authorities were transferred to the U.S. Department of Justice, effective January 24, 2003. ATF's name was also changed to the Bureau of Alcohol, Tobacco, Firearms and Explosives. ATF continues to have the authority to administer and enforce Federal firearms laws. The Department of State retained its authority over the enforcement of the export provisions of the AECA that relate to firearms.

Section 1.4 What are regulations and rulings?

1.4.1 Regulations. Regulations interpret the statutes (the law) and explain the procedures for compliance. The Administrative Procedure Act (APA) generally requires agencies to publish proposed regulations in the Federal Register as a notice of proposed rulemaking, giving the public the opportunity to comment on the proposals before they may be issued as final regulations. The APA provides no specific comment period for proposed rules under the NFA.[8] As specifically provided for in the GCA, GCA regulations require a comment period of at least 90 days.[9] An exception in the APA eliminates the need to provide any notice or comment period with respect to AECA regulations. Regulations have the force and effect of law. Courts will uphold a regulation if they find reasonable legal basis for it and if it generally is within the scope of the statute.

1.4.2 Rulings. ATF publishes rulings in its periodic bulletins and posts them on the ATF website. These contain ATF's interpretation of the law and regulations as they pertain to a particular fact situation. Rulings do not have the force and effect of law but may be cited as precedent with respect to substantially similar fact situations. Courts will recognize and apply such rulings if they are determined to correctly interpret the law and regulations.

Section 1.5 Other ATF publications

1.5.1 ATF's internet website. This is the best source for up to date information on ATF's firearms administration and enforcement activities, including amendments to the law, rulings, regulations, and open letters to firearms industry members. The website address is http://www.atf.gov.

1.5.2 ATF P 5300.4. This is ATF's publication, "Federal Firearms Regulations Reference Guide." ATF supplies the publication to all FFLs and SOTs. It contains all Federal firearms laws and regulations (except those pertaining to the firearms and ammunition excise tax and State Department export regulations), ATF firearms rulings, articles on various firearms issues, and questions and answers. The publication can be found on ATF's website, http://www.atf.gov, and downloaded.

---

[8] 5 U.S.C. 552
[9] 18 U.S.C. 926(b)

Section 1.6 ATF points of contact

Chief, National Firearms Act Branch
Bureau of Alcohol, Tobacco, Firearms and Explosives
244 Needy Road
Martinsburg, WV 25405
Phone: (304) 616-4500
Fax: (304) 616-4501

Chief, Federal Firearms Licensing Center
Bureau of Alcohol, Tobacco, Firearms and Explosives
244 Needy Road
Martinsburg, WV 25405

Phone: (304) 616-4600 or 1-866-662-2750
Fax: (304) 616-4501 or 1-866-257-2749

Chief, Firearms & Explosives Imports Branch
Bureau of Alcohol, Tobacco, Firearms and Explosives
244 Needy Road
Martinsburg, WV 25405
Phone: (304) 616-4550
Fax: (304) 616-4551

Chief, Firearms Technology Branch
Bureau of Alcohol, Tobacco, Firearms and Explosives
244 Needy Road
Martinsburg, WV 25405
Phone: (304) 260-5476
Fax: (304) 260-1701

Section 1.7 ATF Forms

ATF forms may be ordered from ATF's Distribution Center by use of the Center's order form on ATF's website at http://www.atf.gov. After entering the website, click on "Forms." They may also be obtained by calling the Center at (301) 583-4696 or writing the ATF Distribution Center at 1519 Cabin Branch Drive, Landover, MD 20785-3816.

CHAPTER 2. WHAT ARE "FIREARMS" UNDER THE NFA?

Section 2.1 Types of NFA firearms

The NFA defines the specific types of firearms subject to the provisions of the Act. These definitions describe the function, design, configuration and/or dimensions that weapons must have to be NFA firearms. In addition to describing the weapon, some definitions (machinegun, rifle, shotgun, any other weapon) state that the firearm described also includes a weapon that can be readily restored to fire. A firearm that can be readily restored to fire is a firearm that in its present condition is incapable of expelling a projectile by the action of an explosive (or, in the case of a machinegun, will not in its present condition shoot automatically) but which can be restored to a functional condition by the replacement of missing or defective component parts. Please be aware that case law is not specific but courts have held that the "readily restorable" test is satisfied where a firearm can be made capable of renewed automatic operation, even if it requires some degree of skill and the use of tools and parts.

2.1.1 Shotgun A shotgun is a firearm designed to be fired from the shoulder and designed to use the energy of the explosive in a fixed shotgun shell to fire through a smooth bore either a number of projectiles or a single projectile for each pull of the trigger.[10] A shotgun subject to the NFA has a barrel or barrels of less than 18 inches in length.

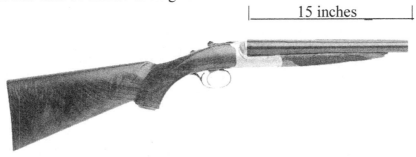

The ATF procedure for measuring barrel length is to measure from the closed bolt (or breech-face) to the furthermost end of the barrel or permanently attached muzzle device. <u>Permanent methods of attachment include full-fusion gas or electric steel-seam welding, high-temperature (1100°F) silver soldering, or blind pinning with the pin head welded over.</u> Barrels are measured by inserting a dowel rod into the barrel until the rod stops against the bolt or breech-face. The rod is then marked at the furthermost end of the barrel or permanently attached muzzle device, withdrawn from the barrel, and measured.

---

[10] 26 U.S.C. 5845(d)

2.1.2 Weapon made from a shotgun. A weapon made from a shotgun is a shotgun type weapon that has an overall length of less than 26 inches or a barrel or barrels of less than 18 inches in length.

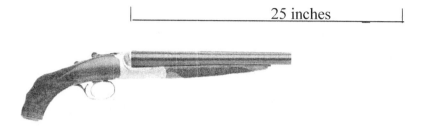

The overall length of a firearm is the distance between the muzzle of the barrel and the rearmost portion of the weapon measured on a line parallel to the axis of the bore.

2.1.3 Rifle. A rifle is a firearm designed to be fired from the shoulder and designed to use the energy of an explosive in a fixed cartridge to fire only a single projectile through a rifled barrel for each single pull of the trigger.[11] A rifle subject to the NFA has a barrel or barrels of less than 16 inches in length.

The ATF procedure for measuring barrel length is to measure from the closed bolt (or breech-face) to the furthermost end of the barrel or permanently attached muzzle device. <u>Permanent methods of attachment include full-fusion gas or electric steel-seam welding, high-temperature (1100°F) silver soldering, or blind pinning with the pin head welded over.</u> Barrels are measured by inserting a dowel rod into the barrel until the rod stops against the bolt or breech-face. The rod is then marked at the furthermost end of the barrel or permanently attached muzzle device, withdrawn from the barrel, and measured.

---

[11] 26 U.S.C. 5845(c)

2.1.4 Weapon made from a rifle. A weapon made from a rifle is a rifle type weapon that has an overall length of less than 26 inches or a barrel or barrels of less than 16 inches in length.

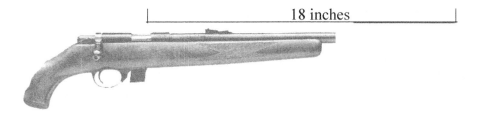

The overall length of a firearm is the distance between the muzzle of the barrel and the rearmost portion of the weapon measured on a line parallel to the axis of the bore.

2.1.5 Any other weapon. Firearms meeting the definition of "any other weapon" are weapons or devices capable of being concealed on the person from which a shot can be discharged through the energy of an explosive. Many "any other weapons" are disguised devices such as penguns, cigarette lighter guns, knife guns, cane guns and umbrella guns.

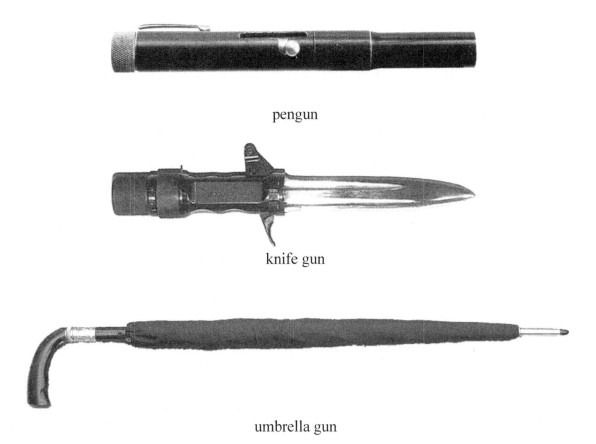

Also included in the "any other weapon" definition are pistols and revolvers having smooth bore barrels designed or redesigned to fire a fixed shotgun shell.

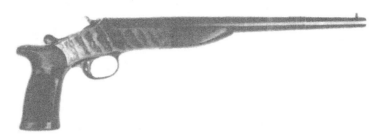

H&R Handy Gun

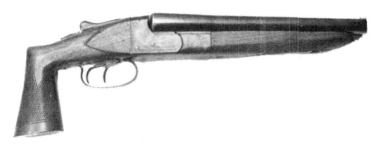

Ithaca Auto & Burglar Gun

While the above weapons are similar in appearance to weapons made from shotguns, they were originally manufactured in the illustrated configuration and are not modified from existing shotguns. As a result, these weapons do not fit within the definition of shotgun[12] or weapons made from a shotgun[13].

The "any other weapon" definition also includes specifically described weapons with combination shotgun and rifle barrels 12 inches or more but less than 18 inches in length from which only a single discharge can be made from either barrel without manual reloading. The firearm most commonly associated with this portion of the definition is the Marble's Game Getter.

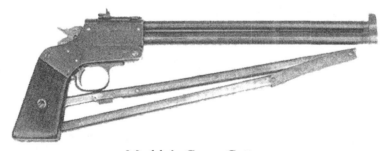

Marble's Game Getter

---

[12] 26 U.S.C. 5845(d)
[13] 26 U.S.C. 5845(a)(2)

NOTE: One version of the Marble's Game Getter was produced with 18-inch barrels and a folding shoulder stock. This model of the Game Getter, as manufactured, is not subject to the provisions of the NFA because it has barrels that are 18 inches in length and the overall length of the firearm, with stock extended, is more than 26 inches. *However, if the shoulder stock has been removed from the 18-inch barrel version of the Game Getter, the firearm has an overall length of less than 26 inches and is an NFA weapon.* Specifically, the firearm is classified as a weapon made from a rifle/shotgun.

The "any other weapon" definition excludes weapons designed to be fired from the shoulder that are not capable of firing fixed ammunition or a pistol or revolver having a rifled bore. However, certain alterations to a pistol or revolver, such as the addition of a second vertical handgrip, create a weapon that no longer meets the definition of pistol or revolver.[14] A pistol or revolver modified as described is an "any other weapon" subject to the NFA because the weapon is not designed to be fired when held in one hand.

semiautomatic pistol with second vertical handgrip

As stated above, a pistol or revolver having a rifled bore does not meet the definition of "any other weapon" and is not subject to the NFA. It is important to note that any pistol or revolver having a barrel without a rifled bore does not fit within the exclusion and is an "any other weapon" subject to the NFA.

2.1.6 Machinegun. Firearms within the definition of machinegun include weapons that shoot, are designed to shoot, or can be readily restored to shoot, automatically more than one shot without manual reloading by a single function of the trigger.

---

[14] 27 CFR 479.11

STEN MK II submachinegun

The definition of machinegun also includes the frame or receiver of a machinegun.

STEN MK II submachinegun receiver

Of all the different firearms defined as NFA weapons, machineguns are the only type where the receiver of the weapon by itself is an NFA firearm. As a result, it is important that the receiver of a machinegun be properly identified. Many machineguns incorporate a "split" or "hinged" receiver design so the main portion of the weapon can be easily separated into upper and lower sections. Additionally, some machineguns utilize a construction method where the receiver is composed of a number of subassemblies that are riveted together to form the complete receiver.

The following table lists specific models of machineguns incorporating the above designs and the portion of the weapon that has been held to be the receiver. This list is not all-inclusive. For information concerning a split or hinged receiver type machinegun not listed below, contact FTB at (304) 260-1699.

Model	**Receiver**
Armalite AR10	lower
Armalite AR15 (all variations)	lower
Armalite AR18	lower
Beretta AR70	lower
British L1A1	upper
Browning M1917	right side plate
Browning M1919 (all variations)	right side plate
Browning M2 & M2HB	right side plate
Colt M16 (all variations)	lower
Czech Vz 61	lower
FN FNC	lower
Model	**Receiver**
FN CAL	upper
FN FAL	upper

French MAT 49	upper
German MP38 & MP40	upper
H&K G3 (all variations)	upper
H&K MP5 (all variations)	upper
IMI UZI	upper
M61 Vulcan	outer housing
M134 Minigun	outer housing
Maxim MG08 and 08/15	right side plate
SIG AMT	upper
SIG STG 57	upper
SIG 550 Series (all variations)	upper
Soviet PPsH 41	upper
Soviet PPS 43	upper
Steyr MPi 69	upper
Steyr MPi 81	upper
Thompson submachinegun (all variations)	upper
Vickers water cooled machineguns	right side plate

The "designed to shoot automatically more than one shot without manual reloading by a single function of the trigger" portion of the definition relates to the characteristics of the weapon that permit full automatic fire. ATF has also held that the "designed" definition includes those weapons which have not previously functioned as machineguns but possess design features which facilitate full automatic fire by simple modification or elimination of existing component parts. ATF has published rulings concerning specific firearms classified as machineguns based on this interpretation of the term "designed."[15]

Included within the definition of machinegun is any part designed and intended solely and exclusively, or combination of parts designed and intended, for use in converting a weapon into a machinegun. This portion of the machinegun definition addresses what are commonly referred to as conversion kits. The "any part designed and intended solely and exclusively" language refers to a part that was produced for no other reason than to convert a weapon into a machinegun. Illustrated below are examples of such parts.

conversion sear for H&K semiautomatic firearms

---

[15] Appendix B (ATF Rulings 82-2, 82-8, 83-5)

Drop in Auto Sear for AR15 type semiautomatic firearms

The above parts are designed solely and exclusively for use in converting a weapon into a machinegun and are classified as machineguns.

The "combination of parts designed and intended for use in converting a weapon into a machinegun" language refers to a group of parts designed and intended to be used in converting a weapon into a machinegun. A typical example is those M2 carbine parts that are only used to permit fully automatic fire in a US Carbine M1 or M2.

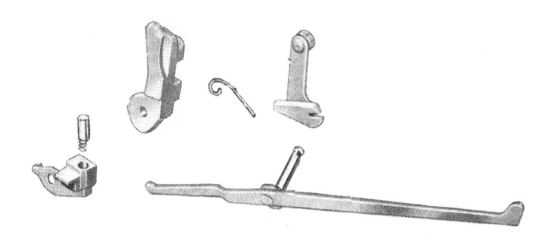

M2 Carbine conversion kit

The above parts consisting of an M2 selector lever, selector lever spring, disconnector lever assembly, M2 disconnector, disconnector spring, disconnector plunger and M2 hammer are classified as a machinegun. These parts are used specifically for fully automatic fire and have no application in a semiautomatic carbine. While other parts such as an M2 sear, operating slide, trigger housing and stock are used in the fully automatic carbine, these parts are also appropriate for use in semiautomatic M1 carbines.[16]

Therefore, the M2 sear, operating slide, trigger housing and stock are not a combination of parts designed and intended for use in converting a weapon into a machinegun. Other commonly encountered

---

[16] TM9-1267, Cal. .30 Carbines M1, M1A1, M2, and M3, United States Government Printing Office, 1953

conversion kits include modified trigger housings and/or trigger paks for Heckler & Koch (HK) type semiautomatic firearms. As originally manufactured, semiautomatic HK firearms (HK, 41, 43, 91, 93 and SP89) were specifically designed such that they will not accept fully automatic trigger housings or trigger paks for HK selective fire weapons such as the G3 and MP5. If selective fire trigger paks or trigger housings are modified so that they will function with semiautomatic HK firearms, the modified components are classified as parts designed and intended solely and exclusively, or combination of parts designed and intended for use in converting a weapon into a machinegun. These modified parts are also machineguns as defined.

The following illustration shows a selective fire HK trigger pak with a selective fire trigger housing that has been modified to function with a HK semiautomatic firearm by removing the forward pivot point or "ears" from the trigger housing.

modified HK selective fire trigger housing

Illustrated below is a selective fire HK trigger pak that has been modified by notching the forward lower corner of the pak so that it will fit into a standard semiautomatic HK trigger housing.

modified HK selective fire trigger pak

NOTE: standard selective fire HK trigger housings and trigger paks as originally manufactured are component parts for machineguns. These unmodified parts, in and of themselves, are not subject to the NFA. However, when adapted to function with a semiautomatic HK firearm the modified parts have been redesigned and are intended for use in converting a weapon into a machinegun.

The following illustration shows a semiautomatic HK trigger pak with HK conversion sear installed.

HK semiautomatic trigger pak with conversion sear installed

For the conversion sear to function the trigger or the trigger pak must be modified to increase the rearward travel of the trigger. When the trigger is modified a notch is cut into the trailing leg to provide more travel before the trigger contacts the upper trigger stop. When the trigger pak is modified, the upper trigger stop is either removed or relocated. *IMPORTANT NOTE: should the conversion sear be removed from the trigger pak and the modified pak left in the firearm, the weapon will still be capable of fully automatic fire. Therefore, it is important that registered HK conversion sears be kept with their respective trigger paks. This is particularly important in instances where HK type firearms are sold as being "sear ready" or "sear host guns". If these weapons contain semiautomatic trigger paks modified to function with conversion sears the firearms are capable of fully automatic fire (without the conversion sear) and as such are machineguns as defined.*

Concerning the installation of conversion kits in semiautomatic firearms, it must be pointed out that the receiver of the firearm may not be modified to permit fully automatic fire. Such modification results in the making of a machinegun which is prohibited by 18 U.S.C. 922(o).

The definition of machinegun also includes a combination of parts from which a machinegun can be assembled if such parts are in the possession or under the control of a person. An example of a firearm meeting this section of the definition is a semiautomatic AR15 rifle possessed with an M16 bolt carrier, hammer, trigger, disconnector and selector. If the semiautomatic AR15 is assembled with the described M16 parts and the rifle is capable of fully automatic fire, the weapon possessed in conjunction with the M16 parts, whether assembled or not, is a machinegun as defined.[17]

---

[17] ATF P 5300.4 (9/05), Federal Firearms Regulations Reference Guide – 2005, p. 155

An additional example of a combination of parts from which a machinegun can be assembled is a STEN submachinegun "parts kit" possessed with a length of metal tube to be used as a replacement receiver and instructions for assembling the parts into a functional machinegun. The parts kit as sold does not contain a firearm receiver although remnants of the destroyed receiver may be present. A machinegun parts kit in this condition is not subject to the GCA or the NFA.

Unfinished receiver tubes with instructions and/or templates for use in the assembly of a functional machinegun are also commercially available. These tubes with instructions/templates, in and of themselves, are not subject to the GCA or NFA.

When the parts kit is possessed in conjunction with the above described unfinished receiver tube, a combination of parts from which a machinegun can be assembled exists and is a machinegun as defined.

2.1.7 Silencer. A firearm silencer and a firearm muffler are defined as any device for silencing, muffling, or diminishing the report of a portable firearm.[18] Firearm silencers are generally composed of an outer tube, internal baffles, a front end cap, and a rear end cap.

complete firearm silencer

The definition of a silencer also includes any combination of parts, designed or redesigned, and intended for use in assembling or fabricating a firearm silencer or firearm muffler.

The following illustration depicts parts that are designed and intended for use in assembling a firearm silencer. Another example of parts redesigned and intended for use in assembling or fabricating a firearm silencer are automotive engine freeze plugs that have been modified by drilling a hole through their center to permit passage of a bullet.

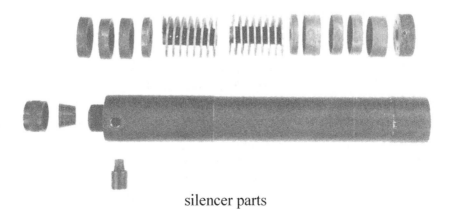

silencer parts

---

[18] 18 U.S.C. 921(a)(24)

Also included within the silencer definition is any part intended only for use in the assembly or fabrication of a firearm silencer.

silencer baffle

Any of the above illustrated components meet the definition of a firearm silencer and are subject to the NFA. *NOTE: the language in the definition of silencer contains no provisions that permit an owner of a registered silencer to possess spare or replacement components for the silencer. However, licensed manufacturers who are SOTs may possess spare silencer components in conjunction with their manufacturing operations.*

2.1.8 Destructive device. The destructive device definition contains different categories that address specific types of munitions. Each category describes the devices subject to the definition based on the material contained in the item, the dimensions of the bore of certain weapons, and a combination of parts for use in converting the described items into destructive devices.

2.1.8.1 Explosive devices. The first portion of the definition deals with explosive, incendiary and poison gas munitions. The definition specifies that any explosive, incendiary or poison gas bomb, grenade, mine or similar device is a destructive device.

explosive bomb

explosive grenade

This portion of the definition includes a rocket having a propellant charge of more than four ounces and a missile (projectile) having an explosive or incendiary charge of more than one-quarter ounce.

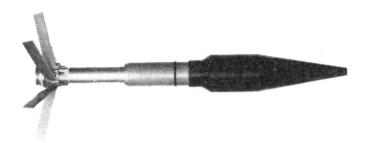

rocket with more than 4 ounces of propellant

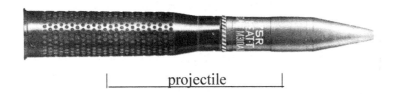

|_____projectile_____|

NOTE: Missiles (projectiles) less than caliber 20mm generally are not large enough to accommodate more than one-quarter ounce of explosive or incendiary material. In the case of 20mm high explosive (HE) or high explosive incendiary (HEI) projectiles, it is imperative to determine the model designation of the specific item as some 20mm HE and HEI projectiles contain more than one-quarter ounce of explosive or incendiary material and are destructive devices. Other 20mm HE and HEI projectiles do not contain more than one-quarter ounce of explosive and are not destructive devices. Therefore, it is incumbent upon persons interested in 20mm HE and HEI ammunition to determine the amount of explosives contained in a specific projectile. HE and HEI missiles (projectiles) larger than 20mm generally contain more than one-quarter ounce of explosive or incendiary material and are destructive devices.

2.1.8.2 Large caliber weapons. The second section of the definition states that any type of weapon by whatever name known which will, or which may be readily converted to, expel a projectile by the action of an explosive or other propellant, the barrel or barrels of which have a bore diameter of more than one-half inch in diameter is a destructive device. This portion of the definition specifically excludes a shotgun or shotgun shell which the Attorney General finds is generally recognized as particularly suitable for sporting purposes. ATF has issued rulings classifying specific shotguns as destructive devices because they have a bore of more than one half inch in diameter and were found to not be particularly suitable forfor sporting purposes.[19]

The majority of weapons covered by this portion of the destructive device definition are large caliber military weapons such as rocket launchers, mortars and cannons.

---

[19] Appendix B (ATF Rulings 94-1, 94-2)

RPG 7 launcher (bore diameter 1.57 inches)

120mm mortar (bore diameter 4.7 inches)

It is important to note that the large caliber firearms covered by this section are defined as weapons that expel a projectile by the action of an explosive *or other propellant*. This is the only place in the GCA and NFA where a propellant other than an explosive must be considered when classifying a weapon. Examples of weapons having a bore diameter of more than one-half inch in diameter and that expel a projectile by means other than an explosive are mortars that utilize compressed air as a propellant and some rocket launchers.

Certain destructive devices may also meet the definition of machinegun because in addition to having a bore diameter of more than one-half inch the weapons are capable of fully automatic fire. ATF treats NFA firearms of this type as both machineguns and destructive devices. The weapons are coded as machineguns in the NFRTR with an annotation that they are also destructive devices. Any such weapons manufactured on or after May 19, 1986 are subject to 18 U.S.C. 922(o). In instances where a weapon of this type is being transferred, it is imperative that State and local laws where the weapon is being transferred do not prohibit possession of destructive devices or machineguns.

M61 20mm full automatic cannon

In addition to defining destructive devices, the definition also specifically excludes certain items from that classification. As previously stated, any shotgun or shotgun shell which the Attorney General finds is generally recognized as particularly suitable for sporting purposes is not a destructive device. Additionally, the following items are also excluded from the definition:

- Any device which is neither designed nor redesigned for use as a weapon.

- Any device, although originally designed for use as a weapon, which is redesigned for use as a signaling, pyrotechnic, line throwing, safety or similar device.

- Surplus ordnance sold, loaned or given by the Secretary of the Army pursuant to the provisions of 10 U.S.C. 4684(2), 4685, or 4686.

- Any other device which the Attorney General finds is not likely to be used as a weapon, or is an antique, or is a rifle which the owner intends to use solely for sporting purposes.

It should not be assumed that any device meeting the above descriptions is automatically excluded from the definition of a destructive device. ATF has ruled that certain pyrotechnic devices are destructive devices.[20] ATF should be contacted to confirm the classification of any items that appear to meet the above exclusions. Additionally, many of the items excluded from the definition of destructive device may contain a firearm receiver and would still be a firearm as defined in the GCA.

2.1.9 Unserviceable firearm. An unserviceable firearm is a firearm that is incapable of discharging a shot by the action of an explosive and is incapable of being readily restored to a firing condition. The most common method for rendering a firearm unserviceable, and that recommended by ATF, is to weld the chamber of the barrel closed and weld the barrel to the receiver.[21] The chamber of the barrel should be plug welded closed and all welds should be full fusion, deep penetrating, and gas or electric steel welds. In instances where the above procedure cannot be employed to render a firearm unserviceable, FTB should be contacted for alternate methods.

It is important to remember that rendering a firearm unserviceable does not remove it from the definition of an NFA firearm. An unserviceable NFA firearm is still subject to the import, registration, and transfer provisions of the NFA. However, there is no tax imposed on the transfer of an unserviceable

---

[20] Appendix B (ATF Ruling 95-3)
[21] ATF Form 5 (5320.5), Instruction 6a

firearm as a "curio or ornament." See 26 U.S.C. 5852(e). *NOTE: "curio or ornament" is only descriptive of unserviceable firearms transferred exempt from transfer tax. An unserviceable firearm transferred as a "curio or ornament" is not necessarily a "curio or relic" firearm for purposes of the GCA unless the weapon is classified as a curio or relic under the GCA.* For further information on curio or relic classification see section 2.2.

Section 2.2 Antique firearm. Firearms defined by the NFA as "antique firearms" are not subject to any controls under the NFA.[22] The NFA defines antique firearms based on their date of manufacture and the type of ignition system used to fire a projectile. Any firearm manufactured in or before 1898 that is not designed or redesigned for using rimfire or conventional center fire ignition with fixed ammunition is an antique firearm. Additionally, any firearm using a matchlock, flintlock, percussion cap or similar type ignition system, irrespective of the actual date of manufacture of the firearm, is also an antique firearm.

NFA firearms using fixed ammunition are antique firearms only if the weapon was actually manufactured in or before 1898 *and* the ammunition for the firearm is no longer manufactured in the United States and is not readily available in the ordinary channels of commercial trade. To qualify as an antique firearm, a fixed cartridge firing NFA weapon must meet both the age and ammunition availability standards of the definition.

Concerning ammunition availability, it is important to note that a specific type of fixed ammunition that has been out of production for many years may again become available due to increasing interest in older firearms. Therefore, the classification of a specific NFA firearm as an antique can change if ammunition for the weapon becomes readily available in the ordinary channels of commercial trade.

Section 2.3 Curios or relics. Curios or relics are firearms that are of special interest to collectors.[23] NFA firearms can be classified as curios or relics under the same criteria used to classify conventional firearms as curios or relics.[24]

An NFA firearm that is recognized as a curio or relic is still an NFA "firearm" and is still subject to the registration and transfer provisions of the NFA. The primary impact of a curio or relic classification is that a properly registered NFA firearm classified as a curio or relic may be lawfully transferred interstate to, or received interstate by, a person licensed as a collector of curios or relics under the GCA.

Section 2.4 Applications to remove firearms from the scope of the NFA as collector's items.

Certain NFA weapons can be removed from the provisions of the NFA as collector's items.[25] The procedures for requesting removal of an NFA firearm are the same as used for requesting a destructive device determination.[26]

---

[22] 26 U.S.C. 5845(a), (g)
[23] 27 CFR 478.11
[24] 27 CFR 478.26
[25] 26 U.S.C. 5845(a)
[26] 27 CFR 479.24 - 479.25

An NFA firearm removed from the NFA as a collector's item is no longer subject to any of the provisions of the NFA. In most cases, the weapon will still be a firearm as defined in the GCA and subject to regulation under the GCA. In some situations, the weapon that is removed from the NFA as a collector's item will be an antique firearm as defined in the GCA.[27] In these instances, the weapon would no longer be a firearm as defined in Federal law.

The Attorney General does not have the authority to remove a machinegun or a destructive device from the provisions of the NFA as collector's items.[28] Therefore, applications to remove machineguns or destructive devices from the NFA as collector's items cannot be approved.

Section 2.5 Removal of firearms from the scope of the NFA by modification/elimination of components.

Firearms, except machineguns and silencers, that are subject to the NFA fall within the various definitions due to specific features. If the particular feature that causes a firearm to be regulated by the NFA is eliminated or modified, the resulting weapon is no longer an NFA weapon.

For example, a shotgun with a barrel length of 15 inches is an NFA weapon. If the 15- inch barrel is removed and disposed of, the remaining firearm is not subject to the NFA because it has no barrel. Likewise, if the 15 inch barrel is modified by permanently attaching an extension such that the barrel length is at least 18 inches and the overall length of the weapon is at least 26 inches, the modified firearm is not subject to the NFA. *NOTE: an acceptable method for permanently installing a barrel extension is by gas or electric steel seam welding or the use of high temperature silver solder having a flow point of 1100 degrees Fahrenheit.*

A shot pistol ("any other weapon") such as an H&R Handy Gun may be removed from the NFA by either disposing of the smooth bore barrel or permanently installing a rifled sleeve chambered to accept a standard pistol cartridge into the smooth bore barrel. Modified by sleeving the barrel, an H&R Handy Gun is no longer an NFA weapon because it now has a rifled bore.

Large caliber destructive devices that are not also machineguns can be removed from the NFA by disposing of the barrel. If the barrel of a 37mm cannon is removed and disposed of, the remaining weapon has no barrel or bore diameter. As an alternative, the barrel of a destructive device may be functionally destroyed. To destroy the barrel of a destructive device the following operations must be performed:

- Cut a hole, equal to the diameter of the bore, on a 90-degree angle to the axis of the bore, through one side of the barrel in the high pressure (chamber) area.
- Weld the barrel to the receiver of the weapon.
- Weld an obstruction into the barrel to prevent the introduction of a round of ammunition.

2.5.1 Removal of machineguns and silencers from the scope of the NFA. Machineguns are defined to include the receiver of a machinegun and the definition of silencer includes each component of a

---

[27] 18 U.S.C. 921(a)(16)
[28] 26 U.S.C. 5845(a)

silencer. Therefore, to remove these weapons from the provisions of the NFA, the receiver of a machinegun or all the components of a silencer must be destroyed.

The preferred method for destroying a machinegun receiver is to completely sever the receiver in specified locations by means of a cutting torch that displaces at least one-quarter inch of material at each cut location. ATF has published rulings concerning the preferred destruction of specific machineguns.[29]

A machinegun receiver may also be properly destroyed by means of saw cutting and disposing of certain removed portions of the receiver. To ensure that the proposed saw cutting of a particular machinegun receiver is acceptable, FTB should be contacted for guidance and approval of any alternative destruction proposal. *Note: a machinegun receiver that is not properly destroyed may still be classified as a machinegun, particularly in instances where the improperly destroyed receiver is possessed in conjunction with other component parts for the weapon.*

A silencer may be destroyed by completely severing each component by means of a cutting torch that has a tip of sufficient size to displace at least one-quarter inch of material at each cut location.

Concerning the outer tube(s) of a silencer, these components may be destroyed by crushing them flat in lieu of cutting with a torch.

Anyone interested in destroying an NFA weapon by means other than described above should contact FTB to discuss possible alternatives.

---

[29] Appendix B (ATF Rulings 2003-1, 2003-2, 2003-3, 2003-4)

CHAPTER 3. REGISTRATION OF NFA FIREARMS

Section 3.1 The National Firearm Registration and Transfer Record (NFRTR)

The NFRTR is the central registry of all NFA firearms in the U.S. which are not in the possession or under the control of the U.S. Government. The registry includes (1) the identification of the firearm, (2) date of registration, and (3) identification and address of the person entitled to possession of the firearm (the person to whom the firearm is registered).[30]

Section 3.2 Who may register NFA firearms

3.2.1 Amnesty registration. When the NFA was amended in 1968, a 30-day amnesty period immediately following the law's effective date was established during which persons possessing unregistered firearms could register them in the NFRTR.[31]

The 1968 amendments also provided for the establishment of additional amnesty periods not exceeding 90 days per period.[32] To date, no additional amnesty periods have been declared. Requests for further amnesty periods have been denied, principally because additional periods could jeopardize pending ATF investigations and prosecutions of NFA violations.

3.2.2 Registration by State and local agencies. To be lawfully possessed by States and political subdivisions of the States (for example, local police departments), NFA firearms must be registered in the NFRTR. The regulations permit State and local police organizations acquiring unregistered NFA firearms for official use, by seizure, forfeiture, or abandonment, to register them in the NFRTR by filing ATF Forms 10. Appendix C contains a copy of the form. Firearms registered on Forms 10 are for official use only and subsequent transfers will be approved only to other government agencies for official use.[33] For example, they may not be traded to an FFL/SOT in exchange for other firearms or police equipment.

3.2.3 Registration by makers. Persons other than FFLs and SOTs desiring to make an NFA firearm are required to first register the firearm by filing Form 1 with ATF and obtaining approval of the form and registration of the firearm. Appendix C contains a copy of the form. ATF will approve a making application on Form 1 if the maker pays the $200 making tax required by the NFA, identifies the firearm as the form requires, includes his/her fingerprints and photographs if the maker is an individual, and if the making and the maker's possession of the firearm would not place the maker in violation of any Federal, State or local law.[34] A law enforcement certification is also required if the maker is an individual. Note also that ATF will not approve the making of a machinegun it determines would violate 18 U.S.C. 922(o). Section 922(o) generally prohibits the possession of machineguns manufactured on or after May 19, 1986.

---

[30] 26 U.S.C. 5841(a)
[31] Section 207(b) of the Gun Control Act of 1968, Public Law 90-618, approved October 22, 1968
[32] Section 207(d), ibid
[33] 27 CFR 479.104
[34] 26 U.S.C 5822; 27 CFR 479.62, 479.63, 479.64

3.2.4 Registration by importers. FFLs/SOTs qualified as importers must register imported firearms by filing ATF Forms 2, Notice of Firearms Manufactured or Imported, no later than 15 days from the date the imported firearms were released by Customs. Upon timely receipt by ATF of a Form 2 and a copy of Form 6A showing Customs' release of an imported firearm, ATF will register the firearm to the importer.[35] Appendix C contains copies of Forms 2 and 6A. Note that the NFA prohibits importation of NFA firearms unless they are being imported for the use of the United States or a State agency, for scientific or research purposes, or for testing or use as a model by a registered importer or solely for use as a sales sample by a registered importer or registered dealer.[36] In the case of an imported machinegun, Section 922(o) of the GCA would also apply.

3.2.5 Registration by manufacturers. FFLs/SOTs qualified as manufacturers must register manufactured firearms by filing ATF Form 2, Notice of Firearms Manufactured or Imported. All firearms manufactured during a single day must be listed on one Form 2. The form must be filed no later than the close of the next business day. Receipt of the form by ATF will serve to register the listed firearms to the manufacturer.[37] Appendix C contains a copy of Form 2.

3.2.6 Registration to transferees. Registered firearms may be transferred by their registered owners/possessors to transferees. Other than Form 10 registration, there is no mechanism in the NFA to lawfully transfer unregistered NFA firearms.

3.2.6.1 Transfers by persons other than FFLs/SOTs to other such persons. Transferors of registered firearms must file ATF Forms 4, Application for Tax Paid Transfer and Registration of a Firearm, to register the firearm to the transferee and pay the applicable transfer tax.[38] Appendix C contains a copy of the form. The form must be approved by ATF before the transfer may be made.[39] ATF will not approve the form if the transfer, receipt, or possession of the firearm would place the transferee in violation of any Federal, State, or local law.[40] A law enforcement certification is also required on ATF Form 4.

3.2.6.2 Transfers by FFLs/SOTs to persons other than FFLs/SOTs. Transferors of registered firearms must file ATF Forms 4, Application for Tax Paid Transfer and Registration of a Firearm, to register the firearm to the transferee and pay the applicable transfer tax. Appendix C contains a copy of the form. The form must be approved by ATF before the transfer may bemade.[41] ATF will not approve the form if the transfer, receipt, or possession of the firearm would place the transferee in violation of any Federal, State, or local law.[42]

3.2.6.3 Transfers by non-FFLs/SOTs to FFLs/SOTs. Transferors of registered firearms must file ATF Forms 4, Application for Tax Paid Transfer and Registration of a Firearm, to register the firearm to

---

[35] 27 CFR 479.112
[36] 26 U.S.C. 5844
[37] 27 CFR 479.103
[38] 26 U.S.C. 5812(a); 27 CFR 479.84
[39] 26 U.S.C. 5812(b); 27 CFR 479.86
[40] 26 U.S.C. 5812(a); 27 CFR 479.85
[41] 26 U.S.C. 5812(b); 27 CFR 479.86
[42] 26 U.S.C. 5812(a); 27 CFR 479.85

the transferee and pay the applicable transfer tax.[43] Appendix C contains a copy of the form. The form must be approved by ATF before the transfer may be made.[44] ATF will not approve the form if the transfer, receipt, or possession of the firearm would place the transferee in violation of any Federal, State, or local law.

3.2.6.4 Transfers by FFLs/SOTs to other FFLs/SOTs. Transferors must file ATF Forms 3, Application for Tax-Exempt Transfer of Firearm and Registration to Special Occupational Taxpayer, to register the firearm to the transferee.[45] Appendix C contains a copy of the form. In these transactions, the transferor has no liability for the transfer tax. The form must be approved by ATF before the transfer may be made.[46] ATF will not approve the form if the transfer, receipt, or possession of the firearm would place the transferee in violation of any Federal, State, or local law.

3.2.6.5 Transfers to State and local government agencies. Transferors must file ATF Forms 5, Application for Tax Exempt Transfer and Registration of a Firearm, to register the firearm to such agency.[47] Appendix C contains a copy of the form. In these transactions, the transferor has no liability for the transfer tax. The Form must be approved by ATF before the transfer may be made.[48]

Section 3.3 Status of unregistered firearms

Firearms not lawfully registered as required by the NFA may not be registered and legitimized by their possessors. They are contraband and unlawful to possess.[49] However, see Section 2.4 for information on removing NFA firearms from the scope of the NFA because of their status as collectors' items, modification, or elimination of certain component parts.

Section 3.4 ATF disclosure of NFA registration information

3.4.1 Restrictive use of information. The NFA provides that no information or evidence obtained from an application, registration, or records required to be submitted or retained by a natural person (individual) in order to comply with the NFA or the NFA regulations shall be used directly or indirectly as evidence against the person in a criminal proceeding with respect to a violation of law occurring prior to or concurrently with the filing of the application or registration.[50] Filing false information is an exception to this prohibition.[51]

3.4.2 Prohibition on ATF's disclosure of tax returns or tax return information. NFA forms are treated as tax returns and registration information in the NFRTR is considered to be tax return

---

[43] 26 U.S.C. 5812(a); 27 CFR 479.84
[44] 26 U.S.C. 5812(b); 27 CFR 479.86
[45] 26 U.S.C. 5812(a); 27 CFR 479.88
[46] 26 U.S.C. 5812(b); 27 CFR 479.88(b)
[47] 26 U.S.C. 5812(a); 27 CFR 479.90
[48] 26 U.S.C. 5812(b); 27 CFR 479.90(b)
[49] U.S. v. Freed, 401 U.S. 601 (1971)
[50] 26 U.S.C. 5848(a)
[51] 26 U.S.C. 5848(b)

information. ATF is generally prohibited from disclosing tax returns and tax return information.[52] However, firearms registration information may be disclosed to registered owners/possessors of the firearms.

3.4.3 Determining the registration status of an NFA firearm. The situation may arise when a person finds in his or her possession an NFA firearm and is uncertain whether the firearm is lawfully registered. Naturally, the person will want to query the NFA Branch to determine the registration status of the firearm. Because of the restriction on disclosure of NFA registration information discussed in section 3.4.2, ATF will not respond to the person's telephone request for the registration status of the firearm. To communicate with the person, the NFA Branch will respond to the request if the person verifies his or her identity to the Branch in writing. If the firearm is registered to the person in the NFRTR, the Branch will so advise the person and, if the circumstances warrant, provide the person with a copy of the registration. See also Section 3.5 on lost or stolen registration documents.

Section 3.5 Lost or stolen registration documents. A person possessing a firearm registered as required by the NFA must retain proof of registration, that is, the registration form showing registration of the firearm to the person, which must be made available to ATF upon request.[53] If a registrant discovers that a Form 1, 2, 3, 4, 5, 6A, or 10 is stolen, lost or destroyed, the registrant must immediately report the theft, loss, or destruction in writing to the NFABranch.[54] The report must contain the details of the situation. ATF will issue a duplicate copy of the registration document as the circumstances warrant.

Section 3.6 Correcting incorrect registration documents. Occasionally, the registered possessor of an NFA firearm may notice that the registered firearm does not match the registration document. Perhaps the serial number is slightly different. In this situation, the registrant should take a photograph of the markings on the firearm (or a rubbing) and send it to the NFA Branch with a written request to correct the serial number as documented on the NFRTR. ATF will respond to the request by letter stating that the NFRTR has been corrected and advising the registrant to keep the letter with the registration document as evidence of proper registration.

Section 3.7 Maintaining registration documents. A person possessing an NFA firearm registered as required by law must retain proof of registration, that is, the document showing the person's registration, which must be made available to ATF upon request.[55]

---

[52] 26 U.S.C. 6103
[53] 26 U.S.C. 5841(e)
[54] 27 CFR 479.142
[55] 26 U.S.C. 5841(e)

CHAPTER 4. TAXES IMPOSED BY THE NFA

Section 4.1 Taxes

The NFA imposes tax on the making and transfer of firearms. The Act also requires annual payment of a special (occupational) tax (SOT) by licensees engaged in the business of manufacturing, dealing in, or importing NFA firearms. The NFA also provides for exemptions from the making, transfer, and special (occupational) taxes in specific situations.

4.1.1 Making tax. A tax of $200 is imposed on the making of all NFA firearms made by other than qualified manufacturers of firearms.[56] The tax must be paid prior to making the firearm. Payment of the making tax is submitted with the Application to Make and Register a Firearm (ATF Form 1). See Appendix C for a copy of Form 1. The making tax is also imposed when a registered, unserviceable NFA firearm is reactivated.[57] See the exemptions from tax discussed in Section 4.2.1.

4.1.2 Transfer tax. Transfer of a serviceable NFA firearm is subject to the transfer tax.[58] The tax must be paid prior to the transfer. Payment of the tax is submitted with the Application to Transfer and Register a Firearm (ATF Form 4). See Appendix C for a copy of Form 4. ATF will accept payment of the tax from either the transferor or transferee. The tax on the transfer of short barrel shotguns, short barrel rifles, machineguns, silencers and destructive devices is $200. The transfer tax for firearms classified as "any other weapon" is $5. See the exemptions from tax discussed in Section 4.2.2.

NOTE: there is often confusion concerning the tax on "any other weapons." The majority of NFA weapons are subject to a making tax of $200 and a transfer tax of $200. Many individuals have the mistaken belief that the rate of tax for making an "any other weapon" is $5 because the transfer tax on "any other weapons" is $5. As discussed in Section 4.1.1, the making tax on all types of NFA firearms is $200.

4.1.3 Special (occupational) tax. On first engaging in business, each importer, manufacturer, and dealer in NFA firearms must pay a special (occupational) tax for each place of business.[59] Special tax is paid by return, specifically ATF Form 5630.7, Special Tax Registration and Return. Appendix C contains a copy of the return. Subsequent to the initial payment of the SOT, the tax is due on or before July 1 of each year. The rate of tax for importers and manufacturers is $1000 per year. The rate of tax for dealers is $500 per year. The NFA provides a reduced rate of SOT for importers and manufacturers whose gross receipts for the most recent taxable year are less than $500,000.[60] See the exemptions from tax discussed in Section 4.2.3.

---

[56] 26 U.S.C. 5821
[57] ATF Form 1 (5320.1), Instruction k
[58] 26 U.S.C. 5811
[59] 26 U.S.C. 5801
[60] 26 U.S.C. 5801(b)(1)

Section 4.2 Exemptions from tax

4.2.1 Making tax. A manufacturer who has paid the SOT is exempt from payment of the making tax.[61] Likewise, there is no making tax imposed on the making of an NFA firearm by or on behalf of a Federal or State agency.[62]

4.2.2 Transfer tax. Transfers of registered firearms between SOTs are exempt from the transfer tax.[63] Likewise, there is no transfer tax imposed on the transfer of firearms to a Federal or State agency.[64]

4.2.2.1 Unserviceable firearms. An unserviceable firearm may be transferred as a curio or ornament without payment of the transfer tax.[65]

4.2.3 Special (occupational) tax. A person required to pay SOT is exempt from the tax if it is established that the business is conducted exclusively with, or on behalf of, an agency of the United States.[66] This exemption must be obtained by filing a letter application addressed to the NFA Branch setting out the manner in which the applicant conducts business, the type of firearms to be manufactured, and satisfactory proof of the existence of the applicant's contract with the Government.[67] This exemption must be renewed by letter on or before July of each year. Approval of the application entitles the applicant to the exemption.

4.2.4 Exportation of firearms. An NFA firearm may be exported without payment of the transfer tax provided that proof of the exportation is furnished in such form and manner as the regulations prescribe.[68] The form to be filed is ATF Form 9 (Firearms), Application and Permit for Exportation of Firearms.[69] See Appendix C for a copy of the form. Approval of the form by ATF is required before exportation. *NOTE: exportation of NFA firearms without an approved Form 9 will subject their registered owner to NFA transfer tax.*

---

[61] 26 U.S. 5852(c)
[62] 26 U.S.C. 5852(b), 5853(b)
[63] 26 U.S.C. 5852(d)
[64] 26 U.S.C. 5852(a), 5853(a)
[65] 26 U.S.C. 5852(e)
[66] 26 U.S.C. 5851
[67] 27 CFR 479.33
[68] 26 U.S.C. 5854
[69] 27 CFR 479.114

CHAPTER 5. QUALIFYING TO DO BUSINESS IN NFA FIREARMS

Section 5.1 Licensing under the GCA

5.1.1 Application for GCA license. Any "person" intending to engage in the business of importing, manufacturing, or dealing in NFA firearms, which are also defined as "firearms" under the GCA, must first apply for and obtain a license.[70] The license application is ATF Form 7 (5310.12). Appendix C contains a copy of the form. Licenses are issued for a period of 3 years.

> **5.1.1.1 Definition of "person" for GCA purposes.** The GCA defines "person" to include "any individual, corporation, company, association, firm, partnership, society, or joint stock company."[71] ATF recognizes the term to include a limited liability company ("LLC") organized under State law. Thus, an LLC must obtain a GCA license to engage in a GCA firearms business and ATF will issue a license to an LLC meeting the licensing standards.

5.1.2 License fees.[72]

> **5.1.2.1 Manufacturers.** If the applicant is a manufacturer of destructive devices, the fee is $1,000 per year. For firearms other than destructive devices, the fee is $50 per year.

> **5.1.2.2 Importers.** If the applicant is an importer of destructive devices, the fee is $1,000 per year. For firearms other than destructive devices, the fee is $50 per year.

> **5.1.2.3 Dealers.** If the applicant is a dealer in destructive devices, the fee is $1,000 per year. For firearms other than destructive devices, the fee is $200 for 3 years, except that the fee for renewal is $90 for 3 years.

5.1.3 Licensing standards under the GCA.[73]

> **5.1.3.1 Age.** If the applicant is an individual, he or she must be at least 21 years of age.

> **5.1.3.2 Prohibited persons.** Persons who fall within the prohibited persons categories set forth in 18 U.S.C. 922(g) and (n) do not qualify for licensing. The same is true of business entities having "responsible persons" under any one of the disabilities.

> **5.1.3.3 "Responsible persons."** If the applicant is a corporation, partnership, or association (including an LLC), the applicant would not qualify for licensing if the entity itself has GCA disabilities under section 922(g) or (n) or has any individual possessing directly or indirectly the power to direct or cause the direction of the management and policies of the firm under disabilities. These management and policy-making individuals include only those having responsibilities with respect to firearms. For example, they would not include individuals only

---

[70] 18 U.S.C. 923(a); 27 CFR 478.44
[71] 18 U.S.C. 921(a)(1)
[72] 18 U.S.C. 923(a)(1); 27 CFR 478.42
[73] 18 U.S.C. 923(d)(1)

having duties related to administration or personnel. Those having management and policy-making responsibilities with respect to firearms are referred to as "responsible persons" and must be listed on the firm's license application and their fingerprints and photographs must accompany the application. If the firm has a "responsible person" under disabilities, the firm would become eligible for licensing if the person is removed from his or her firearms management or policy-making position.

5.1.3.4 Removing disabilities. The GCA provides a mechanism for ATF to grant relief to persons under Federal firearms disabilities who apply for relief.[74] However, Congress has denied ATF's use of funds to process relief applications or grant relief. An exception was made for corporations. Thus, a corporation convicted of a "crime punishable by imprisonment for a term exceeding one year" may apply for and obtain relief from ATF. Not all disabilities are permanent. *Examples*: a person convicted of a crime in Federal court could get relief by applying to the U.S. Pardon Attorney for a presidential pardon and obtaining a pardon; a person convicted of a State crime may, depending on State law, get relief by a State pardon, expunction or set-aside of the conviction, or restoration of rights if the person would have no remaining firearms disabilities under State law[75]; and a person under a restraining order relating to domestic violence would be relieved from disabilities if the order is terminated.

5.1.3.5 Prior willful violations. The applicant must not have willfully violated any provision of the GCA or the regulations.

5.1.3.6 False statements. The applicant has not willfully failed to disclose any material information required or made any material false statements in connection with the application.

5.1.3.7 Business premises. The applicant must have a permanent premises from which business is to be conducted. The applicant must certify that conducting business from that location is not prohibited by State or local law; that within 30 days after license approval the business will comply with State and local laws applicable to the business and business will not be conducted until State and local requirements have been met; and that the chief law enforcement officer at the proposed business location has been advised of the intent to apply for a license.

5.1.3.8 May a license be obtained to do business solely away from the licensed premises at gun shows? Under the law, a licensee is entitled to do business at gun shows within the State in which the licensed premises is located. However, a person seeking a license to deal in firearms solely away from the licensed premises at gun shows does not qualify for licensing. Licensing in this instance would not meet the requirement discussed in Section 5.1.3.8 that the applicant must have a permanent premises from which business is conducted.

5.1.3.9 Gun storage and safety devices. Applicants for dealers licenses must certify that secure gun storage or safety devices will be available to nonlicensees with certain exceptions: storage or safety devices are temporarily unavailable because of theft, casualty loss, consumer sales, backorders, or similar reasons beyond the licensee's control.

---

[74] 18 U.S.C. 925(c)
[75] 18 U.S.C. 921(a)(20)

5.1.4 Multiple business locations. A separate license must be obtained for each location at which business will be conducted.[76]

> **5.1.4.1 Locations solely for storage.** No license is required to cover a separate warehouse used by the FFL solely for storage of firearms if required records are maintained at the licensed premises served by the warehouse.[77]

5.1.5 Establishing a common expiration date for licenses at multiple locations. For the convenience of FFLs, ATF Ruling 73-9 (see Appendix C) provides that FFLs holding licenses at more than one location may establish a common expiration date for the licenses issued to their several locations. FFLs wishing to establish such a date for all licenses issued to them may apply in writing to the Federal Firearms Licensing Center.

5.1.6 Engaging in business as both an importer and a manufacturer. Persons intending to engage in business as firearms importers and manufacturers, even if the businesses will be conducted from the same premises, must have both an importer's license and a manufacturer's license.[78]

5.1.7 Do importers and manufacturers need a dealer's license to deal in the firearms they import or manufacture? Licensed importers and manufacturers are not required to have a separate dealer's license to deal in firearms they import or manufacture. A license as an importer or manufacturer authorizes the FFL to deal in the types of firearms authorized by the license to be imported or manufactured.[79]

5.1.8 License renewal. Licenses are issued for a 3-year period. Prior to the expiration of a license, the FFL will receive from ATF a license renewal application, ATF Form 8, that should be filed with ATF prior to the expiration date shown on the current license. If a Form 8 is not received 30 days before the expiration date, the FFL should contact ATF's Federal Firearms Licensing Center. It is the responsibility of the FFL to timely obtain and file a renewal application. Appendix C contains a copy of the form. ATF has 60 days within which to act on an original or renewal license application.[80]

> **5.1.8.1 Right to operate while renewal application is pending; "letters of continuing operations."** ATF's approval of a license renewal application may occur after the expiration date shown on the current license. If a license renewal application is timely filed, but not acted upon until after the expiration date of the applicant's current license, may the applicant lawfully conduct the business after that date? The law, 5 U.S.C. 558, allows an FFL to continue to lawfully conduct business under a current license until a timely filed renewal application is acted upon. To show the FFL's current suppliers that the license is still valid while the renewal application is pending, the FFL may obtain a "letter of continuing operations" from the Federal Firearms Licensing Center, showing that the transferee's license is still valid even though it appears on its face to have expired.

---

[76] 27 CFR 478.50
[77] Ibid
[78] 27 CFR 478.41(b)
[79] Ibid
[80] 27 CFR 478.45

Section 5.2 Payment of special (occupational) tax to do business in NFA firearms. See also Section 4.1.3.

5.2.1 Every "person" who engages in the business of importing, manufacturing, or dealing in firearms (including pawnbrokers) shall pay a special tax.[81] The tax must be paid on or before the date of commencing the taxable business and every year thereafter on or before July 1. The tax is not prorated and is computed for the entire tax year (July 1 through June 30), regardless of the portion of the year during which the taxpayer engages in business. Persons commencing business at any time after July 1 in any year are liable for the tax for the entire tax year.

> **5.2.1.1 Definition of "person" for NFA purposes.** For purposes of the NFA, "person" is defined as a "partnership, company, association, trust, estate, or corporation, as well as a natural person."[82] ATF recognizes the term to include a limited liability company ("LLC") organized under State law. Thus, an LLC engaged in an NFA firearms business must pay the NFA special tax.

5.2.2 Tax must be paid for each business location. The special tax must be paid for each premises where business will be conducted.[83]

5.2.3 Rate of tax.

> **5.2.3.1 Importers and manufacturers.** The tax is generally $1,000 a year or fraction thereof.[84] See 26 U.S.C. 5801(b) and 27 CFR 479.32a for the reduced tax rate for certain "small importers and manufacturers." Those entitled to the reduced tax rate are subject only to a $500 tax per year.

> **5.2.3.2 Dealers.** The tax is $500 a year or fraction thereof.[85]

5.2.4 How to pay special tax. Special tax must be paid by filing ATF Form 5630.7, Special Tax Registration and Return, together with a check or money order for the amount of the tax. The form and tax payment must be sent to the Bureau of ATF, Attention NFA, P.O. Box 403269, Atlanta, Ga. 30384-3269. Upon filing a properly completed Form 5630.7 and payment of the special tax, the taxpayer will be issued a special tax stamp as evidence of tax payment.[86]

> **5.2.4.1 Employer identification number (EIN).** The tax return, Form 5630.7, must contain a valid EIN number issued by the Internal Revenue Service (IRS). If the taxpayer does not have an EIN number, the IRS in the taxpayer's locality should be contacted to obtain a number. The number may also be obtained by contacting the IRS on-line.

---

[81] 26 U.S.C. 5801
[82] 27 CFR 479.11
[83] 27 CFR 479.38
[84] 26 U.S.C 5801(a)(1)
[85] 26 U.S.C. 5801(a)(2)
[86] 27 CFR 479.36

5.2.4.2 Renewal of special tax. In May of each year, ATF will send a renewal tax return, ATF Form 5630.5R (NFA Special Tax Renewal Registration and Return) and ATF Form 5630.5RC (NFA Special Tax Location Registration Listing) to each person who paid the special tax for the current tax year. The taxpayer should make any necessary changes to the information pre-printed on the forms and return the forms with remittance to ATF as directed on the forms.

5.2.5 Exemption from special tax. Any person required to pay special tax shall be relieved from tax payment if it is established that the business is conducted exclusively on behalf of the U.S. Government.[87] The exemption may be obtained by filing with the NFA Branch a letter stating the manner in which business is conducted, the type of firearms to be manufactured, and proof of the person's contract with the U.S.[88] The exemption must be renewed on or before July 1 of each year.

5.2.6 Collectors acquiring NFA firearms for their personal collections by acquiring dealers' licenses and paying NFA special tax. Some NFA firearms collectors, who are not engaged in any firearms business, have been known to acquire a GCA license to deal in firearms and pay the NFA special tax to acquire NFA firearms for their personal firearms collections. They do so for a number of reasons: (1) to acquire firearms from nonlicensees residing out-of-state; (2) to circumvent requirements imposed on individuals to provide their fingerprints and photographs in order to receive NFA firearms and law enforcement certifications authorizing their receipt of such firearms; and (3) to avoid NFA transfer tax on firearms they receive from FFLs/SOTs.

Warning: These transactions violate the law and can only lead to trouble for the collector. In these instances, the collector has committed Federal felonies by falsely stating on a license application and special tax return that the collector intends to conduct a firearms business. Any NFA firearms received tax free by the collector are subject to transfer tax and the collector's receipt of the firearms tax free violated the NFA. As held in ATF Ruling 76-22, these transfers are unlawful and the firearms received are subject to seizure and forfeiture.

Section 5.3 Registration by firearms manufacturers and exporters with the U.S. Department of State (DOS). DOS has the responsibility of enforcing the provisions of the Arms Export Control Act (AECA) relating to the export of firearms and other defense articles on the U.S. Munitions List. Nevertheless, any person engaged in the U.S. in the business of manufacturing or exporting firearms or other defense articles is required to register with DOS's Directorate of Defense Trade Controls.[89] The regulations expressly state that "Manufacturers who do not engage in exporting must nevertheless register."

5.3.1 How manufacturers should register. DSP-9 (Registration Statement) and a transmittal letter required by DOS regulations at 22 CFR 122.2(b) must be submitted to DOS by the registrant with a check or money order payable to DOS of one of the fees prescribed by 22 CFR 122.3(a).[90] Appendix C contains a copy of Form DSP-9. The registration and transmittal letter must be signed by a senior officer who has been empowered by the registrant to sign the documents. The registrant must also

---

[87] 26 U.S.C. 5851
[88] 27 CFR 479.33
[89] 22 CFR 122.1
[90] 22 CFR 122.2(a)

submit documentation demonstrating that it is incorporated or otherwise authorized to do business in the U.S.

Section 5.4 Registration by firearms importers with ATF. Persons engaged in the business in the U.S. of importing firearms and other articles enumerated on the U.S. Munitions Import List must register with ATF's Director.[91]

5.4.1 How importers should register. An application to register must be filed on ATF Form 4587, in duplicate, with the Director and be accompanied with the registration fee at the rate prescribed by the regulations at 27 CFR 447.32(b).[92] Appendix C contains a copy ATF Form 4587. Fees paid in advance for whole future years of a multiple year registration will be refunded upon request if the registrant ceases to engage in importing such firearms or other articles on the List. A request for refund must be submitted to ATF's Director, attention Firearms and Explosives Imports Branch, prior to the beginning of any year for which refund is claimed.

Sec. 5.5 Filing by Facsimile Transmission. The NFA Branch allows an FFL who is qualified to import, manufacture, or deal in NFA to file certain registration forms by facsimile transmission (fax) directly to the NFA Branch. The forms are: Form 2, Form 3, Form 5 (where the application is not accompanied by fingerprint cards), and Form 9. However, before the FFL can file by fax, the FFL must first submit an affidavit, in original, to the Chief, NFA Branch. The affidavit concerns who files the forms, the treatment of the signature on the fax as original, and that the copies are to be treated as originals. The format for the affidavit and a discussion of the procedure is in an ATF memo to Federal Firearms Licensees and NFA Special (Occupational) Taxpayers, dated January 31, 2006, and can be found in Appendix B.

---

[91] 27 CFR 447.31
[92] 27 CFR 447.32

CHAPTER 6. MAKING NFA FIREARMS BY NONLICENSEE

Section 6.1 Requirements for making NFA firearms. Persons not otherwise prohibited from possessing firearms may submit an application to make an NFA firearm, other than a machinegun.[93] The application process requires submission of ATF Form 1, Application to Make and Register a Firearm, in duplicate, along with FBI FD-258, Fingerprint Card, in duplicate, and payment of the $200 making tax. Appendix C contains a copy of Form 1.

Section 6.2 Preparation of Form 1. Every person (other than a licensed manufacturer who has also paid the required SOT to manufacture NFA weapons) must complete the Form 1.[94] Two identical copies of the application must be prepared. All entries must be made in ink. All required signatures must be original and entered in ink. Photocopies or other facsimile or carbon copy signatures are not acceptable. Under no circumstances will a form filled in by use of a lead pencil be accepted. All changes made on the form must be initialed and dated by the applicant.

6.2.1 Description of firearm. If an existing firearm or firearm receiver is being used, the name and location of the original manufacturer of the weapon should be entered in Block 4(a). If the applicant is making a completely new firearm, the applicant's name and location should be entered in Block 4(a). The type of firearm being made, i.e., short barrel rifle, short barrel shotgun, any other weapon, silencer or destructive device, is to be entered in Block 4(b). The caliber or gauge of the firearm is to be entered in Block 4(c). If a model designation has been assigned to the firearm, that designation is to be placed in Block 4(d). If the weapon has no model designation, enter "none" in Block 4(d). The length of the barrel is to be entered, in inches, in Block 4(e) and the overall length of the firearm is to be entered, in inches, in Block 4(f).

All NFA firearms must be identified by a serial number and other specified markings[95]. If an existing firearm is being used in the making of the NFA weapon, and that firearm is serialized, the existing serial number should be used (unless it duplicates a serial number already used by the maker on Form 1) and entered in Block 4(g). If the weapon is of new manufacture, the applicant must assign a unique serial number and enter it in Block 4(g). For example, a unique serial number could be composed of at least 4 digits preceded by the initials of the maker. *NOTE*: alpha characters, e.g., a name, will not be accepted as a serial number. If a name is to be used, there must be at least one numeric character in addition to the alpha characters.

The serial number must be engraved or stamped on the receiver of the firearm and the caliber, model, and identification of the maker must be engraved on the barrel or frame or receiver of the weapon.[96] The marking and identification requirements for a maker are the same as for a manufacturer. Refer to section 7.4 for a detailed discussion of the requirements.

---

[93] 18 U.S.C. 922(o)
[94] 26 U.S.C. 5822
[95] 27 CFR 479.102
[96] Ibid

6.2.2 Photograph of applicant. An unmounted photograph of the applicant approximately 2 x 2 inches and taken within the past year must be affixed to the indicated space on each copy of the application. The photograph must be original. Photocopies of photographs are not accepted.

6.2.3 FBI Form FD-258, fingerprint card. A completed Form FD-258 containing the fingerprints of the applicant must be submitted in duplicate with the Form 1. The fingerprints should be taken by someone qualified to do so and must be clear, unsmudged and classifiable. The person taking the fingerprints must also enter the identification data regarding the applicant and must complete the fingerprint cards by signing as the person taking the fingerprints. *NOTE*: If the fingerprint cards are not properly prepared or the fingerprints are not legible, the application cannot be acted upon. If this situation occurs, ATF will contact the applicant for a new set of fingerprint cards.

6.2.4 Law enforcement certification. As provided by the regulations, the law enforcement certification located on the back of Form 1 must be completed and signed by the local chief of police or county sheriff, the head of the State police, the State or local district attorney or prosecutor, "or such other person whose certificate may in a particular case be acceptable to the Director."[97] Examples of certifying officials, other than those specifically mentioned in the regulations, who have been found to be acceptable are State attorneys general, heads of district State police offices and certain State court judges. Judges' certifications have been accepted if the judges preside over courts of general jurisdiction having original jurisdiction in all civil and criminal cases or the authority to conduct criminal jury trials in felony cases. Generally, State magistrates and constables do not have such authority. *NOTE: no official's certification will be accepted unless the official has jurisdiction over the place where the applicant resides.* The signature on each copy of the certification must be an original signature in ink. *NOTE: if the Form 1 being submitted is to reactivate a properly registered unserviceable firearm, the law enforcement certification is not required.* See Section 6.6.

>**6.2.4.1 What if the proposed maker is unable to find any official in his or her jurisdiction willing to sign the law enforcement certification?** The inability to find any official to sign the certification will not excuse the requirement for the certification. In that event, the proposed maker will not be able to obtain an approved Form 1 to lawfully make an NFA firearm.

Section 6.3 Submission of Form 1. The completed Form 1, in duplicate, with fingerprint cards, photographs of the applicant, and payment of the $200 making tax should be mailed to:

National Firearms Act Branch
Bureau of Alcohol, Tobacco, Firearms and Explosives
244 Needy Road
Martinsburg, West Virginia 25405

Payment of the making tax is to be in the form of a check or money order payable to the Bureau of Alcohol, Tobacco, Firearms and Explosives.

6.3.1 State permit or license for possession of an NFA weapon. If the applicant's state of residence

---
[97] 27 CFR 479.63

requires a permit or license for the possession of an NFA weapon before the applicant takes possession, a certified copy of the license or permit should be submitted with the Form 1 application.

Section 6.4 Approval of Form 1. Non-FFL/SOT's may seek approval to manufacture an NFA firearm (e.g., short-barreled rifles, short-barreled, shotguns, wallet guns, etc.) via submission of an ATF Form 1. Upon receipt of the completed Form 1, ATF will process the application and, if approved, a tax stamp will be affixed to the original of the form and the approved application will be returned to the applicant. Approval by ATF will effect registration of the firearm to the applicant. Upon receipt of the approved application, the applicant may make the firearm described on the approved Form 1. The approved form must be retained by the applicant and made available at all times for inspection by ATF officers or investigators. *Note: Under no circumstances may the firearm in question be made prior to receipt of the approved Form 1.*

The approval of the Form 1 application authorizes the applicant to make the firearm. The approval does not authorize the applicant to convey or ship the firearm to another person to manufacture the NFA firearm. If another person will manufacture the NFA firearm, the other person would be the maker and the application must be submitted by that person. Subsequent to the making, the firearm could then be transferred, subsequent to an approved Form 4 application, to the person who wanted the modification to be made.

If the applicant on the Form 1 lacks the skill, ability, and/or equipment to manufacture the NFA firearm, the applicant, after receipt of the approved Form 1, can have the firearm created or modified at a premises other than shown on the approved Form 1 as long as the creation or modification was done under the direct oversight of the applicant, thus having the applicant retain custody and control of the firearm. If the location is outside the applicant's State and the firearm being made is a short barreled rifle, short barreled shotgun, destructive device, or an unserviceable machinegun which is being reactivated, the applicant will also need to request permission to transport the firearm interstate as required by 27 CFR 478.28.

Section 6.5 Disapproval of Form 1. If the submitted application is disapproved, ATF will advise the applicant, provide a reason(s) for the disapproval, and return the making tax payment.

Section 6.6 Reactivation of a registered unserviceable NFA firearm. The Form 1 may be used to reactivate a properly registered unserviceable firearm, including registered unserviceable machineguns. Block 4(i) of the form should indicate that a registered unserviceable weapon is being reactivated. The remainder of the form should be prepared and submitted with the making tax in the same manner as described above except that a law enforcement certification is not required. The existing serial number on the unserviceable firearm should be used. If the reactivation will be performed by a Class 2 manufacturer, see Chapter 7 for additional information.

Section 6.7 Incorrect Description of Firearm. If the original registration document for the unserviceable firearm contains incorrect descriptive information for the weapon, a letter should be written to the NFA Branch providing the proper description and/or indicating what portions of the description need to be changed. The letter should contain photographs of the actual markings on the firearm. If a correction of the recorded serial number is needed, a photograph or pencil rubbing of the serial number is required. ATF will provide a response indicating that the NFRTR has been amended to reflect the correct information. This confirmation from ATF should be retained with the registration document for the firearm.

Section 6.8 Withdrawal or Cancellation of an ATF Form 1 and Refund of Making Tax. The Form 1 applicant may withdraw the application by submitting a request, in writing, to the Chief, NFA Branch. The applicant may also cancel an approved Form 1 application by submitting a request, in writing, to the Chief, NFA Branch. The request for cancellation must state that the firearm was not made and must include the approved Form 1 with the stamp affixed. The NFA Branch will amend the NFRTR to reflect the withdrawal or cancellation of the application and arrange for the refund of the making tax. A request for cancellation may only be done if the firearm has not already been manufactured. If the firearm is made, the tax liability is incurred and the applicant cannot seek a cancellation.

CHAPTER 7. MANUFACTURING NFA FIREARMS

Section 7.1 Qualifying to manufacture NFA firearms

7.1.1 Licensing under the GCA. Persons intending to engage in the business of manufacturing NFA firearms that also meet the definition of "firearm" in the GCA must first apply for and obtain a GCA manufacturer's license.[98] The license application is ATF Form 7 (5310.12).[99] Appendix C contains a copy of the form. Licenses are issued for a period of 3 years. See Section 5.1 for a discussion of the license fees, licensing standards, and other provisions of the GCA relating to licensing.

> **7.1.1.1 Engaging in business at multiple locations.** A separate license must be obtained for each location where business will be conducted.[100]
>
> **7.1.1.2 Engaging in business as both an importer and a manufacturer.** Persons intending to engage in business as firearms importers and manufacturers, even if the business will be conducted from the same premises, must have both an importer's license and a manufacturer's license.[101]
>
> **7.1.1.3 Do importers and manufacturers need a dealer's license to deal in the firearms they import or manufacture?** Licensed importers and manufacturers are not required to have a separate dealer's license to deal in firearms they import or manufacture.[102] A license as an importer or manufacturer authorizes the FFL to deal in the types of firearms authorized by the license to be imported or manufactured.
>
> **7.1.1.4 Manufacturers of destructive devices.** Manufacturers are reminded that if the firearms they manufacture include destructive devices, or if they solely manufacture destructive devices, they must apply for and obtain a license as a manufacturer of destructive devices. They should also note that the fee for such license is generally $1,000 per year, rather than $50 per year for a license to manufacture firearms other than destructive devices. A license is issued for a period of 3 years. Qualifying to manufacture destructive devices also entitles the FFL to manufacture and deal in firearms other than destructive devices.[103]

7.1.2 Payment of special (occupational) tax to do business in NFA firearms. Every person who engages in the business of manufacturing NFA firearms must pay a special tax.[104] The tax must be paid on or before the date of commencing the taxable business and every year thereafter on or before July 1. The tax is paid by filing ATF Form 5630.7, Special Tax Registration and Return, together with a check or money order for the amount of the tax.[105] Appendix C contains a copy of the form. The special tax

---

[98] 18 U.S.C. 923(a)
[99] 27 CFR 478.44(a)
[100] 27 CFR 478.50
[101] 27 CFR 478.41(b)
[102] ibid
[103] ibid
[104] 26 U.S.C 5801
[105] 27 CFR 479.34(a)

must be paid for each premises where business will be conducted.[106] See Section 5.2 for a more thorough discussion of NFA's requirements relating to the special tax.

7.1.3 Registration by firearms manufacturers with the U.S. Department of State. The State Department has the responsibility of enforcing the provisions of the Arms Export Control Act (AECA) relating to the export of firearms and other defense articles on the U.S. Munitions List. Nevertheless, any person engaged in the U.S. in the business of manufacturing or exporting firearms or other defense articles is required to register with the State Department's Directorate of Defense Trade Controls (DDTC).[107] The regulations expressly state that "Manufacturers who do not engage in exporting must nevertheless register." Form DSP-9 (Registration Statement) and a transmittal letter must be submitted to DDTC by the registrant with a check or money order payable to the State Department of one of the fees prescribed by State Department regulations.[108] Appendix C contains a copy of Form DSP-9. See Section 5.3 for a more detailed discussion of the registration requirement.

> **7.1.3.1 Registration exemption for fabricating articles for "research and development."** State Department regulations in 22 CFR 122.1(b)(4) exempt from the registration requirement persons who fabricate articles for experimental or scientific purpose, including research and development. The regulations do not define "experimental or scientific purpose" or "research and development." Consequently, manufacturers who believe they may be entitled to the exemption should contact DDTC to determine if they are entitled to the exemption.

Section 7.2 What is a "manufacturer"?; What is "manufacturing"?

7.2.1 "Manufacturer". As defined by the GCA, a "manufacturer" is any person engaged in the business of manufacturing firearms or ammunition for purposes of sale or distribution.[109] Similarly, NFA defines the term to mean any person "who is engaged in the business of manufacturing firearms", that is, firearms subject to the NFA.[110] To determine who is a "manufacturer" of firearms, we must look to see whether the person manufactures firearms as discussed in Section 7.2.2.

7.2.2 "Manufacturing". "Manufacturing" is not defined by the law, regulations, or any formal ATF ruling. Nevertheless, the term has been interpreted by ATF to cover activities other than producing a firearm from scratch. As interpreted by ATF, the term covers virtually any work performed on a firearm during the process of preparing the firearm for subsequent sale. For example, a person having a contract with a manufacturer to apply finishing or other work on firearms, or firearms frames or receivers, to prepare them for subsequent sale by the manufacturer would be a "manufacturer" required to qualify as such. Of course, if the person produced firearms parts other than frames or receivers for the manufacturer or performed work on firearms parts not defined as "firearms," the person would not be a "manufacturer."

---

[106] 27 CFR 479.31(b)
[107] 22 CFR 122.1
[108] 22 CFR 122.2(a)
[109] 18 U.S.C 921(a)(10)
[110] 26 U.S.C. 5845(m)

7.2.3 What is the difference between manufacturing and gunsmithing? Performing the work of a gunsmith requires a dealer's license under the GCA, not a manufacturer's license.[111] Nevertheless, a license as an importer or manufacturer also entitles the licensee to conduct business as a gunsmith. The term "dealer" under the GCA includes a gunsmith, that is, "any person engaged in the business of repairing firearms or fitting special barrels, stocks, or trigger mechanisms to firearms." However, gunsmiths occasionally perform the work of a manufacturer and do so without the required manufacturer's license. Indeed, there is no distinction between the activities of a gunsmith and a manufacturer in terms of the physical things done to a firearm. What distinguishes gunsmithing from manufacturing is the purpose for which the work is done. If a gunsmith performs work on a customer's personal gun for the customer's personal use, the function is lawfully performed pursuant to the gunsmith's license as a dealer under the GCA. However, if the gunsmith performs work on guns as a step in the process of preparing them for subsequent sale, the work is "manufacturing" requiring a manufacturer's license and, if the firearm is an NFA firearm, a special tax stamp under the NFA. Here are some examples:

> (1) John Doe has a personal firearm and takes it to a gunsmith, a licensed dealer, for modification. The work performed in this instance is the legitimate work of a gunsmith and may be performed pursuant to the gunsmith's dealer's license. The gunsmith need not be licensed as a manufacturer, or hold a special tax stamp in the case of an NFA firearm, to perform the work.

> (2) Company A is a licensed manufacturer, but contracts with other licensees to perform finishing work on NFA firearms it manufactures. One such contractor is a gunsmith, a licensed dealer. After receiving the finished firearms, Company A offers the firearms for sale. In this instance, the gunsmith, as well as Company A, is engaged in business as an NFA firearms manufacturer and needs a manufacturer's license and special tax stamp to do so.

7.2.4 Do you know how ATF would classify your product? There is no requirement in the law or regulations for a manufacturer to seek an ATF classification of its product prior to manufacture. Nevertheless, a firearms manufacturer is well advised to seek an ATF classification before going to the trouble and expense of producing it. Perhaps the manufacturer intends to produce a GCA firearm but not an NFA firearm. Submitting a prototype of the item to ATF's Firearms Technology Branch (FTB) for classification in advance of manufacture is a good business practice to avoid an unintended classification and violations of the law.

> **7.2.4.1 ATF classification letters.** ATF letter rulings classifying firearms may generally be relied upon by their recipients as the agency's official position concerning the status of the firearms under Federal firearms laws. Nevertheless, classifications are subject to change if later determined to be erroneous or impacted by subsequent changes in the law or regulations. To make sure their classifications are current, FFLs/SOTs should stay informed by periodically checking the information published on ATF's website, particularly amendments to the law or regulations, published ATF rulings, and "open letters" to industry members.

---
[111] 18 U.S.C. 921(a)(11)(B)

Section 7.3 Registering the manufacture of NFA firearms. A manufacturer qualified to engage in business under the GCA and NFA may make NFA firearms without payment of the making tax.[112] However, the manufacturer must report and register each firearm made by filing with the NFA Branch an accurate notice of the manufacture on ATF Form 2, Notice of Firearms Manufactured or Imported, executed under the penalties of perjury.[113] Appendix C contains a copy of Form 2. The NFA Branch's receipt of the form effectuates the registration of the firearms listed on the form.[114] See Section 7.4.6 on the manufacture of silencer parts.

7.3.1 Preparation of ATF Forms 2. The form and its contents are prescribed by ATF regulation.[115] The regulation states that the form must set forth the name and address of the manufacturer, identify the manufacturer's special tax stamp and license, and show the date of manufacture, the type, model, length of barrel, overall length, caliber, gauge or size, serial numbers and other marks of identification, and place where the firearms are kept.

7.3.2 Filing ATF Forms 2. All firearms manufactured during a single day must be included on one Form 2 and must be filed by the manufacturer no later than the close of the next business day. The manufacturer must prepare the form in duplicate, file the original with the NFA Branch, and keep the copy with the records required to be kept.

> **7.3.2.1 Existing firearms modified into NFA firearms or reactivated.** If an existing firearm is modified into an NFA firearm or reactivated, the existing serial number of the firearm must be entered into Block 8g on Form 2 and the name and address of the original manufacturer or importer must be entered into Block 8b. It is unlawful for any person knowingly to transport, ship, or receive in interstate or foreign commerce any firearm which has had the importer's or manufacturer's serial number removed, obliterated, or altered, or to receive or possess any such firearm that has at any time been shipped or transported in interstate or foreign commerce.[116]

7.3.3 Reactivation of a registered unserviceable NFA firearm. Although unserviceable NFA firearms are "firearms" required to be registered under the NFA, the reactivation of such firearm is considered to be the making or manufacture of an NFA firearm. Consequently, a qualified NFA manufacturer who reactivates an unserviceable firearm must file a Form 2 with ATF showing the reactivation.[117] The existing serial number on the unserviceable firearm should be used.

> **7.3.3.1 Incorrect description of firearm.** If the original registration document for the unserviceable firearm contains incorrect descriptive information for the weapon, a letter should be written to the NFA Branch providing the proper description and/or indicating what portions of the description need to be changed. The letter should contain photographs of the actual markings on the firearm. If a correction of the recorded serial number is needed, a photograph or pencil rubbing of the serial number is required. ATF will provide a response indicating that the

---

[112] 27 CFR 479.68
[113] 27 CFR 479.103
[114] ibid
[115] ibid
[116] 18 U.S.C. 922(k)
[117] See Instruction "c" on Form 2.

NFRTR has been amended to reflect the correct information. This confirmation from ATF should be retained with the registration document for the firearm.

7.3.3.2 Reactivation of a registered unserviceable NFA firearm. From time to time, a qualified manufacturer may receive a registered, unserviceable NFA firearm from a nonlicensee for reactivation. To lawfully do so, the firearm should be received pursuant to an approved ATF Form 5 for tax-exempt transfer (the transfer of a registered unserviceable firearm is not subject to the NFA transfer tax).[118] Upon reactivating the firearm, the manufacturer must file Form 2 with ATF to register the manufacture or reactivation. To return the firearm to its owner, the manufacturer must obtain an approved Form 4 from ATF to transfer the firearm.[119] Since the firearm is no longer unserviceable, the return of the firearm pursuant to an approved Form 4 would be subject to the $200 NFA transfer tax, except that the transfer tax for a firearm defined as "any other weapon" is $5. In these instances, Forms 4 need not contain law enforcement certifications.

Manufacturers may also receive unserviceable NFA firearms from FFLs/SOTs for reactivation. Receipt of the firearms must be pursuant to approved Form 3. Upon reactivation, the manufacturer must file Form 2 to register the manufacture or reactivation. Approved Forms 3 must also be used to return reactivated firearms to the FFLs/SOTs.

Section 7.4 The identification of firearms.

7.4.1 Serial numbers. Each manufacturer of a firearm must legibly identify it by engraving, stamping (impressing), or otherwise conspicuously placing on the firearm's frame or receiver an individual serial number not duplicating any serial number placed by the manufacturer on any other firearm.[120] The requirement that the marking be "conspicuously" placed on the firearm means that the marking must be wholly unobstructed from plain view. For firearms manufactured on or after January 30, 2002, the serial number must be to a minimum depth of .003 inch and in a print size no smaller than 1/16 inch.

7.4.1.1 What is an acceptable serial number? Alpha characters (letters), for example a name, are not acceptable as a serial number. A proper serial number may contain such characters or letters, but it must have at least one numeric character (number). ATF takes the view that marking "legibly" means using exclusively Roman letters (A, B, C, and so forth) and Arabic numerals (1, 2, 3, and so forth).[121] Deviations from this requirement have been found to seriously impair ATF's ability to trace firearms involved in crime.

7.4.2 Additional information. Certain additional information must also be conspicuously placed on the frame, receiver, or barrel of the firearm by engraving, casting, stamping (impressing), that is, they must be placed in such a manner that they are wholly unobstructed from plain view. For firearms manufactured on or after January 30, 2002, this information must be to a minimum depth of .003 inch. The additional information includes:

---

[118] 27 CFR 479.91
[119] 27 CFR 479.84
[120] 27 CFR 479.102
[121] ATF Ruling 2002-6

(1) The model, if such designation has been made;

(2) The caliber or gauge;

(3) The manufacturer's name (or recognized abbreviation); and

(4) The city and State (or recognized abbreviation) where the manufacturer maintains its place of business.[122]

7.4.3 Measuring the depth of markings. The depth of all markings is measured from the flat surface of the metal and not the peaks or ridges. The height of serial numbers is measured as the distance between the latitudinal ends of the character impression bottoms (bases).

7.4.4 Obtaining variances to the marking requirements. Requests for variances from the marking requirements of 27 CFR 478.92 and 27 CFR 479.102 should be submitted by letter to ATF's Firearms Technology Branch (FTB). The letter can be sent via mail to Chief, Firearms Technology Branch, 244 Needy Road, Martinsburg, WV 25405. The letter can also be sent to the marking variance e-mail address at: marking_variances@atf.gov. The marking variance request may be submitted by any of the parties involved in the variance. However, if the primary manufacturer is in possession of all the information including the names of the identity of the secondary manufacturers and the manufacturing processes they may be performing on the firearm, it is preferred that the primary manufacturer submit the request to FTB.

The marking variance letter of request should clearly state the following information:

- manufacturer, importer, or maker of the firearm(s),
- recipient of the firearm(s),
- identify the name, city and State that will be displayed on the firearm(s),
- model designation, if designated,
- identify the type/style of firearm (pistol, machinegun, short-barreled rifle, etc.),
- caliber or gauge if assigned, and
- serial number scheme.

In identifying the serial number scheme to be used, you must supply a different serial scheme for each model and you must state the exact beginning serial number of the serial scheme you wish to use. Although letters and characters may be used, the serial number must use at least one number it the scheme. Please note, using the letter X, or the use of characters (#, *, etc.) as digit/character holders is unacceptable. For example, an incorrectly submitted serial scheme would be ALZXXXX. A correctly submitted serial scheme would be ALZ0001. You do not need to provide an ending serial number when submitting your serial number scheme.

7.4.4.1 Variances in the name and location of the manufacturer. As stated above, the regulations require firearms to be marked with the manufacturer's name, city and State or recognized abbreviation of the information. FTB will only grant marking variances for

---

[122] 27 CFR 479.102

abbreviations regarding city and State names that are commonly recognized by the United States Postal Service. If you intend to use a name or abbreviation other than your licensed name or recognized abbreviation, you must contact the Federal Firearms Licensing Center and complete ATF Form 5300.38 to have your Federal Firearms License amended to reflect the addition of a trade name or a "doing business as" name to your license. You may not use a name or abbreviation until it is approved.

7.4.4.2 Variances for manufacturers' contractors. As pointed out in Section 7.2.2, some manufacturers contract with other entities to perform certain work on their firearms prior to their ultimate sale. In those instances the contractors are also "manufacturers" who must be licensed as a Type 07 Manufacturer or as a Type 10 Manufacturer of Destructive Devices in order to perform any manufacturing function on the firearm. Additionally, the regulations require that the secondary manufacturer mark the firearm with their identifying information to include name, city and State. A qualified, secondary manufacturer may request a variance to adopt the markings of the initial manufacturer. If a manufacturer is working with a secondary manufacturer, either the manufacturer or the secondary manufacturer can submit a letter of request to FTB for a marking variance.

You should be aware that marking variances for the manufacturer of machineguns is limited to the making of the receiver from one special (occupational) taxpayer manufacturer to another. The machinegun can be made on behalf of a manufacturer who intends on making the machineguns for stockpile for future sale to other dealers as sales samples, or for sale to law enforcement and the military. A machinegun cannot be transferred to a secondary manufacturer such as a bluer, Parkerizer, heat treater etc. In order to have a machinegun receiver blued, Parkerized or heat treated, etc., the possessor of the machinegun must transport the machinegun and remain in possession of the machinegun while it is being blued, Parkerized or heated treated by the secondary manufacturer.

7.4.4.3 Marking Destructive Devices. In the case of a destructive device, FTB may authorize an alternate means of identification upon receipt of a manufacturer's letter of request. The letter of request should indicate that the engraving, casting or stamping the weapons would be dangerous or impracticable[123] The variance would allow an alternate *method* of marking such devices. For example, ATF may permit the required markings to be placed on the device by paint or stencil. A variance in this format will contain the information that is proscribed by the regulations. For example, lot numbers of ammunition classified as destructive devices would be acceptable in lieu of the information required by the regulations.

7.4.4.4 Marking parts, other than frames or receivers, defined as NFA firearms. FTB may authorize alternate means of identifying such parts upon receipt of the manufacturer's letter application showing that such other identification is reasonable and will not hinder the effective administration of the regulations.[124] See Section 7.4.6 for information on marking silencer parts.

---

[123] ibid
[124] ibid

7.4.5 Marking frames or receivers that are not complete weapons at the time of disposition. Firearms frames or receivers that are not components of complete firearms at the time of disposition must be identified with all the required markings, that is, serial numbers and all the additional markings discussed in Sections 7.4.1 and 7.4.2.[124]

7.4.6 Marking silencer parts. Some FFLs/SOTs assemble silencers, for subsequent sale, from parts acquired from their contractors (*NOTE*: this activity is the "manufacture" of NFA firearms requiring the assembler and the contractor to qualify as manufacturers under the GCA and the NFA). Under these circumstances, ATF takes the position that contractors are not required to place identifying markings on silencer parts. They may, however, place an assembler's markings on these parts if the assembler so desires. It should also be noted that these contractors are not required to register the parts they produce by filing Forms 2, nor are they required to obtain approved Forms 3 to transfer the parts to assemblers.

Section 7.5 Manufacturing machineguns. Section 922(o), Title 18, U.S.C., makes it unlawful to possess or transfer a machinegun, except for transfers to or possession by Federal and State agencies or the transfer or possession of a machinegun lawfully possessed before the effective date of the statute, May 19, 1986. So, machineguns "lawfully possessed" before the effective date are those manufactured before May 19, 1986 and registered in the NFRTR. See also Section 7.6 on the manufacture of machineguns by contractors of FFLs/SOTs.

7.5.1 Manufacture of machineguns for sale to government agencies or as "sales samples". Notwithstanding the prohibition in Section 922(o), qualified manufacturers may manufacture machineguns on or after May 19, 1986 for sale to Federal and State agencies or to FFLs/SOTs as "sales samples" for demonstration to prospective governmental customers.[125] The weapons may be manufactured and stockpiled in contemplation of future sales, but their registration and subsequent transfer are conditioned upon and restricted to sales only to government agencies or as sales samples. See Chapter 9 for a discussion of the required documentation supporting these sales. See also Section 7.6.1 on the manufacture of machineguns by contractors of FFLs/SOTs.

7.5.2 Manufacture of machineguns for exportation. Notwithstanding the prohibition in Section 922(o), qualified manufacturers may manufacture machineguns on or after May 19, 1986 for exportation in compliance with the Arms Export Control Act and Department of State regulations.[126] The weapons may be manufactured and stockpiled for future exportation.

7.5.3 May machineguns be manufactured for distribution to U.S. Government contractors? As interpreted by ATF, Section 922(o) contains no exception that would permit the lawful manufacture and stockpiling of machineguns for transfer to Government contractors. The only exceptions to the machinegun transfer and possession prohibitions in the statute are for machineguns manufactured for sale to Federal and State agencies, for distribution and use as sales samples, or for exportation.

---

[125] ibid
[125] 27 CFR 479.105(c)
[126] ibid

7.5.4 May machinegun receivers be manufactured and used as replacement parts for machineguns lawfully registered and possessed prior to May 19, 1986? As previously stated, 18 U.S.C. 922(o) generally makes it unlawful to possess or transfer any machinegun, including a machinegun frame or receiver, manufactured after May 18, 1986. Exceptions are provided for weapons produced by a qualified manufacturer for sale to government entities, as dealer sales samples, or for exportation. There is no exception allowing for the lawful production, transfer, possession, or use of a post-May 18, 1986 machinegun receiver as a replacement receiver on a weapon produced prior to May 19, 1986.

Section 7.6 Manufacture of NFA firearms by contractors. Qualified manufacturers of NFA firearms may contract with other persons to manufacture their NFA firearms. However, contractors who manufacture NFA firearms, or perform work on existing firearms as part of the manufacturing process, must also be qualified to manufacture NFA firearms. They are also subject to all NFA requirements imposed on NFA manufacturers relative to the manufacture, registration, transfer, and marking of NFA firearms. See Section 7.4 on the marking of firearms by manufacturers and variances that may be obtained from marking requirements.

7.6.1 Contractors' manufacture of machineguns. As previously stated, machineguns manufactured in the U.S. on or after May 19, 1986 must be solely for sale to U.S. or State governmental entities, for distribution as "sales samples," or for exportation (see Sections 7.5.1 and 7.5.2). However, a qualified NFA manufacturer may contract with other qualified firms to produce machineguns it intends to distribute only for those purposes. Since the number of machineguns that may be transferred between licensees is limited by 27 CFR 479.105, the parties involved will need to seek an alternate method or procedure under 479.26. For example, manufacturer B contracts with manufacturer A to build B's machinegun receivers and applies for and receives a variance that allows A to identify the receivers with B's identifying marks. A is to provide the receivers for assembly and distribution. However, since A is manufacturing the machineguns and must register them on a Form 2, the transfer is limited due to the provisions of 922(o) and 479. 105. Both parties would need to apply for an alternate procedure or method that would allow A to transfer these machineguns to B.

7.6.2 Manufacture of machineguns solely for purposes of testing. The manufacture of machineguns solely for testing or research purposes is not recognized as a legitimate exception to the ban on possession or transfer of firearms under 18 U.S.C. 922(o). As previously stated, manufacturers may only manufacture machineguns on or after May 19, 1986 and stockpile the same if they are manufactured and held for sale to Federal or State agencies, for distribution as "sales samples," or for exportation.

Section 7.7 Manufacturing NFA firearms exclusively for the United States. A person or entity engaged in the business of manufacturing NFA firearms exclusively for the United States or any agency of the U.S. may be relieved from compliance with any provision of the NFA regulations, 27 CFR Part 479, with respect to such firearms.[127] This exemption may be obtained by filing with the NFA Branch a letter application setting out the manner in which the applicant conducts business, the type of firearm to be manufactured, and satisfactory proof of the existence of the manufacturer's Government contract

---

[127] 26 U.S.C. 5851(a)

under which the applicant intends to under which the applicant intends to operate.[128] Approval of the application entitles the applicant to the exemption. The manufacture of weapons for the U.S. *and* other customers (for example, manufacture for exportation to overseas customers) would not qualify for the exemption. The exemption must be renewed with another approved letter application on or before July 1 of each year.[129]

Section 7.8 Locations. Your licensed premises is where your manufacturing must be done. ATF is often asked by a manufacturer whether he or she can conduct a manufacturing operation elsewhere, such as a nearby machine shop. While, in general, component parts can be made at a site other than the licensed premises, if the part being made is a receiver, silencer part, or a procedure is being performed (such as shortening of the barrel of a rifle or shotgun) where the complete firearm is there, the operation must be done on the licensed manufacturing premises. If components are modified or fabricated at a location where all other parts for a complete firearm are present, the location must be licensed as a manufacturer.

---

[128] 27 CFR 479.33(b)
[129] 26 U.S.C 5851(b)

CHAPTER 8. IMPORTING NFA FIREARMS

Section 8.1 Qualifying to import NFA firearms

8.1.1 Licensing under the GCA. Persons intending to engage in the business of importing NFA firearms that also meet the definition of "firearm" in the GCA must first apply for and obtain a GCA importer's license.[130] The license application is ATF Form 7.[131] Appendix C contains a copy of the form. Licenses are issued for a period of 3 years. See Section 5.1 for a discussion of the license fees, licensing standards, and other provisions of the GCA related to licensing.

> **8.1.1.1 Engaging in business at multiple locations.** A separate license must be obtained for each location where business will be conducted.[132]
>
> **8.1.1.2 Engaging in business as both an importer and a manufacturer.** Persons intending to engage in business as firearms importers and manufacturers, even if the business will be conducted from the same premises, must have both an importer's license and a manufacturer's license.[133]
>
> **8.1.1.3 Do importers and manufacturers need a dealer's license to deal in the firearms they import or manufacture?** Licensed importers and manufacturers are not required to have a separate dealer's license to deal in firearms they import or manufacture. A license as an importer or manufacturer authorizes the FFL to deal in the types of firearms authorized by the license to be imported or manufactured.[134]
>
> **8.1.1.4 Importers of destructive devices.** Importers are reminded that if the firearms they import include destructive devices, or if they solely import destructive devices, they must apply for and obtain a license as an importer of destructive devices. They should also note that the fee for such license is $1,000 per year, rather than $50 per year for a license to import firearms other than destructive devices. Qualifying to import destructive devices also entitles the FFL to import and deal in firearms other than destructive devices.[135]

8.1.2 Payment of special (occupational) tax to do business in NFA firearms. Every person who engages in the business of importing NFA firearms must pay a special tax.[136] The tax must be paid on or before the date of commencing the taxable business and every year thereafter on or before July 1. The tax is paid by filing ATF Form 5630.7, Special Tax Registration and Return, together with a check or money order for the amount of the tax.[137] Appendix C contains a copy of the form. The special tax

---

[130] 18 U.S.C. 923(a)
[131] 27 CFR 478.44(a)
[132] 27 CFR 478.50
[133] 27 CFR 478.41(b)
[134] ibid
[135] ibid
[136] 26 U.S.C. 5801
[137] 27 CFR 479.34(a)

must be paid for each premises where business will be conducted.[138] See Section 5.2 for a more thorough discussion of NFA's requirements relative to the special tax.

8.1.3 Registration by importers of U.S. Munitions Import List articles with ATF. ATF has the responsibility of enforcing the provisions of the Arms Export Control Act (AECA) relating to the importation of firearms and other defense articles on the U.S. Munitions Import List. Any person engaged in the U.S. in the business of importing firearms or other defense articles is required to register with ATF. Form 4587, Application to Register as an Importer of U.S. Munitions Import List Articles, must be submitted to ATF by the registrant with a check or money order payable to the Bureau of Alcohol, Tobacco, Firearms and Explosives of one of the fees prescribed by 27 CFR 447.32. Appendix C contains a copy of Form 4587. See Section 5.4 for a more detailed discussion of the registration requirement.

Section 8.2 What is an "importer?"; What is "importation?"

8.2.1 "Importer." As defined by the GCA, an "importer" is any person engaged in the business of importing or bringing firearms or ammunition into the United States for purposes of sale or distribution."[139] Similarly, the NFA defines the term to mean any person "who is engaged in the business of importing firearms into the United States, that is, firearms subject to the NFA.[140]

8.2.2 "Importation." Importation is defined in the regulations as the bringing of a firearm within the limits of the United States or any territory under its control or jurisdiction, from a place outside thereof (whether such place be a foreign country or territory subject to the jurisdiction of the United States), with the intent to unlade.[141] However, bringing a firearm from a foreign country or a territory subject to the jurisdiction of the United States into a Foreign Trade Zone (FTZ) for storage pending shipment to a foreign country or subsequent importation into this country shall not be deemed importation.

Section 8.3 Importation of NFA firearms.

With certain exceptions, NFA firearms may only be imported for the use of the United States or any State or possession or political subdivision thereof such as a law enforcement agency; for scientific or research purposes; solely for testing or use as a model by a registered manufacturer; or solely for use as a sample by a registered importer or registered dealer.[142] Importers may not import NFA firearms for stockpiling or warehousing them at their licensed premises for the purpose of filling future orders from qualifying agencies or dealers requesting sales samples. Imported NFA firearms may be stored in a Customs Bonded Warehouse (CBW) or a Foreign Trade Zone (FTZ). NFA firearms may only be withdrawn from these facilities to fill specifically approved purchase requests.

8.3.1 Importation of machineguns. Section 922(o), Title 18, U.S.C., makes it unlawful to possess or transfer a machinegun, except for transfers to or possession by Federal and State agencies or the transfer or possession of a machinegun lawfully possessed before the effective date of the statute, May 19, 1986.

---

[138] 27 CFR 479.31(b)
[139] 18 U.S.C. 921(a)(9)
[140] 26 U.S.C. 5845(i)
[141] 27 CFR 479.11
[142] 26 U.S.C. 5844

So, machineguns "lawfully possessed" before the effective date are those manufactured before May 19, 1986 and registered in the NFRTR. Notwithstanding the prohibition in Section 922(o), licensed importers may import machineguns on or after May 19, 1986 for sale to Federal and State agencies or to FFLs/SOTs as "sales samples" for demonstration to prospective governmental customers. The weapons may be imported and stockpiled in CBWs or in FTZs in contemplation of future sales, but their registration and subsequent transfer are conditioned upon and restricted to sales only to government agencies or as "sales samples." See Chapter 9 for a discussion of the required documentation supporting these sales. Due to the restrictions in Section 922(o), machineguns may not be imported for other purposes, such as transfer to government defense contractors, security purposes, testing, research or use as a model by registered manufacturers.

8.3.2 Importation for use of the United States, qualifying political subdivisions, and law enforcement agencies. NFA firearms may be imported for sale to Federal, State, or local government agencies. To import NFA firearms for this purpose, an ATF Form 6, Application and Permit for Importation of Firearms, Ammunition and Implements of War, must be submitted to ATF in triplicate. Appendix C contains a copy of Form 6. The Form 6 must include the agency's letter or purchase order reflecting the purchase of the firearms.[143] Appendix E contains a sample letter for use by an agency ordering imported firearms.

8.3.3 Importation for use by Nuclear Regulatory Commission (NRC) licensees and authorized contractors. Congress recently amended the Atomic Energy Act of 1954 with passage of the Energy Policy Act of 2005.[144] Although the new provision does not amend the GCA or the NFA, it does allow for the possession of machineguns by NRC licensees and authorized contractors that provide security to these licensees at nuclear facilities. This new provision, 42 U.S.C. 2201a, is a departure from legal restrictions in Federal firearms laws that do not allow for machineguns to be imported for, transferred to, or possessed by non-government entities. The law states that before the new statute may take effect, the NRC must establish guidelines for implementation that are approved by the Attorney General. As of January 30, 2006, the guidelines have not been prepared or approved. Therefore, ATF does not yet have the authority to process import or transfer applications filed pursuant to 42 U.S.C. 2201a.

8.3.4 Importation for authorized scientific or research purposes. NFA firearms, except machineguns, may be imported for authorized scientific or research purposes. To import NFA firearms for this purpose, a Form 6 must be submitted in triplicate. The Form 6 must include a statement describing the specific scientific or research purpose for which the firearm is needed.[145] The statement must also include a detailed explanation of why the importation of the firearm is needed for scientific or research purposes

8.3.5 Importation for use as a model by a registered manufacturer. NFA firearms, except machineguns, may be imported for use as a model by a registered manufacturer. To import NFA firearms for this purpose, a Form 6 must be submitted in triplicate. The Form 6 must include a detailed explanation of why the importation of the firearm is needed for use as a model.[146]

---

[143] 27 CFR 479.111
[144] Public Law 109-58
[145] 27 CFR 478.112(b)(vii)(A)
[146] 27 CFR 479.111

8.3.6 Importation for use as a "sales sample." NFA firearms may be imported for use as sales samples by qualified NFA importers and dealers to demonstrate the firearms to government agencies and generate possible future sales to such agencies. To import NFA firearms for this purpose, a Form 6 must be submitted to ATF, in triplicate. Information must be submitted with the Form 6 establishing that the firearm is suitable or potentially suitable for an agency's use; the expected governmental customers requiring a demonstration of the firearm; information as to the availability of the firearm to fill subsequent orders; and letters from agencies expressing a need for a particular model or interest in seeing a demonstration of a particular firearm.[147] Appendix D contains sample letters for use in acquiring imported sales samples.

8.3.7 Importing multiple quantities of the same model firearm as sales samples. An application to import two or more NFA firearms of a particular model for use as a sales sample by the importer or a qualified dealer will be approved if documentation shows the necessity for demonstration to government agencies.[148] A Form 6 must be submitted to ATF, in triplicate, along with documentation that the firearm is needed by the importer or dealer to demonstrate the weapon to all of the officers of a police department, SWAT team, or special operations unit. ATF may authorize the importation of more than 2 of the same model if an importer provides specific documentation to justify the need for additional weapons.

8.3.8 Importation of NFA weapons classified as curios or relics. An NFA firearm may not be imported as a sales sample for demonstration to a law enforcement agency if it is a curio or relic unless it is established that it is particularly suitable for use as a law enforcement weapon.[149] Suitability for law enforcement use may be established by providing detailed information as to why the weapon is particularly suitable for such use, the expected customers who would require a demonstration of the weapon, and information as to the availability of such firearms to fill subsequent orders. To import NFA firearms classified as curios or relics, a Form 6 must be submitted to ATF, in triplicate, including a statement showing that the weapons meet the above discussed criteria.

8.3.9 Conditional importation. ATF may impose conditions upon any application to import firearms.[150] In most cases, a conditional import permit is issued for the purpose of examining and testing a firearm to determine whether the weapon in question will be authorized for importation. The conditions to the permit will normally authorize only one sample of a particular firearm and require that the firearm be shipped directly from Customs to FTB for testing and examination. The importer must agree to either export or destroy the weapon if a final determination is made that the weapon may not be imported. If the weapon is found to qualify for importation for one of the authorized purposes, the firearm will be returned to Customs for release to the importer.

8.3.10 Temporary importation of NFA firearms. ATF has adopted an alternate procedure for importers to use when temporarily importing NFA weapons for inspection, testing, calibration, repair, or incorporation into another defense article.[151] This procedure requires that importers:

---

[147] 27 CFR 479.105(d)
[148] ATF Ruling 2002-5
[149] ATF Ruling 85-2
[150] 27 CFR 479.113
[151] ATF Rul. 2004-2

1. Must be qualified under the GCA and NFA to import the type of firearms at issue.

2. Obtain a temporary import license, DSP-61, from the Department of State in accordance with the ITAR (22 CFR 122.3) or qualify for a temporary import license exemption pursuant to 22 CFR 123.4.

3. Within 15 days of the release of the firearms from Customs custody, file an ATF Form 2. The DSP-61 must be attached to the Form 2. If the importation is subject to a licensing exemption under 22 CFR 123.4, the importer must submit with the Form 2 a statement, under penalties of perjury, attesting to the exemption and stating that the weapon will be exported within four years of its importation.

4. Maintain the firearm(s) in a secure place and manner to ensure that the firearm(s) is not diverted to criminal or terrorist use.

5. Export the firearm(s) within four years of importation.

NFA weapons temporarily imported may be temporarily provided to a contractor in the United States for the purposes stated above by obtaining advance approval of an ATF Form 5, Application for Tax Exempt Transfer and Registration of Firearm. As an alternative, the transfer may be accomplished with a letter from the importer to the contractor, who must be qualified to engage in an NFA firearms business, stating the following:

1. The weapon is being temporarily conveyed for inspection, testing, calibration, repair, or incorporation into another defense article; and

2. The approximate time period the weapon will be in the contractor's possession.

The above alternate procedure became effective on April 7, 2004.

8.3.11 Re-importation of NFA firearms temporarily exported from the United States by nonlicensees. A properly registered NFA firearm that has been temporarily exported from the United States may be re-imported by the same person who temporarily exported the firearm. The firearm may be returned to the United States without submission of a Form 6 or Form 2, provided that ATF Form 5320.20, Application to Transport Interstate or to Temporarily Export Certain National Firearms Act Weapons, has been submitted to and approved by ATF prior to the temporary exportation of the firearm. The firearm must be registered to the person who is re-importing the weapon.[152]

8.3.12 What is the difference between a Customs Bonded Warehouse (CBW) and a Foreign Trade Zone (FTZ)?

8.3.12.1 Customs Bonded Warehouse. A Customs Bonded Warehouse is a building or other secured area in which dutiable goods may be stored without payment of duty. Bringing items into a CBW is an importation. To bring NFA firearms into a CBW for storage requires an

---

[152] 27 CFR 479.111(c)

approved ATF Form 6, Application and Permit for Importation of Firearms, Ammunition and Implements of War. NFA weapons stored in a CBW may be manipulated, destroyed or otherwise altered in the CBW. To withdraw stored NFA firearms stored from a CBW, an additional Form 6 is required. NFA weapons may only be withdrawn from a CBW for the purposes discussed in Section 8.3.

8.3.12.2 Foreign Trade Zone. A Foreign Trade Zone is a specially designated area, in or adjacent to a U.S. Customs Port of Entry, which is considered to be outside the Customs Territory of the United States. For the purposes of the GCA and NFA, bringing items into an FTZ is not treated as an import because the FTZ is considered foreign soil. However, under the import provisions of the AECA, an FTZ is considered to be part of the United States. As a result, a Form 6 is required by AECA regulations to bring NFA firearms into an FTZ. Firearms stored in an FTZ may be manipulated, repackaged, destroyed, otherwise altered or exported. Moving an NFA firearm from an FTZ to a CBW for storage or for delivery to a qualifying customer is an "importation" requiring an additional approved Form 6.

8.3.13 Preparation of ATF Forms 6. The form and its contents are prescribed by ATF regulations.[153] The importer must also establish to the satisfaction of ATF that the importation is for one of the purposes authorized by the statute. A detailed explanation of why the importation falls within the standards must be attached to the application. Acceptable documentation may include purchase orders from government agencies, a letter from a government agency requesting a demonstration of the firearm, or a letter from a dealer requesting an NFA weapon as a sales sample. Examples of the above letter requests can be found in Appendix D. The Form 6 must be submitted in triplicate.

8.3.14 "eForm6." eForm6 is the system used to electronically file the Form 6 and track the status of permit applications submitted for approval. In order to use the eFrom6 system a user ID and password must be obtained from ATF. To register for eForm6, a registration form, eForm6 Access Request (ATF E-form 5013.3),[154] must be submitted to the following address:

> Firearms & Explosives Imports Branch
> Bureau of Alcohol, Tobacco, Firearms and Explosives
> 244 Needy Road
> Martinsburg, West Virginia 25405

Additional information concerning eForm6 may also be found on the ATF website, www.atf.gov .

8.3.15 Preparation of ATF Forms 6A. This form and its contents are also prescribed by ATF regulations.[155] Upon release of the firearm(s) from Customs custody, the importer will prepare ATF Form 6A, in duplicate, and furnish the original to the Customs officer releasing the firearm(s). The Customs officer will, after certification, forward the Form 6A to the address specified on the form. Within 15 days of the date of release from Customs, the importer must forward to the address specified

---

[153] 27 CFR 478.112(b)
[154] See Appendix C
[155] 27 CFR 478.112(c)

on the form a copy of the Form 6A on which must be reported any error or discrepancy appearing on the Form 6A certified by Customs and serial numbers if not previously provided on Form 6A.

Section 8.4 Registering the importation of NFA firearms. The importer must report and register each firearm imported by filing with the NFA Branch an accurate notice of the importation on ATF Form 2, Notice of Firearms Manufactured or Imported, executed under the penalties of perjury.[156] Appendix C contains a copy of Form 2. ATF's receipt of the form effectuates the registration of the firearms listed on the form.[157]

8.4.1 Preparation of ATF Forms 2. The form and its contents are prescribed by ATF regulation.[158] The regulation states that the form must set forth the name and address of the importer, identify the importer's special tax stamp and license, import permit number, the date of release of the firearm from Customs custody, the type, model, length of barrel, overall length, caliber, gauge or size, serial numbers and other marks of identification, and place where the firearms are kept. The Form 2 should list only firearms imported on one specifically approved Form 6.

8.4.2 Filing ATF Forms 2. A Form 2 must be filed by the importer no later than 15 days from the date the firearm was released from Customs custody. If the importation involves more than one import permit, a separate Form 2 must be filed to report those firearms imported under each permit. The importer must prepare the form in duplicate, file the original with the NFA Branch, and keep the copy with the records required to be kept.

Section 8.5 The identification of firearms.

8.5.1 Serial numbers. Each importer of a firearm must legibly identify it by engraving, stamping (impressing), or otherwise conspicuously placing on the firearm's frame or receiver an individual serial number not duplicating any serial number placed by the importer on any other firearm.[159] An importer may adopt the serial number placed on the firearm by the foreign manufacturer provided that such serial number does not duplicate a number previously adopted or assigned by the importer to any other firearm. The requirement that the marking be "conspicuously" placed on the firearm means that the marking must be wholly unobstructed from plain view. For firearms imported on or after January 30, 2002, the serial number must be marked to a minimum depth of .003 inch and in a print size no smaller than 1/16 inch.

> **8.5.1.1 What is an acceptable serial number?** Alpha characters (letters), for example a name, are not acceptable as a serial number. A proper serial number may contain such characters or letters, but it must have at least one numeric character (number). ATF takes the view that marking "legibly" means using exclusively Roman letters (A, B, C, and so forth) and Arabic numerals (1, 2, 3, and so forth).[160] Deviations from this requirement have been found to seriously impair ATF's ability to trace firearms involved in crime.

---

[156] 27 CFR 479.112(a)
[157] 27 CFR 112(a)
[158] ibid
[159] 27 CFR 479.102
[160] ATF Ruling 2002-6

8.5.2 Additional information. Certain additional information must also be conspicuously placed on the frame, receiver, or barrel of the firearm by engraving, casting, stamping (impressing), that is, they must be placed in such a manner that they are wholly unobstructed from plain view. For firearms imported on or after January 30, 2002, this information must be marked to a minimum depth of .003 inch. The additional information includes:

(1) The model, if such designation has been made;

(2) The caliber or gauge;

(3) The name of the importer;

(4) The name of the foreign manufacturer;

(5) The country in which the firearm was manufactured;

(6) The city and State (or recognized abbreviation) where the importer maintains its place of business.[161]

8.5.3 Measuring the depth of markings. The depth of all markings is measured from the flat surface of the metal and not the peaks or ridges. The height of serial numbers is measured as the distance between the latitudinal ends of the character impression bottoms (bases).

8.5.4 Obtaining variances to the marking requirements. Requests for variances from the marking requirements should be submitted by letter to ATF's Firearms Technology Branch (FTB) in duplicate. The requests should state the proposed variance and the reasons for the variance.

8.5.4.1 Variances in the name and location of the importer. As stated above, the regulations require firearms to be marked with the importer's name, city, and State or a recognized abbreviation of the information. If other than complete names or recognized abbreviations are proposed to be used, a variance must be obtained from ATF.

8.5.4.2 Marking frames or receivers that are not complete weapons at the time of disposition. Firearms frames or receivers that are not components of complete firearms at the time of disposition must be identified with all the required markings, that is, serial numbers and all the additional markings discussed in Sections 8.5.1 and 8.5.2.[162]

8.5.4.3 Marking destructive devices. In the case of a destructive device, ATF may authorize alternate means of identification upon receipt of an importer's letter application, in duplicate. The application should show that engraving, casting, or stamping the weapons would be dangerous or impractical.[163]

---

[161] 27 CFR 479.102
[162] ibid
[163] ibid

8.5.4.4 Marking parts, other than frames or receivers, defined as NFA firearms. ATF may authorize alternate means of identifying such parts, for example, parts defined as mufflers or silencers, upon receipt of the importer's letter application, in duplicate, showing that such other identification is reasonable and will not hinder the effective administration of the regulations.[164]

8.5.5 When must markings be applied to imported NFA firearms? All of the markings discussed in this section must be applied to imported NFA firearms no later than 15 days from the date the firearms were released from Customs custody. If the required markings cannot be applied within the 15 day period due to the quantity of weapons being imported or other factors, ATF may grant a variance extending the time for application of the markings. A request for an extension of the time should be submitted in the same manner as discussed in Section 8.5.4.

---

[164] 27 CFE 479.102

CHAPTER 9. TRANSFERS OF NFA FIREARMS

Section 9.1 Definition of "transfer." The term "transfer" is broadly defined by the NFA to include "selling, assigning, pledging, leasing, loaning, giving away, or otherwise disposing of" an NFA firearm.[165] The lawful transfer of an NFA firearm generally requires the filing of an appropriate transfer form with ATF, payment of any transfer tax imposed, approval of the form by ATF, and registration of the firearm to the transferee in the NFRTR. Approval must be obtained before a transfer may be made. See Section 9.5 for a discussion of certain NFA transactions not considered by ATF to be "transfers."

Section 9.2 Only previously registered firearms may be lawfully transferred. ATF will not approve the transfer of an NFA firearm unless it has been registered to the transferor in the NFRTR. NFA firearms may only be registered upon their lawful making, manufacture, or importation, or upon the transfer of firearms already registered. Generally, unregistered firearms may not be lawfully received, possessed, or transferred. They are contraband subject to seizure and forfeiture. Violators are also subject to criminal prosecution. However, see Sections 2.4 and 3.3 on removing NFA firearms from the scope of the NFA because of their status as collectors' items, modification, or elimination of certain component parts.

Section 9.3 Interstate transfers of NFA firearms. ATF will not approve the transfer of an NFA firearm to a non-FFL/SOT residing in a State other than the State in which the transferor's licensed business is located or the transferor resides. Such interstate transfers would violate the GCA. However, See section 9.5.4 regarding the custody of firearms by employees of FFLs/SOTs.

Section 9.4 ATF forms for use in transferring NFA firearms

9.4.1 ATF Form 3. Transfers by FFLs/SOTs to other FFLs/SOTs require the filing of ATF Forms 3, Application for Tax Exempt Transfer and Registration of a Firearm, to register firearms to the transferees.[166] See also Section 3.2.6.4. Appendix C contains a copy of the form. In these transactions, transferors have no liability for the transfer tax. As previously stated, Forms 3 must be approved by ATF before transfers may be made.

9.4.2 ATF Form 4. Forms 4, Application for Tax Paid Transfer and Registration of a Firearm, are for use in transferring serviceable NFA firearms in the following instances: transfers by non-FFLs/SOTs to other such persons; transfers by non-FFLs/SOTs to FFLs/SOTs; and transfers by FFLs/SOTs to non-FFLs/SOTs.[167] Appendix C contains a copy of the form. See also Sections 3.2.6.1 through 3.2.6.3. These transfers are subject to the NFA transfer tax, so the forms must be accompanied by the appropriate tax payment. Forms 4 transferring firearms to individuals other than FFLs/SOTs must also be accompanied by transferees' fingerprints and photographs on FBI Forms FD-258. If the individual's receipt or possession of the firearm would violate Federal, State, or local law, the form would be disapproved. In addition, an individual transferee must have an appropriate law enforcement official execute the certification on the form.[168] See Section 9.8 for more information on law enforcement

---

[165] 26 U.S.C. 5845(j)
[166] 27 CFR 479.88(b)
[167] 27 CFR 479.84
[168] 27 CFR 479.85

certifications. Forms 4 must be approved by ATF before the transfers may be made. The completed Form 4, in duplicate, with fingerprint cards, photographs of the transferee, and payment of the applicable transfer tax should be mailed to:

National Firearms Act Branch
Bureau of Alcohol, Tobacco, Firearms and Explosives
P.O. Box 530298
Atlanta, GA 30353-0298

Payment of the transfer tax is to be in the form of a check or money order payable to the Bureau of Alcohol, Tobacco, Firearms and Explosives.

9.4.2.1 Copies of transferees' State or local licenses or permits. If State or local law requires the transferee to have a State or local license or permit to possess the firearm and the requirement is imposed upon the person prior to receipt, the Form 4 application should also be accompanied by a copy of the license or permit.

9.4.2.2 Transfers of NFA firearms to persons other than an individual or an FFL and special (occupational) taxpayer. Section 479.85 of the Code of Federal Regulations requires the ATF Form 4 or Form 5 application to properly identify the transferee. Although transfers to natural persons (individuals) must include a recent photograph, duplicate fingerprint cards, and a certification from law enforcement, the NFA also defines a person to include a partnership, company, association, trust, estate, or corporation. The requirements for fingerprints, photographs, and the law enforcement certificate specified in § 479.85 are not applicable for transferee who is not an individual.

When an ATF Form 4 or Form 5 application is submitted to transfer a firearm to a partnership, company, association, trust, estate, or corporation (collectively, an entity), the transferee entity must be identified on the Form 4 using the complete, formal name of the entity, along with the entity's street address, city, and state. The Form 4 or Form 5 must not include an individual's proper name, unless the proper name is a part of the entity's name (e.g., The Irrevocable Trust of John Doe, John Smith, Inc., etc.). ATF requires that the Form 4 or Form 5 include documentation evidencing the existence of the entity. This documentation would include, without limitation, partnership agreements, articles of incorporation, corporate registration, a complete copy of the declaration of trust, schedules or attachments referenced in the trust, etc. If the firearm being transferred is a machinegun, short barreled rifle, short barreled shotgun, or destructive device and the transfer is from an FFL, a person authorized to act on behalf of the entity must complete item 15 of the Form 4 and Form 5.

Please see section 9.12 for information regarding the NICS background check.

9.4.3 ATF Form 5. Transferors of NFA firearms to government entities, Federal, State, or local, must file ATF Forms 5, Application for Tax Exempt Transfer and Registration of a Firearm, to transfer the firearms to such entities.[169] *(Note: The applicant may wish to include details regarding the receiving*

---

[169] 27 CFR 479.90

agency if the agency is obscure. Note also that there are no transfers to task forces.) Although Forms 5 are generally required to be filed and approved for transfer of firearms to U.S. agencies, firearms owned or possessed by Federal agencies are not required to be registered. Appendix C contains a copy of the form. In these transactions, the transferor has no liability for the transfer tax. As previously stated, the form must be approved by ATF before the transfer may be made. As discussed in more detail below, Forms 5 are also used to transfer unserviceable firearms tax free, transfer firearms to FFLs for repair and for their return, and for distribution of estate firearms to lawful heirs.

Section 9.5 Conveyances of NFA firearms not treated as "transfers" under the NFA

9.5.1 Repair of firearms. ATF does not consider the temporary conveyance of an NFA firearm to an FFL for repair to be a "transfer" under the NFA. Thus, a transfer application is not required to convey the firearm for repair or to return the repaired firearm to its owner/possessor. Nevertheless, in order to avoid any appearance that a "transfer" has taken place, ATF recommends that a Form 5 application be submitted for approval prior to conveying the firearm for repair. It is also recommended that the FFL making repairs obtain an approved Form 5 to return a repaired firearm. If Forms 5 are not used to convey a firearm for repair or return the repaired firearm to the owner, the parties should maintain documentation showing that the conveyance was for purposes of repair, identifying the firearm, and showing the anticipated time for repair. Approved Forms 5, or the recommended documentation, will show that an unlawful "transfer" did not take place and that the FFL making the repairs is not in unlawful possession of the firearm. A non-FFL who proposes to transport a destructive device, machinegun, or short-barrel shotgun or rifle interstate to an FFL for repair should first obtain an approved ATF Form 5320.20 before transporting the firearm.[170]

    9.5.1.1 Repair of firearm silencers. ATF published FAQs on April 17, 2008, regarding the repair and replacement of silencers and silencer components. These FAQs are published on the ATF website and are included in Appendix B.

9.5.2 Possession of firearms by employees of FFLs/SOTs for employers' business purposes. No "transfer" under the NFA occurs when an FFL/SOT permits a bona fide employee to take custody of its registered NFA firearms for purposes within the employee's scope of employment and for the business purposes of the FFL/SOT. Therefore, no approved ATF transfer form is required when employees take custody of firearms under these circumstances. In addition, the interstate delivery of a firearm to the employee and the employee's receipt of the firearm would not violate the GCA.

9.5.3 Distribution of estate firearms. A decedent's registered NFA firearms may be conveyed tax-exempt to lawful heirs. These distributions are not treated as voluntary "transfers" under the NFA. Rather, they are considered to be involuntary "transfers by operation of law." Under this concept, ATF will honor State court decisions relative to the ownership and right to possess NFA firearms. So, when State courts authorize the distribution of estate firearms to decedents' lawful heirs, ATF will approve the distribution and registration to the heirs if the transactions are otherwise lawful. A lawful heir is anyone named in the decedent's will or, in the absence of a will, anyone entitled to inherit under the laws of the State in which the decedent last resided.

---

[170] 18 U.S.C. 922(a)(4); 27 CFR 478.28

9.5.3.1 Distributions to heirs. Although these distributions are not treated as "transfers" for purposes of the NFA, Form 5 must be filed by an executor or administrator to register a firearm to a lawful heir and the form must be approved by ATF prior to distribution to the heir. The form should be filed as soon as possible. However, ATF will allow a reasonable time to arrange for the transfer. This generally should be done before probate is closed. When a firearm is being transferred to an *individual* heir, his or her fingerprints on FBI Forms FD-258 must accompany the transfer application. The application will be denied if the heir's receipt or possession of the firearm would violate Federal, State, or local law. The law enforcement certification on the form need not be completed. The form should also be accompanied by documentation showing the executor's or administrator's authority to distribute the firearm as well as the heir's entitlement to the firearm. Distributions to heirs should not be made until Forms 5 are approved. Executors and administrators are not required to have estate firearms registered to them prior to distribution to lawful heirs.

9.5.3.2 Distributions to persons outside the estate. Distributions of NFA firearms by executors or administrators to persons outside the estate (not beneficiaries) are "transfers" under the NFA and require an ATF-approved transfer form. Transfers of serviceable firearms to other entities or persons require an approved Form 4. Form 4 applications must be accompanied by the applicable transfer tax, and, if the transferee is an individual, the transferee's fingerprints on FBI Forms FD-258. Applications will be denied if transferees' receipt or possession of the firearms would violate Federal, State, or local law. Also, Form 4 applications to transfer firearms to individuals must contain the law enforcement certification of an appropriate law enforcement official. See Section 9.8 for further information on these certifications. Form 4 applications to transfer firearms to non-FFLs residing outside the State in which the estate is being administered will be denied. Form 4 transfers should not be made until the transfers are approved.

9.5.3.3 Uncertainty about the registration status of decedents' firearms In some cases, an executor or administrator of an estate may be uncertain whether the decedent's firearms are registered to the decedent in the NFRTR. Perhaps the executor or administrator is unable to locate the decedent's registration documents. As discussed in Section 9.2, if the decedent's firearms are not registered to him/her in the NFRTR, the firearms are contraband and may not be lawfully possessed or transferred. If the executor or administrator cannot locate the decedent's registration documents, he/she should contact the NFA Branch in writing and inquire about the firearms' registration status. This inquiry should be accompanied by documents showing the executor's or administrator's authority under State law to represent the decedent and dispose of the decedent's firearms. Although ATF is generally prohibited from disclosing tax information, including the identity of persons to whom NFA firearms are registered, ATF may disclose such information to persons lawfully representing registrants of NFA firearms.

9.5.3.4 Unregistered estate firearms. Should an estate contain NFA firearms not registered to the decedent, these firearms are contraband that may not be lawfully possessed or transferred. Where these are found within an estate, the executor or administrator should contact his/her local ATF office and arrange for their disposal.

9.5.3.5 Distribution of decedents' "sales samples." If NFA firearms in a decedent's estate are "sales samples," that is, they were imported and distributed to the decedent as sales samples or were domestically manufactured machineguns distributed to the decedent as sales samples, the sale sample restriction continues in effect and lawful possession of the firearms requires that the firearms be held as "sales samples" for demonstration to government agencies.[171] Therefore, these firearms within an estate must be transferred to government agencies or FFLs/SOTs as sales samples for demonstration to such agencies.

Section 9.6 Manufacturers' use of contractors to perform work on firearms. As part of the manufacturing process to produce firearms for subsequent sale, some manufacturers contract with other persons to perform steps in the manufacturing process. As discussed in Chapter 7, these contractors are also manufacturers subject to licensing as firearms manufacturers and payment of NFA special tax. In addition, a manufacturer's transfer of an NFA firearm to such a contractor and the return of the firearm to the manufacturer are transfers required to be approved by ATF. These transfers require approved Forms 3.

Section 9.7 Transfers of unserviceable NFA firearms. "Unserviceable firearms" are firearms "incapable of discharging a shot by means of an explosive and incapable of being readily restored to a firing condition."[172] They are still "firearms" for purposes of the NFA and must be registered in the NFRTR to be lawfully possessed and transferred. However, their transfer is not subject to transfer tax.[173] To lawfully transfer unserviceable firearms, Form 5 transfer applications must be filed with ATF and approved. Appendix C contains a copy of the form. Form 5 applications to transfer the firearms to individuals must be accompanied by transferees' fingerprints and photographs on FBI Forms FD-258. Applications will be disapproved if receipt or possession of the firearms would place transferees in violation of Federal, State, or local law. In the case of transfers to individuals, the transferees must have an appropriate law enforcement official sign the law enforcement certification on the form. See Section 9.9 for further information on the law enforcement certification. A Form 5 transfer application will not be approved if the transferee is an individual residing outside the State in which the transferor resides; however, as previously discussed, there is an exception for FFLs' over-the-counter transfers of rifles and shotguns to non-residents if the laws of the transferors' and transferees' States are complied with. Transfers pursuant to Forms 5 may not be made until approved.

Section 9.8 U.S. Government-owned firearms. Conveyances of U.S. Government-owned NFA firearms to FFLs/SOTs for repair, modification, or performing other work such as incorporating the firearms into a weapons system require no approved ATF transfer or registration. The same is true for the return of the firearms to U.S. Government entities.

Section 9.9 Law enforcement certifications. These certifications on Forms 1 and 4 must be signed by an appropriate law enforcement official when the forms seek the transfer or making of an NFA firearm to or by an individual. However, as stated in Section 9.5.4.1, the certifications are not required when estate firearms are distributed to lawful heirs. As provided by regulations, the certificate must state that the certifying official is satisfied that the individual's fingerprints and photographs accompanying the

---

[171] 26 U.S.C. 5844(3)
[172] 26 U.S.C. 5845(h)
[173] 27 CFR 479.91

application are those of the applicant and that the official has no information indicating that the receipt or possession of the firearm would place the transferee in violation of State or local law or that the transferee will use the firearm for other than lawful purposes. Acceptable certifying officials include chiefs of police, county sheriffs, heads of State police, State or local district attorneys, or "such other persons whose certificates may in a particular case be acceptable to the Director."[174] Examples of other officials whose certifications have been found acceptable include State attorneys general and judges of State courts having authority to conduct jury trials in felony cases.

If another official is proposed as an acceptable certifying official, the transferor may, in advance of filing the transfer form, submit a written request to the NFA Branch whether the official is an acceptable certifying official. Alternatively, the transfer form may be filed with the official's certificate. If the certification is unacceptable, ATF would disapprove the form and return it to the proposed transferor.

9.9.1 Is a law enforcement officer required to sign the certification? In some jurisdictions, officers whose certifications on a transfer form would be acceptable will not sign the certifications for reasons of their own. These officials cannot be compelled to sign the certifications.

9.9.2 Is a law enforcement certification acceptable if signed by an official outside the jurisdiction where the transferee resides? No. The certification must be signed by an official having jurisdiction where the transferee resides.

Section 9.10 Transfers of imported NFA firearms

9.10.1 Firearms imported for government agencies. As discussed in Chapter 8, NFA firearms may be imported for sale to Federal, State, or local government agencies. For approval of these imports, the importer's Form 6 permit application must be accompanied by the agency's letter or purchase order reflecting the purchase of the firearms. Appendix D contains a sample letter for use by an agency ordering imported firearms. Transfer of the firearms to the purchasing agency requires an approved Form 5. If a qualified NFA dealer received the agency's order and placed it with the importer, the importer may transfer the firearms to the dealer on an approved Form 3 and the dealer, in turn, would use an approved Form 5 to transfer the firearms to the agency.

9.10.2 "Sales samples." As discussed in Chapter 8, NFA firearms may be imported for use as sales samples by qualified NFA importers and dealers to demonstrate the firearms to government agencies and generate possible future sales to such agencies. As provided by the regulations, a Form 6 application to import such sample will be approved if it is established by specific information attached to the application that the firearm is suitable or potentially suitable for an agency's use; the expected governmental customers requiring a demonstration of the firearm; information as to the availability of the firearm to fill subsequent orders; and letters from agencies expressing a need for a particular model or interest in seeing a demonstration of a particular firearm.[175] Appendix D contains sample letters for use in acquiring imported sales samples, including a qualified NFA dealer's letter ordering a sales sample from an importer and an agency's letter requesting a demonstration of a sales sample. An importer's transfer of a sales sample to a dealer requires an approved Form 3.

---

[174] 27 CFR 479.85
[175] 27 CFR 479.112(c) and (d)

9.10.3 Transferring multiple quantities of the same firearm model as "sales samples." As provided by the regulations, applications to import or transfer more than one firearm of a particular model for use as a sales sample by an importer or dealer must establish the importer's or dealer's need for the quantity of samples sought to be imported.[176] In the case of machineguns imported on or after May 19, 1986 (as well as machineguns domestically manufactured after that date), ATF Ruling 2002-5 holds that if an FFL needs to demonstrate a particular model of machinegun to an entire police department or SWAT team, ATF will approve the transfer of two machineguns of that model to the dealer as sales samples. Additional quantities will be allowed if an FFL can document the need for more than two machineguns of a particular model.

Section 9.11 Transfers of machineguns imported or manufactured on or after May 19, 1986

9.11.1 Machinegun prohibition in 18 U.S.C. 922(o). This statute makes it unlawful to transfer or possess a machinegun, except for transfers to or by, or possession by or under the authority of, the United States or a State, or machineguns lawfully possessed before May 19, 1986 (that is, machineguns in the U.S. and registered in the NFRTR). Regulations implementing the statute allow domestic manufacturers to lawfully manufacture and stockpile machineguns for future sale to Federal and State agencies, for distribution to FFLs/SOTs as sales samples for demonstration to such agencies, or for exportation.[177] The procedures discussed in Section 9.8 for transferring imported firearms to government agencies or to FFLs for use as sales samples apply as well to domestically manufactured machineguns.

9.11.2 May machineguns subject to section 922(o) be transferred to government contractors? The statute provides no exception for the lawful possession of these machineguns by government contractors for use in testing, research, design, or other work in fulfilling government contracts. One specific exception to this general rule appears in the Atomic Energy Act of 1954, 42 U.S.C. 2201a. This recently enacted provision allows for machinegun possession by security personnel engaged in the protection of Nuclear Regulatory Commission facilities or radioactive materials. Note also that although the NFA provides for the importation of NFA firearms for scientific or research purposes or for testing or use as a model by a registered manufacturer, the prohibition in Section 922(o) contains no exception that would permit the lawful possession of machineguns in the U.S. for those purposes; thus, applications to import machineguns for those purposes would be denied.

Section 9.12 Are FFLs/SOTs required to initiate a background check of the transferee under the Brady Law in connection with the transfer of an NFA firearm? No. Although 18 U.S.C. § 922(t) requires an FFL to complete a National Instant Criminal Background Checks System (NICS) check of the firearm recipient prior to completing the transfer, subsection 922(t)(3)(B) removes ATF-approved transfers of NFA firearms from the NICS requirement for individuals.

>**9.12.1 NFA Transfers to other than individuals.** Subsequent to the approval of an application requesting to transfer an NFA firearm to, or on behalf of, a partnership, company, association, trust, estate, or corporation, the authorized person picking up the firearm on behalf of, a

---

[176] Ibid. See also 27 CFR 479.105(d)
[177] 27 CFR 479.105(c)

partnership, company, association, trust, estate, or corporation from the FFL must complete the Form 4473 with his/her personal information and undergo a NICS check. See also, question P60 in the ATF FAQs.

9.12.2 NFA transfer with other GCA firearm. An application to transfer an NFA firearm that includes a firearm regulated by the GCA, (e.g., silencer with a pistol, wallet-holster with pistol, etc.), requires the completion of a Form 4473 and NICS check prior to transfer of the GCA firearm. This includes the transfer of a firearm where the suppressor is permanently attached to the firearm. The GCA firearm can only be transferred after the required NICS check is completed. The serial number of the GCA firearm and the permanently attached NFA firearm must be included on the ATF form 4473. FFL/SOT payers are also responsible for and adhering to all applicable State and local requirements for NFA transfers. If the FFL/SOT is awaiting ATF approval of the transfer application, the unattached GCA firearm can be transfer prior to the completion of the NFA transfer, however, an additional NICS check may be necessary if the transfer is to a non-individual.

Section 9.13 May an FFL/SOT transfer a personally owned destructive device without qualifying to do business in destructive devices? Persons engaged in the business of dealing in firearms must have a GCA license authorizing them to deal in the type of firearms in which they deal. If they engage in the business of dealing in destructive devices, they must have a license to do so as required by 18 U.S.C. 923(a)(3)(A). However, ATF recognizes that persons licensed to deal in firearms other than destructive devices may lawfully maintain a personal collection of destructive devices and *occasionally* dispose of them as personal firearms on Forms 4 without having a license to deal in such devices. But if the dealer's receipt and disposition of these devices become *repetitive*, ATF may infer that the dealer is engaged in the business of dealing in the devices and require him/her to be licensed as a dealer in such devices. There is no precise number of transactions that would trigger the license requirement.

Section 9.14 Transferable Status and the Form 10. Unregistered firearms obtained by State or local government agencies through abandonment or forfeiture are registered on an ATF Form 10. See 27 CFR § 479.104. Upon registration the Form 10 is marked "official use only," and subsequent transfer and registration is limited to the official use of other State or local government entities. The firearms may not enter ordinary commercial channels. NFA firearms which were registered on Form 10 but were transferred to an FFL or individual prior to the effective date of ATF Ruling 74-8 may continue to be possessed in commercial or private channels. If the firearm was still registered to the State or local entity on Form 10 at the time of the effective date of ATF Ruling 74-8, the firearm may only be transferred to another government entity for "official use only."

CHAPTER 10. COLLECTORS OF NFA FIREARMS

Section 10.1 Curios or relics

10.1.1 Definition of curio or relic. Curios or relics include firearms which are of special interest to collectors by reason of some quality other than is associated with firearms intended for sporting use or as offensive or defensive weapons.[178] To be recognized as curios or relics firearms must fall within one of the following categories:

- Firearms which were manufactured at least 50 years prior to the current date, but not including replicas thereof.

- Firearms which are certified by the curator of a municipal, State, or Federal museum which exhibits firearms to be curios or relics of museum interest.

- Any other firearms which derive a substantial part of their monetary value from the fact that they are novel, rare, bizarre, or because of their association with some historical figure, period or event. Proof of qualification of a particular firearm under this category may be established by evidence of present value and evidence that like firearms are not available except as collector's items, or that the value of like firearms available in ordinary commercial channels is substantially less.

10.1.2 Curio or relic classification. A formal ATF classification of a firearm as a curio or relic is not required by the law or regulations, however, such official determination is recommended. By obtaining a curio or relic classification, a firearm is officially recognized as a curio or relic and the weapon is added to the ATF Firearms Curios or Relics List.[179] Firearms classified as curios or relics are still firearms as defined. A curio or relic classification may be obtained by submitting a written request, in duplicate, to ATF's Firearms Technology Branch (FTB).[180] The request must be executed under the penalties of perjury, contain a complete and accurate description of the firearm and documentation showing that the firearm fits within one of the qualifying categories listed in Section 10.1.1. FTB may require submission of the firearm for examination and evaluation. If submission of the firearm is impractical, the person requesting the determination must advise FTB and designate the place where the firearm will be available for examination and evaluation.

In the case of firearms that are more than 50 years old, ATF has determined that a collector need not request a classification for such weapons.[181] Firearms 50 years or older automatically qualify as curios or relics.

A request for curio or relic determination should be submitted to:

---

[178] 27 CFR 478.11
[179] ATF P 5300.11
[180] 27 CFR 478.26
[181] FFL Newsletter, Vol. 1, Issue 2

Firearms Technology Branch
Bureau of Alcohol, Tobacco, Firearms and Explosives
244 Needy Road
Martinsburg, West Virginia 25405

10.1.3 NFA firearms classified as curios or relics. NFA firearms may be classified as curios or relics under the same requirements discussed in Section 10.1.1. NFA firearms classified as curios or relics are still subject to the provisions of the NFA.

10.1.4 The Firearms Curios or Relics List (ATF P 5300.11). This publication contains a listing of those firearms that have been officially classified as curios or relics. The list contains the following sections:

1. Ammunition classified as curios or relics prior to the 1986 amendments of the GCA.

2. Firearms classified as curios or relics subject to the provisions of the GCA.

3. Weapons removed from the NFA as collector's items which are determined to be curios or relics subject to the provisions of the GCA.

4. Weapons removed from the NFA as collector's items which are antiques not subject to the provisions of the GCA.

5. NFA weapons classified as curios or relics subject to the provisions of the GCA and NFA.

The most recent edition of the Curios or Relics List is available on the ATF website www.ATF.gov. Periodic updates to the list are also available on the website.

10.1.5 DEWATS. Deactivated War Trophy (DEWAT) firearms are still firearms under the NFA, but have been rendered unserviceable (i.e., incapable of discharging a shot by means of an explosive and incapable of being readily restored to a firing condition). The deactivation may have been accomplished by various means such as (but not limited to) welding of the chamber, cutting the barrel/chamber/breech, plugging the barrel, welding the bolt to the chamber, or some combination of these actions which rendered the firearm incapable of firing a shot.

Regardless of being unserviceable, the DEWAT firearm must be registered and approved for transfer as any other NFA firearm. The process to transfer a DEWAT is set forth in §479.90. Because the DEWAT is unserviceable, it is transferred tax-exempt as a curio or ornament on an ATF Form 5. The Form 5 must identify the transferee and transferor, FFL/SOT, any importer, type, model, caliber, overall length, gauge, size, serial number or other marks of identification. Additionally, the transferor must check the block in item 1 of the Form 5 indicating the unserviceable status of the firearm and answer item 4(i) confirming how the firearm has been rendered unserviceable.

10.1.5.1 Reactivation of DEWATS. Deactivated War Trophy (DEWAT) firearms may be returned to a serviceable condition. A DEWAT that has been returned to a serviceable condition (or reactivated) is often referred to as Reactivated War Trophy (REWAT). The act of returning a DEWAT to a serviceable condition is considered the "making" or "manufacturing" of a firearm by ATF. The procedures for reactivation by a non-FFL or FFL with other than a manufacturer's SOT status or with no SOT status on Form 1 are found in section 6.6 of the handbook. The procedures for reactivation by an FFL with SOT status as a manufacturer are found in section 7.3.3 of the handbook.

Curio or Relic status: When the DEWAT firearm being reactivated is a curio and relic (C&R), the C&R status is retained. Please see 27 CFR 478.11 for the definition of curios and relics.

Section 10.2 Licensed collector

10.2.1 Collector of curios or relics license. There is no requirement to have a Federal license for the purpose of collecting firearms. However, the GCA has a license category for collectors of curios or relics.[182] The collector of curios or relics license serves one purpose - it enables the holder to receive curio or relic firearms interstate under the GCA. A collector's license does not authorize the holder to engage in the business of dealing in firearms. If a collector wants to deal in curio or relic firearms, a dealer's license must be obtained. In the case of dealing in NFA curio or relic firearms, the SOT must also be paid. Further, with respect to firearms other than curios or relics, a licensed collector is in the same position as a nonlicensee. That is, the licensed collector may not lawfully receive them in interstate commerce.

10.2.2 Receipt of NFA curios or relics by a licensed collector. A licensed collector may receive an NFA curio or relic firearm directly from any person in any State. Such receipt requires an approved Form 4 (or in the case of an unserviceable firearm, an approved Form 5) with law enforcement certification and fingerprint cards. If the NFA curio or relic firearm being transferred is not specifically listed on the Curios or Relics List, the applicant or transferee should submit documentation that the firearm in question has been classified as a curio or relic. Including this information can reduce delays in processing a transfer application.

10.2.3 Transfer of NFA curios or relics by a licensed collector. A licensed collector may transfer an NFA curio or relic firearm in interstate commerce only to a licensed collector, licensed dealer, licensed importer or licensed manufacturer. Such transfer requires an approved Form 4 (or in the case of an unserviceable firearm, an approved Form 5). If the transferee is not an SOT, the law enforcement certification and fingerprint cards are also required. A licensed collector may transfer an NFA curio or relic firearm directly to a nonlicensee who resides in the same State as the licensed collector. A transfer of this type requires an approved Form 4 or Form 5, a law enforcement certification, and fingerprint cards.

---

[182] 18 U.S.C. 923(b)

Section 10.3 Recordkeeping requirements

10.3.1 Acquisition and disposition records. Licensed collectors must maintain a record of the acquisition and disposition of curio or relic firearms.[183] The regulations specify the format and information required to be maintained. Only firearms classified as curios or relics should be listed in the required records. A licensed collector is not required to execute a Form 4473, Firearms Transaction Record, or initiate a NICS background check when disposing of a curio or relic firearm.

10.3.2 Termination of a collector's license. A licensed collector who decides not to renew a collector's license is not required to surrender the acquisition and disposition records for curio or relic firearms to ATF.

---

[183] 27 CFR 478.125(f)

CHAPTER 11. EXPORTATION OF NFA FIREARMS

Section 11.1 Arms Export Control Act (AECA), 22 U.S.C. 2778. The AECA regulates the exportation of "defense articles," including firearms and firearm parts. Authority to administer and enforce the exportation provisions of the AECA rests with the U.S. State Department. The articles subject to AECA control are listed under various categories in the State Department's U.S. Munitions List contained in the regulations in 22 CFR 121.1. Firearms and component parts of firearms are listed under Categories I and II.

11.1.1 State Department regulations implementing the AECA. State Department's regulations implementing the AECA are known as the International Traffic in Arms Regulations (ITAR) (22 CFR Parts 120-130). The regulations can be found on the internet by querying "U.S. State Department" and then "Directorate of Defense Trade Controls." A hardcopy of the regulations is published annually and includes all amendments made to the ITAR from April 1 through March 31 of each year. The hardcopy can be obtained from the Government Printing Office.

11.1.2 Firearms and firearm component parts subject to the AECA. As stated in Section 11.1, firearms and component parts of firearms are included in Categories I and II of the U.S. Munitions List.

11.1.2.1 Category I. Category I covers nonautomatic and semi-automatic firearms to caliber .50 inclusive (12.7 mm), as well as fully automatic firearms to .50 caliber inclusive. This category also covers silencers, mufflers, sound and flash suppressors, and rifle scopes manufactured to military specifications. Excluded from Category I are non-combat shotguns with barrel lengths of 18 inches or longer. In other words, sporting shotguns not subject to the NFA are not defense articles subject to State Department export controls. Category I also covers components, parts, accessories and attachments for firearms. However, it excludes rifle scopes and sighting devices not manufactured to military specifications, as well as accessories and attachments (for example, belts, slings, after market rubber grips, cleaning kits) for firearms that do not enhance the usefulness, effectiveness, or capabilities of the firearm, components, and parts. The Department of Commerce regulates the export of firearms and parts not covered by Category I. Therefore, see the Commerce's regulations in 15 CFR Parts 730-799 for export controls over those items.

11.1.2.2 Category II. This category covers guns over caliber .50, as well as all other components, parts, accessories, attachments and associated equipment specifically designed or modified for such guns.

Section 11.2 Registration of exporters and manufacturers under the AECA. As required by regulations in 22 CFR 122.1(a), any person engaged in the United States in the business of manufacturing or exporting defense articles on the U.S. Munitions List is required to register with State Department's Directorate of Defense Trade Controls (DDTC). Persons engaged in the business of manufacturing firearms and other defense articles must register even if they do not export such items. Certain exceptions to the registration requirement are listed in Section 122.1(b).

11.2.1 Submission of registration form, DSP-9. As provided by 22 CFR 122.2, Department of State Form DSP-9 must be submitted by the registrant with a check or money order payable to the Department of State of one of the fees prescribed in section 122.3(a).

11.2.2 Transmittal letter must accompany Form DSP-9. Form DSP-9 must be accompanied by a transmittal letter signed by a senior officer, as well as documentation showing that the registrant is incorporated or otherwise authorized to do business in the United States. The letter must contain the statements required by section 122.2(b). In summary, the letter must state whether any senior officer or member of the board of directors:

(1) Has ever been indicted or convicted of violating any criminal statute enumerated in 22 CFR 120.27;

(2) Is ineligible to contract with, or to receive a license or other approval to import defense articles from, or receive an export license or other approval from, any U.S. agency; and

(3) Whether the registrant is owned or controlled by foreign persons (as defined in 22 CFR 120.16). If the registrant is owned or controlled by foreign persons, the letter must also state whether the registrant is incorporated or otherwise authorized to engage in business in the United States. See Section 122.2(c) for definitions of "ownership" and "control."

11.2.3 Notification of changes in information furnished by registrants. See 22 CFR 122.4 for the requirement to report changes to DDTC in the information provided in registering with the State Department on Form DSP-9.

Section 11.3 License requirement for permanent export of a defense article. Any person or entity intending to permanently export a defense article must obtain approval of DDTC prior to the export. Approval must be obtained by filing with DDTC Form DSP-5. For more detailed information, see State Department regulations in 22 CFR 123.1.

Section 11.4 License requirement for temporary export of a defense article. Any person or entity intending to temporarily export a defense article must obtain approval of DDTC prior to the export. Approval must be obtained by filing with Form DSP-73. No ATF approval is required for a temporary exportation. For more detailed information, see State Department regulations in 22 CFR 123.5.

Section 11.5 Prohibited exports and sales to certain countries. It is the policy of the United States to deny licenses to export defense articles destined for certain countries. Therefore, the State Department will deny applications for licenses to export such articles, including firearms, to those countries. A list of these countries can be found in State Department's regulations in 22 CFR 126.1, for example, Cuba, Iran, Libya, North Korea, and Vietnam. This policy also applies to countries with respect to which the United States maintains an arms embargo, for example, Burma, China, and Liberia.

Section 11.6 ATF requirements relative to the exportation of firearms. Any person or entity desiring to permanently export an NFA firearm without payment of the transfer tax must file with ATF an application for a permit to export the firearm on ATF Form 9. Shipment may not be made until the permit is received. ATF will not act on the application unless it contains the information required by the regulations in 27 CFR 479.114. See ATF's regulations in 27 CFR 479.114 – 479.121 for detailed information on ATF's exportation requirements.

11.6.1 Applying for an export permit on ATF Form 9. Any person desiring to export an NFA firearm without paying the transfer tax must file with ATF a permit application to export the firearm on Form 9. Appendix C contains a copy of Form 9. The application requires submission of the following information:

(1) Name and address of the foreign consignee;

(2) Number of firearms covered by the application;

(3) The intended port of exportation;

(4) A complete description of each firearm to be exported (an attached list of serial numbers/descriptions may be used);

(5) The name, address, State Department export license number (or date of application if not issued), and identification of the special (occupational) tax stamp of the transferor; and

(6) The application must be supported by a certified copy of a written order or contract of sale or other evidence showing that the firearm is to be shipped to a foreign destination. However, a copy of a State Department export license on DSP-5 is acceptable in lieu of such certification.

11.6.2 Transfers to another person for export. Where is desired to make a transfer free of tax to another person who in turn will export the firearm, the transferor must likewise file an application on Form 9 supported by evidence that the transfer will start the firearm in the course of exportation. However, where both the transferor and exporter are FFLs/SOTs, the transferor is not required to file a Form 9 application.

11.6.3 Proof of exportation. Within a six-month period from the date of issuance of the permit on Form 9, the exporter must provide ATF with the evidence of exportation specified by the regulations in 27 CFR 479.118. Where such evidence is not furnished, the exporter will be assessed the transfer tax on the firearm.

CHAPTER 12. RECORDKEEPING

Section 12.1 Maintaining proof of registration. The NFA requires that a person possessing a firearm registered in the National Firearms Registration and Transfer Record (NFRTR) retain proof of registration which must be made available to the Attorney General, specifically an ATF agent or investigator, upon request.[184] Proof of registration would be on a Form 1 registering a firearm to its maker, Form 2 registering a firearm to an importer or manufacturer, or a Form 3, 4, or 5 showing registration of a firearm to a transferee.

12.1.1 Manner in which registration documents must be kept. NFA regulations require FFLs/SOTs maintain their registration documents in chronological order at their place of business.[185]

12.1.2 Recordkeeping where registered firearms are kept on premises other than the registered owner's place of business. If the registered firearms are kept at a location other than the place of business shown on the registrant's special tax stamp, the forms showing the firearm's registration must be annotated to reflect the place where the firearms are kept or stored. ATF has advised in the past that documents (such as a statement, file card, or office form indicating the current location) may be kept with the registration records to show such off-premises location. In addition, an FFL/SOT's notation in the A & D Records disposition line is also acceptable to show such location if a notice is kept with the registration document stating "See bound book for storage location." ATF will clarify this policy in the near future.

Section 12.2 Verifying the description of firearms on registration documents. It is important to verify that the information on a registration document accurately describes the registered firearm. Where firearms were registered prior to the amended NFA in 1968 or during the 1968 amnesty period, it was not uncommon for these firearms to have been inaccurately described on the registration forms. Owners of registered firearms should carefully compare each field in the "Description of Firearm" section on the registration document with their firearm. Of particular importance are the fields recording the type of firearm, model, and serial number. Concerning the serial number, it is important to ensure that digits in the number have not been transposed, or, if the serial number contains letters as a prefix or suffix, that those letters are properly shown as part of the number.

Section 12.3 Correcting an error in the description of a registered firearm. If errors are found in the description of a firearm in the owner's registration document, the owner should write a letter to the Chief, NFA Branch and request the registration record for the firearm be corrected. The letter should describe the problem and provide the correct information. If the error being reported involves an incorrect serial number, ATF will require that close-up photographs or a pencil rubbing of the actual serial number be provided. A copy of the registration document should also be included with the letter request. Persons requesting a correction to the description of their registered firearm should also retain a copy of the letter request with their registration document until ATF responds with an acknowledgement that the registration record has been corrected.

---

[184] 26 U.S.C. 5841(e)
[185] 27 CFR 479.131

Section 12.4 Custody of NFA firearms by employees of FFLs/SOTs. It is common for employees of FFLs/SOTs to take firearms registered to the FFLs/SOTs off-premises for display, demonstration, or other purposes on behalf of their registered owners. This does not result in the "transfer" of NFA firearms requiring ATF approval and registration of the firearms to the employees as long as the firearms are possessed for the employer's business purposes and not for employee's personal use. Similarly, employees taking custody of firearms under these circumstances would not constitute a "firearms disposition" that is required to be recorded in FFL/SOT's acquisition and disposition records (A & D Records). Although not legally required, FFLs/SOTs and their employees should consider taking the following actions as a matter of good business practice:

(1) Keep a copy of the NFA registration document with each registered firearm.

(2) If the firearm is located in an area having State or local registration requirements, keep a copy of the State/local registration document with the firearm.

(3) Where the firearm is taken off-premises for display, demonstration, or other purposes on behalf of the registered owner, keep a copy of the NFA and State/local registration documents with the firearm.

(4) Provide an employee having custody of the registered owner's firearm away from the licensed premises with a letter authorizing the employee to possess the firearm on the employer's behalf.

These actions would help convince law enforcement authorities who encounter the firearm that the FFL/SOT's employee is in lawful possession of the firearm and that the firearm is not unlawfully possessed and subject to seizure.

12.4.1 Who is an "employee" of an FFL/SOT? For purposes of this section, an "employee" is a bona fide employee of an FFL/SOT on the FFL/SOT's payroll. An "employee" is not a mere agent of the FFL/SOT appointed temporarily to take possession of the registered owner's firearm for a particular mission. If an agent of an FFL/SOT, rather than a bona fide employee, takes possession of the FFL/SOT's registered firearm, a "transfer" occurs subject to registration, tax, and other provisions of the NFA.

Section 12.5 Firearms acquisition and disposition records. NFA regulations require each manufacturer, importer, and dealer in NFA firearms to maintain the records of the acquisition and disposition of firearms required by GCA regulations in 27 CFR Part 478, Subpart H.[186] The regulations identify specific formats and required information fields for recording and maintaining these records. The records must be maintained on the FFL/SOT's licensed premises.[187]

12.5.1 Commercial records of firearms received. When a commercial record is held by a licensed dealer or collector showing the acquisition of a firearm or curio or relic, and the record contains all acquisition information required to be recorded in the licensee's A & D Records, the licensee may, for a period not exceeding 7 days following the date of receipt, delay making the required entry in the A & D

---

[186] 27 CFR 479.131
[187] 27 CFR 478.121(a)

Records if the commercial record is (1) maintained separate from other commercial documents, and (2) is readily available for inspection on the licensed premises. When disposition is made of the firearm not entered into the A & D Records, the licensee must enter all required information in the A & D Records at the time of the transfer.[188]

12.5.2 Alternate acquisition and disposition records for low volume dealers. This is a little used but available alternative for low-volume firearms dealers to maintain records of the acquisition and disposition of firearms. In lieu of the A&D records discussed in Section 12.5, a licensed dealer contemplating the disposition of not more than 50 firearms within a succeeding 12-month period, whether to other FFLs or to nonlicensees, may maintain a record of the acquisition and disposition of firearms on firearms transaction records, Forms 4473(LV).[189] A dealer maintaining records on these forms, whose firearms dispositions exceed 50 firearms within the 12-month period, must make and maintain the prescribed A&D Records for each firearm exceeding 50. See the regulations in 27 CFR 478.124a for details on maintaining records on Forms 4473(LV).

12.5.2 Variances in the recordkeeping requirements for the acquisition and disposition of firearms. ATF may authorize an FFL to maintain alternate records of the acquisition and disposition of firearms if such records would accurately and readily disclose the required information.[190] To use an alternate method of recordkeeping, an FFL must submit a letter application, in duplicate, to the appropriate Director of Industry Operations (DIO) and describe the proposed alternate records. Alternate records may not be employed by the FFL until approval is received from ATF. With the exception of computerized recordkeeping variance requests presented by FFLs located within one ATF Field Division, DIOs may be required to forward variance requests to the ATF Firearms Programs Division for review and approval.

> **12.5.2.1 Computerized records.** In lieu of the hard-copy, A & D Records required by the regulations, the DIO may authorize FFLs to maintain computerized records of their firearms acquisitions and dispositions records. DIOs will approve the use of a computerized recordkeeping system if:
>
> (1) The system meets the regulatory requirements for recording the information in 27 CFR 478.122, 27 CFR 478.123, and/or 27 CFR 478.125.
>
> (2) The system allows queries by serial number, acquisition date, and name of the manufacturer. Commonly recognized trade names may be used when denoting the manufacturer or importer.
>
> (3) The system has an acceptable daily backup for all databases.
>
> (4) The system must provide periodic printouts of all records at least semiannually, upon request of an ATF officer, when the database is purged, and when the license is

---

[188] 27 CFR 478.125(g)
[189] 27 CFR 478.124a
[190] 27 CFR 478.125(h)

terminated. The printouts must be limited to the information required by 27 CFR 478.122, 27 CFR 478.123, and/or 27 CFR 478.125 only. The printouts must be retained until the next required printout is prepared

(5) The computer printouts contain firearms in inventory, as well as all firearms transferred during the period covered, sequentially by date of acquisition.

(6) The system must record both the manufacturer and the importer of foreign made firearms.

(7) (7) Printouts may include antique firearms, but cannot include other non-firearm merchandise. However, firearms not subject to GCA requirements must be identified as "ANT" in the "firearm type" column.

(8) The name and address (if nonlicensee) or the name and FFL number (if licensee) of both the supplier/consignor and the purchaser/transferee must be included in the computer data. The name and ATF Form transaction number may be used in lieu of the address for recording the transfer of a firearm to a nonlicensee if the Forms 4473 are filed numerically.

(9) The system cannot rely upon invoices or other paper/manual systems to provide any of the required information.

(10) Any changes in an approved system must be reported to the DIO in writing with a copy of the original variance approval attached, for evaluation and consideration prior to implementation.

(11) All acquisition and disposition records must remain at the licensed premises.

Section 12.6 Forms 4473. A licensed firearms importer, manufacturer, or dealer may not sell or dispose of a firearm to a nonlicensee unless the transaction is recorded on ATF Form 4473.[191] See Section 12.6.2 for firearms transfers occurring as a result of the return of a repaired or replacement firearm.

12.6.1 Firearms acquired from an FFL by an organization. An FFL who sells or otherwise disposes of a firearm to a nonlicensee who is other an individual, that is, a corporation, partnership, or association, must obtain a Form 4473 from the individual acquiring the firearm on behalf of the organization.[192] The individual must attach a written statement to the form, executed under the penalties of perjury, stating that the firearm is being acquired for the use of his/her organization and the name and address of the organization. The FFL must also initiate a background check of the individual under the Brady Law.[193]

---

[191] 27 CFR 478.124(a)
[192] 27 CFR 478.124(g)
[193] Q&A P60, ATF Pub. 5300.4, Sept. 2005, p. 195

12.6.2 Return of firearms delivered to an FFL for repair or customizing. A Form 4473 is not required to record the disposition of a firearm delivered to an FFL for the sole purpose of repair or customizing when the firearm or a replacement firearm is returned to the person from whom it was received.[194] See Section 9.5.1 suggesting the use of Forms 5 to document the delivery of a firearm to an FFL for repair (or customizing) and the return of the firearm. The use of an ATF-approved Form 5 for these transactions is beneficial to the registered owner of the firearm and to the FFL having the firearm for repair or customizing. If the registered owner is inspected by ATF while the gun is away for repair or customizing, an ATF-approved Form 5 will satisfy the inspector that the absence of the gun from inventory is lawful and not due to a loss or unlawful transfer. If the FFL having the gun for repair or customizing has an approved Form 5 for receipt of the gun, the FFL can establish to an ATF inspector's satisfaction that the gun is lawfully possessed.

12.6.3 Maintaining Forms 4473. FFLs must retain in alphabetical (by name of purchaser), chronological (by date of disposition), or numerical (by transaction serial number) order, each Form 4473 obtained in the course of transferring firearms.[195] Forms 4473 obtained whereby the sale, delivery or transfer of the firearm did not take place must be separately retained in similar alphabetical, numerical, or chronological fashion.[196]

Section 12.7 Record retention period. The regulations provided under the NFA, specifically 27 CFR 479.131, provide that the retention periods for required records shall be in conformity with the requirements specified under Part 478. As provided by Part 478:

(1) Records of firearms transactions maintained by licensed importers and licensed manufacturers must maintain permanent records of the importation, manufacture, or other acquisition of firearms.[197]

(2) Licensed importer's and manufacturer's records of sales or other disposition of firearms over the age of 20 years may be discarded.[198]

(3) The A & D Records prepared by licensed dealers and licensed collectors over 20 years of age may be discarded.

(4) All FFLs shall retain each Form 4473 and 4473(LV) for a period not less than 20 years from the date of sale or disposition of the firearms. Forms 4473 obtained by FFLs where the NICS check was initiated, but the sale, delivery, or transfer of the firearm was not completed must be retained for a period of not less than 5 years.[199]

---

[194] 27 CFR 478.124(a)
[195] 27 CFR 478.124(b)
[196] 27 CFR 478.129(b)
[197] 27 CFR 478.129(d)
[198] 27 CFR 478.129(a); 478.129(d)
[199] 27 CFR 478.129(b)

(5) Licensees are also required to retain the ATF Form 3310.4, Multiple Sales or Other Disposition of Pistols and Revolvers, as well as ATF Form 3310.11, Federal Firearms Licensee Theft/Loss Report, for a period of not less than 5 years.[200]

(6) Retention of the records relating to transactions in semi-automatic assault weapons must be retained for a period not less 5 years

---

[200] 27 CFR 478.129(c)

CHAPTER 13. REQUIRED REPORTS AND NOTIFICATIONS TO ATF

Section 13.1 Change of business address.

13.1.1 GCA requirements. Technically, a change in an FFL's/SOT's business address does not trigger an ATF "notification" or "reporting" requirement under the GCA. Rather, it requires the FFL to apply for and receive an amended license before business may be resumed at the new business location. GCA regulations require that an application for an amended license, ATF Form 5300.38, be filed not less than 30 days prior to the change with the Chief, Federal Firearms Licensing Center (FFLC).[201] The application must be accompanied by the FFL's original license. The FFLC may also require the applicant to submit an original license application on ATF Form 7, or may issue an amended license if the applicant is determined to be qualified to do business at the new location. The amended license is valid for the remainder of the term of the original license.

> **13.1.1.1 Application for amended license.** Moving a licensed business to a new location requires careful planning. In completing the application for an amended license, the FFL will be asked if there are any restrictions, covenants, or zoning ordinances prohibiting the conduct of business at the new premises. The FFL must also attach to the application copies of any State license or permit required to conduct the business, as well as evidence of payment of any required State or local business tax. The FFL must also certify that notification has been given to the chief law enforcement officer (the sheriff, chief of police, or equivalent officer) at the new location that the FFL intends to file the application. If ATF determines that the firearms business may not be lawfully conducted at the new location, the application will be denied.

13.1.2 NFA requirements. If the FFL is qualified to do business in NFA firearms, the FFL may not lawfully conduct business in NFA firearms at the new location without the approval of the Chief, NFA Branch.[202] The regulations require the FFL/SOT to file Form 5630.7 with ATF, bearing the notation "Removal Registry" and showing the new address to be used. The FFL/SOT must also send the current special tax stamp to ATF, as well as a letter application requesting the amendment of the registration. Upon approval, the NFA Branch will return the special tax stamp, amended to show the new business location.

Section 13.2 Change in trade name

13.2.1 GCA requirements. GCA regulations provide that an FFL is not required to obtain a new license by reason of a mere change in trade name, provided the license is sent for endorsement of the change to the Chief, Federal Firearms Licensing Center within 30 days from the date the business starts using the new name.[203]

13.2.2 NFA requirements. An FFL/SOT may not continue business in these types of firearms under a new trade name without the approval of the Chief, NFA Branch.[204] To obtain approval, the regulations

---

[201] 27 CFR 478.52
[202] 27 CFR 479.46
[203] 27 CFR 478.53
[204] 27 CFR 479.47

require the FFL/SOT to file ATF Form 5630.7 with ATF, bearing the notation "Amended" and showing the new trade name intended to be used. The FFL/SOT must also send the current NFA special tax stamp to ATF, as well as a letter application requesting amendment of the registration as a special (occupational) taxpayer. Upon approval, the NFA Branch will return the amended special tax stamp showing the new trade name.

Section 13.3 Change in control. A "change in control" is defined in GCA regulations as a change in the actual or legal control of a licensed corporation or association, directly or indirectly, whether by reason of a change in stock ownership, by operation of law, or in any other manner.[205] The regulations require the FFL to give written notification of the change, executed under the penalties of perjury, to the Chief, Federal Firearms Licensing Center, within 30 days of the change. Upon expiration of the license, the regulations require the FFL to file an application for an original license on ATF Form 7. Here are some examples of a "change in control:"

(1) In the case of a licensed corporation, an individual's acquisition of 51% of the stock of the corporation.

(2) Corporation A, an FFL, is acquired by Corporation B. That is, Corporation B purchased 100% of the stock of Corporation A. Corporation A continues to exist as a distinct legal entity after the acquisition and may continue to engage in its licensed firearms business.

(3) The entire board of directors or slate of officers of a corporate FFL changes.

13.3.1 Changes in an FFL's "responsible persons." For a business entity such as a corporation, association, or partnership to qualify for a GCA license, it must not have any person responsible for the management or policies of the firearms business under Federal disabilities, for example, felons.[206] Thus, the entity must list its "responsible persons" on the license application and provide ATF with the fingerprints and photographs of such responsible persons. ATF will conduct a background check of these persons prior to issuing a license. Although a change in responsible persons may not result in a "change in control" for the licensed entity, it is advisable that the FFL notify the Chief, Federal Firearms Licensing Center (FFLC) in writing of such a change and provide the FFLC with same identifying information as required for other responsible persons on the ATF Form 7, as well as the new responsible person's photograph and fingerprints.

13.3.2 A "change in control" is distinguishable from the sale or transfer of a firearms business to another person or entity. Where an FFL sells or transfers the firearms business to a different person or entity, the FFL's license is not transferable to the new person or entity.[207] For example, if Corporation A purchases the assets of an FFL, Corporation B, and Corporation A intends to operate the new firearms business, Corporation A may not lawfully operate the business on Corporation B's license. Rather, Corporation A must apply for and receive its own GCA license to lawfully carry on the business. The

---

[205] 27 CFR 478.54
[206] 18 U.S.C 923(d)(1)(B); 27 CFR 478.47
[207] 27 CFR 478.51

NFA would also require Corporation A to pay the NFA special tax by filing ATF Form 5630.7, Special Tax Registration and Return.[208]

Section 13.4 Reporting firearms transaction information. Each licensee must, when required by letter issued by the ATF, submit on ATF Form 4483, Report of Firearms Transactions, for the periods and times specified in the letter, all record information called for by the letter.[209] This includes the requirement for firearms manufacturers to annually report their firearms production on ATF Form 5300.11. Even if there has been no production, the annual report must be filed. See the instructions on the form for more specific information on the reporting requirement. Should a manufacturer's production fall within the following categories, the report would reflect "o" (zero) for firearms produced:

(1) Firearms produced solely for the official use of the Armed Forces of the United States.

(2) Firearms disposed of to another licensed firearms manufacturer for the purpose of final finishing and assembly

(3) Destructive devices as defined in 18 U.S.C. 921(a)(4) and 26 U.S.C. 5845(f).

(4) Antique firearms as defined in 18 U.S.C. 921(a)(16).

(5) Firearms incorporating frames or receivers of foreign manufacture.

(7) Firearms remanufactured or customized and previously in the possession of non-FFLs.

Section 13.5 Reporting thefts or losses of firearms

13.5.1 GCA requirements. Each FFL must report the theft or loss of a firearm from the FFL's inventory (including any firearm that has been transferred from the inventory to the FFL's personal collection and held as a personal firearm for at least 1 year), or from the collection of a licensed collector, within 48 hours after the theft or loss is discovered.[210] Reports must be made by telephoning ATF at 1-888-930-9275 (nationwide toll free number) and by preparing ATF Form 3310.11, Federal Firearms Licensee Theft/Loss Report, in accordance with the instructions on the form. The original of the report must be forwarded to the ATF National Tracing Center at the address specified on the form, and a copy must be retained by the FFL in the FFL's permanent records for a period not less than 5 years.[211] Theft or loss of any firearm must also be reported to appropriate local authorities.

13.5.2 NFA requirements. When any registered firearm is stolen or lost, the person losing possession must, immediately upon discovery of the theft or loss, make a written report to ATF, specifically the NFA Branch, showing the following: (1) name and address of the person in whose name the firearm is

---

[208] 27 CFR 479.31
[209] 18 U.S.C 923(g)(5)(A); 27 CFR 478.126
[210] 18 U.S.C. 923(g)(6); 27 CFR 478.39a
[211] 27 CFR 478.129(c)

registered; (2) kind of firearm; (3) serial number; (4) model; (5) caliber; (6) manufacturer; (7) date and place of theft or loss; and (8) a complete statement of the facts and circumstances surrounding the theft or loss.[212]

Section 13.6 Reporting theft or loss of NFA registration documents. When any Form 1, 2, 3, 4, 5, 6A, or 10 evidencing possession of a firearm is stolen, lost, or destroyed, the person losing possession must immediately upon discovery of the theft, loss, or destruction report the matter in writing to ATF, specifically the NFA Branch.[213] The report must show the circumstances of the theft, loss, or destruction and include all known facts which may serve to identify the document. Upon receipt of the report, ATF may conduct an investigation and issue a duplicate document.

Section 13.7 Reporting information in response to ATF trace requests. The Gun Control Act of 1968 (GCA) requires an FFL to respond immediately, and in no event later than 24 hours after the receipt of, to a request by an ATF officer at the National Tracing Center (NTC) for information contained in the FFL's required GCA records for determining the disposition of one or more firearms in the course of a bona fide criminal investigation. (See 18 U.S.C. 923(g)(7) and 27 CFR 478.25a). The requested information must be provided orally to the ATF officer within the 24-hour period. Verification of the identity and employment of NTC personnel requesting this information may be established by telephoning the toll-free number 1-800-788-7133 or using the toll-free FAX number 1-800-578-7223.

Section 13.8. Requesting permission to transport certain firearms in interstate or foreign commerce. A person, other than an FFL/SOT, may not lawfully transport in interstate or foreign commerce any destructive device, machinegun, short-barreled shotgun, or short-barreled rifle, without prior written approval of ATF, specifically the NFA Branch.[214] For definitions of these firearms and devices, refer to 27 CFR 478.11. Licensed collectors are not required to obtain such approval if the firearms and devices being transported are "curio or relic" firearms under the GCA. Approval for the transportation may be obtained by (1) a written request or (2) an approved application filed with ATF on Form 5320.20.

13.8.1 A written (letter) request. A written (letter) request must contain:

(1) A complete description and identification of the device or firearm to be transported;

(2) A statement whether the transportation involves a transfer of title;

(3) The need for such transportation;

(4) The approximate date the transportation is to take place;

(5) The present location of the device or firearm and the place to which it is being transported.

---

[212] 27 CFR 479.141
[213] 27 CFR 479.37, 479.142
[214] 18 U.S.C. 922(a)(4); 27 CFR 478.28

(6) The mode of transportation to be used (including, if by common or contract carrier, the name and address of the carrier); and

(7) Evidence that the transportation or possession of the device or firearm is not inconsistent with the laws at the place of destination.

13.8.2 Form 5320.20. As stated above, transportation of these firearms and devices may also be approved by completing and filing this form and obtaining ATF approval of the form.

13.8.3 One-year approval. If a person will be transporting his/her firearm(s) to the same location on a continual basis, ATF will approve a transportation request for up to 1 year. *Example*: the person lives in State A, has a farm in State B (State B allows possession of the particular firearm), and wants to take the firearm to the farm throughout the year. The person may request permission for a 1-year period to transport the firearm interstate to the farm. Any other interstate transportation would still require a separate request and approval. *Second example*: the person lives in State A and wants to transport his/her firearm to a site in State B where competitions and shoots occur several times a year (State B allows possession of the particular firearm). The person may request permission for a 1-year period to transport the firearm interstate to the site for competitions and shoots. Any other interstate transportation would still require a separate request and approval.

CHAPTER 14. GOING OUT OF BUSINESS

Section 14.1 Disposition of GCA records.

14.1.1 "Records" for purposes of this section. Reference to the term "records" in this chapter refers to the acquisition and disposition records required by GCA and NFA regulations, Forms 4473, Forms 3310.4 (Report of Multiple Sale or Other Disposition of Pistols and Revolvers), ATF Forms 3310.11 (Federal Firearms Licensee Theft/Loss Report), records of transactions in semiautomatic assault weapons, records of importation (ATF Forms 6 and 6A), and law enforcement certification letters. If the licensee was granted a variance to use a computerized recordkeeping system, this term also refers to the required printout of the all A & D records, as required by the variance approval.[215]   As required by the regulations, these records must be surrendered to the ATF Out-of-Business Records Center (OBRC) or transferred to any successor of the firearms business within 30 days of the discontinuance of such business.[216] [Handwritten changes add cite "27 C.F.R. § 478.129" but may just be the above referenced forms]

14.1.2 Transfer of the firearms business to a new owner. In the event that the firearms business is transferred to a new owner (i.e. successor), the FFL going out of business may dispose of the records in one of two ways: (1) close all open A & D Record disposition entries by recording the date of transfer, as well as the name and FFL of the succeeding licensee (or record that the firearm was transferred to the discontinued FFL's personal inventory), underline the final entry in each bound book, and deliver all records to the business successor; or (2) deliver the records to the ATF Out-of-Business Records Center, 244 Needy Road, Martinsburg, West Virginia 25405, or to any ATF office in the division in which the business was located. A successor licensee, who receives the records from the original licensee, may choose to forward the records to the ATF Out-of-Business Records Center.[217]

14.1.3 Discontinuance of the business. If the firearms business is discontinued and there is no successor, within 30 days of business' discontinuance, the FFL must ship the records to the ATF Out-of-Business Records Center or to any office in the ATF division in which the business was located. If the FFL was granted a variance to use a computerized recordkeeping system, the FFL must provide a complete printout of the acquisition and disposition records as stipulated in the variance approval.[218]

Section 14.2 Disposition of NFA firearms (other than "post-'86 machineguns").

14.2.1 Sole proprietors. FFLs licensed as sole proprietors, who have been qualified to deal in NFA firearms and who go out of the NFA business, may lawfully retain their inventory of these firearms, including imported NFA "sales samples", in their individual capacity. No NFA transfer occurs that would require an ATF-approved transfer because the firearms are still possessed by the same person to whom they were previously transferred and registered. However, any firearm registered to the individual as a "sales sample" would continue to bear the "sales sample" restriction on any subsequent transfer, unless the firearm is being transferred to a government agency. Thus, the transfer of a "sales

---

[215] ATF P 5300.4 (09/05), Question C-7, Page 180
[216] 18 U.S.C. 923(g)(4); 27 CFR 478.127
[217] Ibid.
[218] Ibid.

sample" to other than a government agency will only be approved if the transferee is an FFL/SOT qualified to receive such samples.[219] Since the registered owner of the firearm is no longer an FFL/SOT, the owner's subsequent transfer of the firearm to other than a government agency would be subject to transfer tax and require approval of an ATF Form 4. *NOTE: If an NFA firearm registered to a sole proprietor as a "sale sample" becomes part of the person's estate upon his/her death, the firearm may not be registered to a beneficiary of the estate unless the beneficiary is qualified to deal in NFA sales samples.*

14.2.2 Corporations, partnerships, and associations. FFLs licensed as corporations, partnerships, or associations, who have been qualified to deal in NFA firearms and who go out of the NFA business, may lawfully retain their inventory of these firearms, including imported NFA "sales samples," as long as the entity does not dissolve but continues to exist under State law. No NFA transfer occurs that would require an ATF-approved transfer because the firearms are still possessed by the same entity to which they were previously transferred and registered. However, any firearm registered to the entity as a "sales sample" would continue to bear the "sales sample" restriction on any subsequent transfer, unless the firearm is being transferred to a government agency. Thus, the transfer of a "sales sample" to other than a government agency will only be approved if the transferee is an FFL/SOT qualified such samples.[220]

14.2.2.1 Effect of dissolution of a corporation, partnership, or association. If an FFL licensed as a corporation, partnership, or association goes out of business and dissolves (ceases to exist under State law), the firm's NFA firearms will be considered to have been "transferred" to whomever takes custody of the firearms and possesses them after dissolution. To be lawful, such transfers must be approved in advance by ATF on ATF Forms 4 and are subject to NFA transfer tax. *However, ATF will not approve the transfer of an NFA "sales sample" unless the transfer is to a government agency or to an FFL/SOT qualified to receive such samples.*[221]

14.2.3 Avoiding NFA transfer tax. An FFL/SOT going out of business and contemplating the transfer of an inventory of NFA firearms or NFA "sales samples" should be mindful of the tax consequences of such transfers. If the FFL/SOT wishes to transfer the firearms to another such person or entity, the transfers may be made on approved ATF Forms 3 transfer tax free if both the transferor and transferee are licensed under the GCA and hold NFA special tax stamps. *Thus, a person or entity going out of business who allows his/her FFL or special tax stamp to expire before the transfers would be subject to the transfer tax on each firearm transferred and the transfers would have to be made on ATF-approved Forms 4.*[222]

Section 14.3 Disposition of "post-86 machineguns." Section 479.105(f) requires the FFL/SOT going out of business to transfer machinegun(s) manufactured after May 19, 1986 to a Federal, State or local government entity, qualified manufacturer, qualified importer, or, subject to the provisions of 479.105(d), to a qualified dealer. The transfers must be completed prior to the FFL/SOT going out of business. The transfer to a government entity would be on Form 5 and the transfer to a qualified

---

[219] Item 10g, ATF Pub. 5300.4 (9/05), <u>Federal Firearms Regulations Reference Guide</u>, p. 164
[220] Ibid.
[221] Ibid.
[222] 26 U.S.C. 5852(d)

manufacturer, importer, or dealer would be on Form 3. The transfer of a machinegun manufactured after May 19, 1986 to a qualified manufacturer or qualified importer can be done without the 'law enforcement letters of interest' when the possessing FFL/SOT is going out of business. That fact that the transferring FFL is discontinuing business must be documented with the submission of the transfer applications. Transfer of a machinegun manufactured after May 19, 1986 from an FFL/SOT going out of business to a qualified dealer requires compliance with section 479.105(d).

The FFL/SOT going out of business may also choose to destroy the machinegun(s), transfer them to State or local government agencies, or abandon them to ATF or State or local government agencies. If the firearms will be destroyed, ATF's Firearms Technology Branch can be contacted for procedures to properly destroy a machinegun. Once the destruction has been accomplished, notify the NFA Branch of the destruction in writing, including a description of the machinegun(s) and the means of destruction. For abandonment to ATF, contact the local ATF office. [223]

---

[223] 27 CFR 478.36, 479.105; Item 10g, ATF Pub. 5300.4 (Sept. 2005), p. 164

CHAPTER 15. PENALTIES AND SANCTIONS

Section 15.1 NFA.

15.1.1 Criminal. The acts prohibited by the NFA and prosecutable as Federal offenses are listed in 26 U.S.C. 5861(a) through (l). As provided by 26 U.S.C. 5871, any person who commits an offense shall, upon conviction, be sentenced to imprisonment for not more than 10 years or fined. Although the fine specified in the statute is an amount not exceeding $10,000, an amendment to Federal law provides for a fine of not more than $250,000 in the case of an individual or $500,000 in the case of an organization.[224]

15.1.2 Forfeiture. Any firearm involved in any violation of the NFA is subject to seizure and forfeiture.[225]

15.1.3 Assessment of NFA tax. ATF may assess tax liabilities under the NFA, including penalties and interest, as provided by the Internal Revenue Code.[226]

Section 15.2 GCA.

15.2.1 Criminal. The criminal penalties for violations of the GCA are provided for in 18 U.S.C. § 924. The criminal penalties in the GCA include both felonies and misdemeanors. For misdemeanors, the fines would be not more than $100,000 for individuals or $200,000 in the case of organizations. The criminal provisions of the NFA are found in 26 U.S.C. § 5871. As in the case of NFA offenses, fines for violation of the felony provisions would be not more than $250,000 in the case of an individual or $500,000 in the case of an organization.

15.2.2 Forfeiture. The GCA also provides for the forfeiture of firearms and ammunition involved in certain violations of the GCA and other violations of the criminal laws of the United States in 18 U.S.C. 924(d).

15.2.3 License denial or revocation. ATF may issue a notice of denial of an application for a Federal firearms license where it determines that the applicant fails to meet the licensing requirements of 18 U.S.C. 923(d).[227] It may also issue a notice of revocation of a license when it determines that an FFL has willfully violated the GCA or its implementing regulations.[228] For the applicable procedures, see ATF's regulations in
27 CFR Part 478, Subpart E. Note that the courts have held that a person's conduct was "willful" where the evidence showed that the FFL knew of his legal obligation and disregarded or was plainly indifferent to that obligation.[229]

---

[224] 18 U.S.C. 3571(b) and (c)
[225] 26 U.S.C. 5872
[226] 27 CFR 479.191
[227] 27 CFR 478.47, 478.71
[228] 18 U.S.C. 923(e); 27 CFR 478.73
[229] Bryan V. United States, 524 U.S. 184 (1998) [note: this is criminal case, not civil license revocation.]

Section 15.3 AECA

15.3.1 Criminal. Any person who (1) imports articles on the U.S. Munitions Import List without a permit, (2) engages in the business of importing articles on the List without registering as required, or (3) otherwise violates any provision of the regulations in 27 CFR Part 447 shall, upon conviction, be fined not more than $1,000,000 or imprisoned for not more than 10 years, or both.[230] The same penalties apply to a person who willfully, in a registration or permit application, makes a false statement of a material fact or fails to state a material fact.

15.3.2 Forfeiture. Whoever knowingly imports into the United States contrary to law any article on the U.S. Munitions Import List, or receives, conceals, buys, sells, or in any manner facilitates its transportation, concealment, or sale after importation, knowing the same to have been imported contrary to law, shall be fined not more than $10,000 or imprisoned not more than 5 years, or both; and the merchandise so imported or the value thereof shall be forfeited to the United States.[231]

---

[230] 22 U.S.C. 2778(c)
[231] 27 CFR 447.63

APPENDIX A

NFA, 26 U.S.C. Chapter 53

THE NATIONAL FIREARMS ACT

TITLE 26, UNITED STATES CODE, CHAPTER 53 INTERNAL REVENUE CODE

Editor's Note:

The National Firearms Act (NFA) is part of the Internal Revenue Code of 1986. The Internal Revenue Code, with the exception of the NF A, is administered and enforced by the Secretary of the Treasury. When ATF transferred to the Department of Justice under the Homeland Security Act of 2002, all its authorities, including the authority to administer and enforce the NFA, were transferred to the Attorney General In order to keep all the references throughout the Internal Revenue Code consistent, references to the Secretary of the Treasury in the NFA were left unchanged by the Homeland Security Act. However, section 7801(a)(2), Title 26, V.S.C., provides that references to the term "Secretary" or "Secretary of the Treasury" in the NFA shall mean the Attorney General.

CHAPTER 53 - MACHINE GUNS, DESTRUCTIVE DEVICES, AND CERTAIN OTHER FIREARMS

Subchapter A - Taxes

Part I - Special (occupational) taxes.

§ 5801 Imposition of tax.

§ 5802 Registration of importers, manufacturers, and dealers.

Part II - Tax on transferring firearms.

§ 5811 Transfer tax.

§ 5812 Transfers.

Part III - Tax on making firearms.

§ 5821 Making tax.

§ 5822 Making.

Subchapter B - General Provisions and Exemptions

Part I - General Provisions.

§ 5841 Registration of firearms.

§ 5842 Identification of firearms.

§ 5843 Records and returns.

§ 5844 Importation.

§ 5845 Definitions.

§ 5846 Other laws applicable.

§ 5847 Effect on other laws..

§ 5848 Restrictive use of information.

§ 5849 Citation of chapter.

Part II - Exemptions.

§ 5851 Special (occupational) taxes.

§ 5852 General transfer and making tax exemption.

§ 5853 Transfer and making tax exemption available to certain governmental entities.

§ 5854 Exportation of firearms exempt from transfer tax.

Subchapter C - Prohibited Acts

§ 5861 Prohibited acts.

Subchapter D- Penalties and Forfeitures

§ 5871 Penalties.

§5872 Forfeitures.

SUBCHAPTER A - TAXES

Part I - Special Occupational Taxes

§ 5801 Imposition of tax.

(a) General rule. On first engaging in business and thereafter on or before July 1 of each year, every importer, manufacturer, and dealer in firearms shall pay a special (occupational) tax for each place of business at the following rates:

(1) Importers and manufacturers: $1,000 a year or fraction thereof.

(2) Dealers: $500 a year or fraction thereof.

(b) Reduced rates of tax for small importers and manufacturers.

(1) In general. Paragraph (1) of subsection (a) shall be applied by substituting "$500" for "$1,000" with respect to any taxpayer the gross receipts of which (for the most recent taxable year ending before the 1st day of the taxable period to which the tax imposed by subsection (a) relates) are less than $500,000.

(2) Controlled group rules. All persons treated as 1 taxpayer under section 5061 (e)(3) shall be treated as 1 taxpayer for purposes of paragraph (1).

(3) Certain rules to apply. For purposes of paragraph (1), rules similar to the rules of subparagraphs (B) and (C) of section 448(c)(3) shall apply.

§ 5802 Registration of importers, manufacturers, and dealers.

On first engaging in business and thereafter on or before the first day of July of each year, each importer, manufacturer, and dealer in firearms shall register with the Secretary in each internal revenue district in which such business is to be carried on, his name, including any trade name, and the address of each location in the district where he will conduct such business. An individual required to register under this section shall include a photograph and fingerprints of the individual with the initial application. Where there is a change during the taxable year in the location of, or the trade name used in, such business, the importer, manufacturer, or dealer shall file an application with the Secretary to amend his registration. Firearms operations of an importer, manufacturer, or dealer may not be commenced at the new location or under a new trade name prior to approval of the application by the Secretary.

Part II - Tax on Transferring Firearms.

§ 5811 Transfer tax.

(a) Rate. There shall be levied, collected, and paid on firearms transferred a tax at the rate of $200 for each firearm transferred, except, the transfer tax on any firearm classified as any other weapon under section 5845(e) shall be at the rate of $5 for each such firearm transferred.

(b) By whom paid. The tax imposed by subsection (a) of this section shall be paid by the transferor.

(c) Payment. The tax imposed by subsection (a) of this section shall be payable by the appropriate stamps prescribed for payment by the Secretary.

§ 5812 Transfers.

(a) Application. A firearm shall not be transferred unless (1) the transferor of the firearm has filed with the Secretary a written application, in duplicate, for the transfer and registration of the firearm to the transferee on the application form prescribed by the Secretary; (2) any tax payable on the transfer is paid as evidenced by the proper stamp affixed to the original application form; (3) the transferee is identified in the application form in such manner as the Secretary may by regulations prescribe, except that, if such person is an individual, the identification must include his fingerprints and his photograph; (4) the transferor of the firearm is identified in the application form in such manner as the Secretary may by regulations prescribe; (5) the firearm is identified in the application form in such manner as the Secretary may by regulations prescribe; and (6) the application form shows that the Secretary has approved the transfer and the registration of the firearm to the transferee. Applications shall be denied if the transfer, receipt, or possession of the firearm would place the transferee in violation of law.

(b) Transfer of possession. The transferee of a firearm shall not take possession of the firearm unless the Secretary has approved the transfer and registration of the firearm to the transferee as required by subsection (a) of this section.

Part 111- Tax on Making Firearms.

§ 5821 Making tax.

(a) Rate. There shall be levied, collected, and paid upon the making of a firearm a tax at the rate of $200 for each firearm made.

(b) By whom paid. The tax imposed by subsection (a) of this section shall be paid by the person making the firearm.

(c) Payment. The tax imposed by subsection (a) of this section shall be payable by the stamp prescribed for payment by the Secretary.

§ 5822 Making.

No person shall make a firearm unless

he has (a) filed with the Secretary a written application, in duplicate, to make and register the firearm on the form prescribed by the Secretary; (b) paid any tax payable on the making and such payment is evidenced by the proper stamp affixed to the original application form; (c) identified the firearm to be made in the application form in such manner as the Secretary may by regulations prescribe; (d) identified himself in the application form in such manner as the Secretary may by regulations prescribe, except that, if such person is an individual, the identification must include his fingerprints and his photograph; and (e) obtained the approval of the Secretary to make and register the firearm and the application form shows such approval. Applications shall be denied if the making or possession of the firearm would place the person making the firearm in violation of law.

SUBCHAPTER B GENERAL PROVISIONS AND EXEMPTIONS

Part I - General Provisions.

§ 5841 Registration of firearms.

(a) Central registry. The Secretary shall maintain a central registry of all firearms in the United States which are not in the possession or under the control of the United States. This registry shall be known as the National Firearms Registration and Transfer Record. The registry shall include

(1) identification of the firearm;

(2) date of registration; and

(3) identification and address of person entitled to possession of the firearm.

(b) By whom registered. Each manufacturer, importer, and maker shall register each firearm he manufactures, imports, or makes. Each firearm transferred shall be registered to the transferee by the transferor.

(c) How registered. Each manufacturer shall notify the Secretary of the manufacture of a firearm in such manner as may by regulations be prescribed and such notification shall effect the registration of the firearm required by this section. Each importer, maker, and transferor of a firearm shall, prior to importing, making, or transferring a firearm, obtain authorization in such manner as required by this chapter or regulations issued thereunder to import, make, or transfer the firearm, and such authorization shall effect the registration of the firearm required by this section.

(d) Firearms registered on effective date of this act. A person shown as possessing a firearm by the records maintained by the Secretary pursuant to the National Firearms Act in force on the day immediately prior to the effective date of the National Firearms Act of 1968 shall be considered to have registered under this section the firearms in his possession which are disclosed by that record as being in his possession.

(e) Proof of registration. A person possessing a firearm registered as required by this section shall retain proof of registration which shall be made available to the Secretary upon request.

§ 5842 Identification of firearms.

(a) Identification of firearms other than destructive devices. Each manufacturer and importer and anyone making a firearm shall identify each firearm, other than a destructive device, manufactured, imported, or made by a serial number which may not be readily removed, obliterated, or altered, the name of the manufacturer, importer, or maker, and such other identification as the Secretary may by regulations prescribe.

(b) Firearms without serial number. Any person who possesses a firearm, other than a destructive device, which does not bear the serial number and other information required by subsection (a) of this section shall identify the firearm with a serial number assigned by the Secretary and any other information the Secretary may by regulations prescribe.

(c) Identification of destructive device. Any firearm classified as a destructive device shall be identified in such manner as the Secretary may by regulations prescribe.

§ 5843 Records and returns.

Importers, manufacturers, and dealers shall keep such records of, and render such returns in relation to, the importation, manufacture, making, receipt, and sale, or other disposition, of firearms as the Secretary may by regulations prescribe.

§ 5844 Importation.

No firearm shall be imported or brought into the United States or any territory under its control or jurisdiction unless the importer establishes, under regulations as may be prescribed by the Secretary, that the firearm to be imported or brought in is

(1) being imported or brought in for the use of the United States or any department, independent establishment, or agency thereof or any State or possession or any political subdivision thereof; or

(2) being imported or brought in for scientific or research purposes; or

(3) being imported or brought in solely for testing or use as a model by a registered manufacturer or solely for use as a sample by a registered importer or registered dealer;

except that, the Secretary may permit the conditional importation or bringing in of a firearm for examination and testing in connection with classifying the firearm.

§ 5845 Definitions.

For the purpose of this chapter-

(a) Firearm. The term 'firearm' means (1) a shotgun having a barrel or barrels of less than 18 inches in length; (2) a weapon made from a shotgun if such weapon as modified has an overall length of less than 26 inches or a barrel or barrels of less than 18 inches in length; (3) a rifle having a barrel or barrels of less than 16 inches in length; (4) a weapon made from a rifle if such weapon as modified has an overall length of less than 26 inches or a barrel or barrels of less than 16 inches in length; (5) any other weapon, as defined in subsection (e); (6) a machinegun; (7) any silencer (as defined in section 921 of title 18, United States Code); and (8) a destructive device. The term 'firearm' shall not include an antique firearm or any device (other than a machinegun or destructive device) which, although designed as a weapon, the Secretary finds by reason of the date of its manufacture, value, design, and other characteristics is primarily a collector's item and is not likely to be used as a weapon.

(b) Machinegun. The term 'machinegun' means any weapon which shoots, is designed to shoot, or can be readily restored to shoot, automatically more than one shot, without manual reloading, by a single function of the trigger. The term shall also include the frame or receiver of any such weapon, any part designed and intended solely and exclusively, or combination of parts designed and intended, for use in converting a weapon into a machinegun, and any combination of parts from which a machinegun can be assembled if such parts are in the possession or under the control of a person.

(c) Rifle. The term 'rifle' means a weapon designed or redesigned, made or remade, and intended to be fired from the shoulder and designed or redesigned and made or remade to use the energy of the explosive in a fixed cartridge to fire only a single projectile through a rifled bore for each single pull of the trigger, and shall include any such weapon which may be readily restored to fire a fixed cartridge.

(d) Shotgun. The term 'shotgun' means a weapon designed or redesigned, made or remade, and intended to be fired from the shoulder and designed or redesigned and made or remade to use the energy of the explosive in a fixed shotgun shell to fire through a smooth bore either a number of projectiles (ball shot) or a single projectile for each pull of the trigger, and shall include any such weapon which may be readily restored to fire a fixed shotgun shell.

(e) Any other weapon. The term 'any other weapon' means any weapon or device capable of being concealed on the person from which a shot can be discharged through the energy of an explosive, a pistol or revolver having a barrel with a smooth bore designed or redesigned to fire a fixed shotgun shell, weapons with combination shotgun and rifle barrels 12 inches or more, less than 18 inches in length, from which only a single discharge can be made from either barrel without manual reloading, and shall include any such weapon which may be readily restored to fire. Such term shall not include a pistol or a revolver having a rifled bore, or rifled bores, or weapons designed, made, or intended to be fired from the shoulder and not capable of firing fixed ammunition.

(f) Destructive device. The term 'destructive device' means (1) any explosive, incendiary, or poison gas (A) bomb, (8) grenade, (C) rocket having a propellant charge of more than four ounces, (0) missile having an explosive or incendiary charge of more than one-quarter ounce, (E) mine, or (F) similar device; (2) any type of weapon by whatever name known which will, or which may be readily converted to, expel a projectile by the action of an explosive or other propellant, the barrel or barrels of which have a bore of more than one-half inch in diameter, except a shotgun or shotgun shell which the Secretary finds is generally recognized as particularly suitable for sporting purposes; and (3) any combination of parts either designed or intended for use in converting any device into a destructive device as defined in subparagraphs (1) and (2) and from which a destructive device may be readily assembled. The term 'destructive device' shall not include any device which is neither designed nor redesigned for use as a weapon; any device, although originally designed for use as a weapon, which is redesigned for use as a signaling, pyrotechnic, line throwing, safety, or similar device; surplus ordnance sold, loaned, or given by the Secretary of the Army pursuant to the provisions of section 4684(2), 4685, or 4686 of title 10 of the United States Code; or any other device which the Secretary finds is not likely to be used as a weapon, or is an antique or is a rifle which the owner intends to use solely for sporting purposes.

(g) Antique firearm. The term 'antique firearm' means any firearm not designed or redesigned for using rim fire or conventional center fire ignition with fixed ammunition and manufactured in or before 1898 (including any matchlock, flintlock, percussion cap, or similar type of ignition system or replica thereof, whether actually manufactured before or after the year 1898) and also any firearm using fixed ammunition manufactured in or before 1898, for which ammunition is no longer manufactured in the

United States and is not readily available in the ordinary channels of commercial trade.

(h) Unserviceable firearm. The term 'unserviceable firearm' means a firearm which is incapable of discharging a shot by means of an explosive and incapable of being readily restored to a firing condition.

(i) Make. The term 'make', and the various derivatives of such word, shall include manufacturing (other than by one qualified to engage in such business under this chapter), putting together, altering, any combination of these, or otherwise producing a firearm.

(j) Transfer. The term. 'transfer' and the various derivatives of such word, shall include selling, assigning, pledging, leasing, loaning, giving away, or otherwise disposing of.

(k) Dealer. The term 'dealer' means any person, not a manufacturer or importer, engaged in the business of selling, renting, leasing, or loaning firearms and shall include pawnbrokers who accept firearms as collateral for loans.

(l) Importer. The term 'importer' means any person who is engaged in the business of importing or bringing firearms into the United States.

(m) Manufacturer. The term 'manufacturer' means any person who is engaged in the business of manufacturing firearms.

§ 5846 Other laws applicable.

All provisions of law relating to special taxes imposed by chapter 51 and to engraving, issuance, sale, accountability, cancellation, and distribution of stamps for tax payment shall, insofar as not inconsistent with the provisions of this chapter, be applicable with respect to the taxes imposed by sections 5801, 5811, and 5821.

§ 5847 Effect on other laws.

Nothing in this chapter shall be construed as modifying or affecting the requirements of section 414 of the Mutual Security Act of 1954, as amended, with respect to the manufacture, exportation, and importation of arms, ammunition, and implements of war.

§ 5848 Restrictive use of information.

(a) General Rule. No information or evidence obtained from an application, registration, or records required to be submitted or retained by a natural person in order to comply with any provision of this chapter or regulations issued thereunder, shall, except as provided in subsection (b) of this section, be used, directly or indirectly, as evidence against that person in a criminal proceeding with respect to a violation of law occurring prior to or concurrently with the filing of the application or registration, or the compiling of the records containing the information or evidence.

(b) Furnishing false information. Subsection (a) of this section shall not preclude the use of any such information or evidence in a prosecution or other action under any applicable provision of law with respect to the furnishing of false information.

§ 5849 Citation of chapter.

This chapter may be cited as the 'National Firearms Act' and any reference in any other provision of law to the 'National Firearms Act' shall be held to refer to the provisions of this chapter.

Part II - Exemptions.

§ 5851 Special (occupational) tax exemption.

(a) Business with United States. Any person required to pay special (occupational) tax under section 5801 shall be relieved from payment of that tax if he establishes to the satisfaction of the Secretary that his business is conducted exclusively with, or on behalf of, the United States or any department, independent establishment, or agency thereof. The Secretary may relieve any person manufacturing firearms for, or on behalf of, the United States from compliance with any provision of this chapter in the conduct of such business.

(b) Application. The exemption provided for in subsection (a) of this section may be obtained by filing with the Secretary an application on such form and containing such information as may by regulations be prescribed. The exemptions must thereafter be renewed on or before July 1 of each year. Approval of the application by the Secretary shall entitle the applicant to the exemptions stated on the approved application.

§ 5852 General transfer and making tax exemption.

(a) Transfer. Any firearm may be transferred to the United States or any department, independent establishment, or agency thereof, without payment of the transfer tax imposed by section 5811.

(b) Making by a person other than a qualified manufacturer. Any firearm may be made by, or on behalf of, the United States, or any department, independent establishment, or agency thereof, without payment of the making tax imposed by section 5821.

(c) Making by a qualified manufacturer. A manufacturer qualified under this chapter to engage in such business may make the type of firearm which he is qualified to manufacture without payment of the making tax imposed by section 5821.

(d) Transfers between special (occupational) taxpayers. A firearm registered to a person qualified under this chapter to engage in business as an importer, manufacturer, or dealer may be transferred by that person without payment of the transfer tax imposed by section 5811 to any other person qualified under this chapter to manufacture, import, or deal in that type of firearm.

(e) Unserviceable firearm. An unserviceable firearm may be transferred as a curio or ornament without payment of the transfer tax imposed by section 5811, under such requirements as the Secretary may by regulations prescribe.

(f) Right to exemption. No firearm may be transferred or made exempt from tax under the provisions of this section unless the transfer or making is performed pursuant to an application in such form and manner as the Secretary may by regulations prescribe.

§ 5853 Transfer and making tax exemption available to certain governmental entities.

(a) Transfer. A firearm may be transferred without the payment of the transfer tax imposed by section 5811 to any State, possession of the United States, any political subdivision thereof, or any official police organization of such a government entity engaged in criminal investigations.

(b) Making. A firearm may be made without payment of the making tax imposed by section 5821 by, or on behalf of, any State, or possession of the United States, any political subdivision thereof, or any official police organization of such a government entity engaged in criminal investigations.

(c) Right to exemption. No firearm may be transferred or made exempt from tax under this section unless the transfer or making is performed pursuant to an application in such form and manner as the Secretary may by regulations prescribe.

§ 5854 Exportation of firearms exempt from transfer tax. A firearm may be exported without payment of the transfer tax imposed under section 5811 provided that proof of the exportation is furnished in such form and manner as the Secretary may by regulations prescribe.

SUBCHAPTER C - PROHIBITED ACTS

§ 5861 Prohibited acts.

It shall be unlawful for any person

(a) to engage in business as a manufacturer or importer of, or dealer in, firearms without having paid the special (occupational) tax required by section 5801 for his business or having registered as required by section 5802; or

(b) to receive or possess a firearm transferred to him in violation of the provisions of this chapter; or

(c) to receive or possess a firearm made in violation of the provisions of this chapter; or

(d) to receive or possess a firearm which is not registered to him in the National Firearms Registration and Transfer Record; or

(e) to transfer a firearm in violation of the provisions of this chapter; or

(f) to make a firearm in violation of the provisions of this chapter; or

(g) to obliterate, remove, change, or alter the serial number or other identification of a firearm required by this chapter; or

(h) to receive or possess a firearm having the serial number or other identification required by this chapter obliterated, removed, changed, or altered; or obliterated, or

(i) to receive or possess a firearm which is not identified by a serial number as required by this chapter; or

(j) to transport, deliver, or receive any firearm in interstate commerce which has not been registered as required by this chapter; or

(k) to receive or possess a firearm which has been imported or brought into the United States in violation of section 5844; or

(I) to make, or cause the making of, a false entry on any application, return, or record required by this chapter, knowing such entry to be false.

SUBCHAPTER D - PENALTIES AND FORFEITURES

§ 5871 Penalties.

Any person who violates or fails to comply with any provision of this chapter shall, upon conviction, be fined not more than $10,000, or be imprisoned not more than ten years, or both.

§ 5872 Forfeitures.

(a) Laws applicable. Any firearm involved in any violation of the provisions of this chapter shall be subject to seizure and forfeiture, and (except as provided in subsection (b» all the provisions of internal revenue laws relating to searches, seizures, and forfeitures of unstamped articles are extended to and made to apply to the articles taxed under this chapter, and the persons to whom this chapter applies.

(b) Disposal. In the case of the forfeiture of any firearm by reason of a violation of this chapter, no notice of public sale shall be required; no such firearm shall be sold at public sale; if such firearm is forfeited for a violation of this chapter and there is no remission or mitigation of forfeiture thereof, it shall be delivered by the Secretary to the Administrator of General Services, General Services Administration, who may order such firearm destroyed or may sell it to any State, or possession, or political subdivision thereof, or at the request of the Secretary, may authorize its retention for official use of the Treasury Department, or may transfer it without charge to any executive department or independent establishment of the Government for use by it.

TITLE 27 CFR CHAPTER II

PART 479-MACHINE GUNS, DESTRUCTIVE DEVICES, AND CERTAIN OTHER FIREARMS

(This part was formerly designated as Part 179)

Editor's Note:

Effective January 24, 2003, the Homeland Security Act transferred the Bureau of Alcohol, Tobacco and Firearms from the Department of the Treasury to the Department of Justice. In addition, the agency's name was changed to the Bureau of Alcohol, Tobacco. Firearms and Explosives. The regulations, as printed in this publication, do not yet reflect this change. The regulations will be amended to change the references from the "Bureau of Alcohol, Tobacco and Firearms," the "Department of the Treasury," and the "Secretary of the Treasury" to the "Bureau of Alcohol, Tobacco, Firearms and Explosives," the "Department of Justice" and the "Attorney General," respectively.

Subpart A -Scope of Regulations

§ 479.1 General.

Subpart B - Definitions

§ 479.11 Meaning of terms.

Subpart C - Administrative and Miscellaneous Provisions

§ 479.21 Forms prescribed.

§ 479.22 Right of entry and examination.

§ 479.23 Restrictive use of required information.

§ 479.24 Destructive device determination.

§ 479.25 Collector's items.

§ 479.26 Alternate methods or procedures; emergency variations from requirements.

Subpart D - Special (Occupational) Taxes

§ 479.31 Liability for tax.

§ 479.32 Special (occupational) tax rates.

§ 479.32a Reduced rate of tax for small importers and manufacturers.

§ 479.33 Special exemption

§ 479.34 Special tax registration and return.

§ 479.35 Employer identification number.

§ 479.36 The special tax stamp, receipt for special (occupational) taxes.

§ 479.37 Certification in lieu of stamps lost or destroyed.

§ 479.38 Engaging in business at more than one location.

§ 479.39 Engaging in more than one business at the same location.

§ 479.40 Partnership liability.

§ 479.41 Single sale.

Change of Ownership

§ 479.42 Changes through death of *owner.*

§ 479.43 Changes through bankruptcy of owner.

§ 479.44 Change in partnership or unincorporated association.

§ 479.45 Changes in corporation.

Change of Business Location

§ 479.46 Notice by taxpayer.

Change of Trade Name

§ 479.47 Notice by taxpayer.

Penalties and Interest

§ 479.48 Failure to pay special (occupational) tax.

§ 479.49 Failure to register change or removal.

§ 479.50 Delinquency.

§ 479.51 Fraudulent return.

Application of State Laws

§ 479.52 State regulations.

Subpart E-Tax on Making Firearms

§ 479.61 Rate of tax.

Application to Make a Firearm

§ 479.62 Application to make.

§ 479.63 Identification of applicant.

§ 479.64 Procedure for approval of application.

§ 479.65 Denial of application.

§ 479.66 Subsequent transfer of firearms.

§ 479.67 Cancellation of stamp.

Exceptions to Tax on Making Firearms

§ 479.68 Qualified manufacturer.

§ 479.69 Making a firearm for the United States.

§ 479.70 Certain government entities.

Registration

§ 479.71 Proof of registration.

Subpart F- Transfer Tax

§ 479.81 Scope of tax.
§ 479.82 Rate of tax.
§ 479.83 Transfer tax in addition to import duty.

Application and Order for Transfer of Firearm

§ 479.84 Application to transfer.
§ 479.85 Identification of transferee.
§ 479.86 Action on application.
§ 479.87 Cancellation of stamp.

Exemptions Relating to Transfers of Firearms

§ 479.88 Special (occupational) taxpayers.

§ 479.89 Transfers to the United States.

§ 479.90 Certain government entities.

§ 479.91 Unserviceable firearms.

§ 479.92 Transportation of firearms to effect transfer.

Other Provisions

§ 479.93 Transfers of firearms to certain persons.

Subpart G-Registration and Identification of Firearms

§ 479.101 Registration of firearms

§ 479.102 How must firearms be registered

§ 479.103 Registration of firearms manufactured

§ 479.104 Registration of firearms by certain governmental entities

Machine Guns

§ 479.105 Transfer and possession of machine guns.

Subpart H-Importation and Exportation

Importation

§ 479.111 Procedure.

§ 479.112 Registration of imported firearms.

§ 479.113 Conditional importation.

Exportation

§ 479.114 Application and permit for exportation of firearms.

§ 479.115 Action by Director.

§ 479.116 Procedure by exporter.

§ 479.117 Action by Customs.

§ 479.118 Proof of exportation.

§ 479.119 Transportation of firearms to effect exportation.
§ 479.120 Refunds.

§ 479.121 Insular possessions.
Arms Export Control Act

§ 479.122 Requirements.

Subpart I-Records and Returns

§ 479.131 Records.

Subpart J-Stolen or Lost Firearms or Documents

§ 479.141 Stolen or lost firearms.

§ 479.142 Stolen or lost documents.

Subpart K-Examination of Books and Records

§ 479.151 Failure to make returns: Substitute returns.

§ 479.152 Penalties (records and returns).

Subpart L-Distribution and Sale of Stamps

§ 479.161 National Firearms Act stamps.
§ 479.162 Stamps authorized.
§ 479.163 Reuse of stamps prohibited

Subpart M-Redemption of or Allowance for Stamps or Refunds

§ 479.171 Redemption of or allowance for stamps.

§ 479.172 Refunds.

Subpart N-Penalties and Forfeitures

§ 479.181 Penalties.

§ 479.182 Forfeitures.

Subpart O-Other Laws Applicable

§ 479.191 Applicability of other provisions of internal revenue laws.

§ 479.192 Commerce in firearms and ammunition.

§ 479.193 Arms Export Control Act.
Subpart A-Scope of Regulations

§ 479.1 General.

This part contains the procedural and substantive requirements relative to the importation, manufacture, making, exportation, identification and registration of, and the dealing in, machine guns, destructive devices and certain other firearms under the provisions of the National Firearms Act (26 U.S.C. Chapter 53).

Subpart B-Definitions

§ 479.11 Meaning of terms.

When used in this part and in forms prescribed under this part, where not otherwise distinctly expressed or manifestly incompatible with the intent thereof, terms shall have the meanings ascribed in this section. Words in the plural form shall include the singular, and vice versa, and words importing the masculine gender shall include the feminine. The terms "includes" and "including" do not exclude other things not enumerated which are in the same general class or are otherwise within the scope thereof.

Antique firearm. Any firearm not designed or redesigned for using rim fire or conventional center fire ignition with fixed ammunition and manufactured in or before 1898 (including any matchlock, flintlock, percussion cap, or similar type of ignition system or replica thereof, whether actually manufactured before or after the year 1898) and also any firearm using fixed ammunition manufactured in or before 1898, for which ammunition is no longer manufactured in the United States and is not readily available in the ordinary channels of commercial trade.

Any other weapon. Any weapon or device capable of being concealed on the person from which a shot can be discharged through the energy of an explosive, a pistol or revolver having a barrel with a smooth bore designed or redesigned to fire a fixed shotgun shell, weapons with combination shotgun and rifle barrels 12 inches or more, less than 18 inches in length, from which only a single discharge can be made from either barrel without manual reloading, and shall include any such weapon which may be readily restored to fire. Such term shall not include a pistol or a revolver having a rifled bore, or rifled bores, or weapons designed, made, or intended to be fired from the shoulder and not capable of firing fixed ammunition.

ATF officer. An officer or employee of the Bureau of Alcohol, Tobacco and Firearms (ATF) authorized to perform any function relating to the administration or enforcement of this part.

Customs officer. Any officer of the Customs Service or any commissioned, warrant, or petty officer of the Coast Guard, or any agent or other person authorized by law or designated by the Secretary of the Treasury to perform any duties of an officer of the Customs Service.

Dealer. Any person, not a manufacturer or importer, engaged in the business of selling, renting, leasing, or loaning firearms and shall include pawnbrokers who accept firearms as collateral for loans.

Destructive device. (a) Any explosive, incendiary, or poison gas (1) bomb, (2) grenade, (3) rocket having a propellant charge of more than 4 ounces, (4) missile having an explosive or incendiary charge of more than one-quarter ounce, (5) mine, or (6) similar device; (b) any type of weapon by whatever name known which will, or which may be readily converted to, expel a projectile by the action of an explosive or other propellant, the barrel or barrels of which have a bore of more than one-half inch in diameter, except a shotgun or shotgun shell which the Director finds is generally recognized as particularly suitable for sporting purposes; and (c) any combination of parts either designed or intended for use in converting any device into a destructive device as described in paragraphs (a) and (b) of this definition and from which a destructive device may be readily assembled. The term shall not include any device which is neither designed or redesigned for use as a weapon; any device, although originally designed for use as a weapon, which is redesigned for use as a signaling, pyrotechnic, line throwing, safety, or similar device; surplus ordnance sold, loaned, or given by the Secretary of the Army under 10 U.S.C. 4684(2), 4685, or 4686, or any device which the Director finds is not likely to be used as a weapon, or is an antique or is a rifle which the owner intends to use solely for sporting purposes.

Director. The Director, Bureau of Alcohol, Tobacco and Firearms, the Department of the Treasury, Washington, DC.

Director of the Service Center. A director of an Internal Revenue Service Center in an internal revenue region.

District director. A district director of the Internal Revenue Service in an internal revenue district.

Executed under penalties of perjury. Signed with the prescribed declaration under the penalties of perjury as provided on or with respect to the return, form, or other document or, where no form of declaration is prescribed, with the declaration:

"I declare under the penalties of perjury that this-(insert type of document, such as, statement, application, request, certificate), including the documents submitted in support thereof, has been examined by me and, to the best of my knowledge and belief, is true, correct, and complete."

Exportation. The severance of goods from the mass of things belonging to this country with the intention of uniting them to the mass of things belonging to some foreign country.

Exporter. Any person who exports firearms from the United States.

Firearm. (a) A shotgun having a barrel or barrels of less than 18 inches in length; (b) a weapon made from a shotgun if such weapon as modified has an overall length of less than 26 inches or a barrel or barrels of less than 18 inches in length; (c) a rifle having a barrel or barrels of less than 16 inches in length; (d) a weapon made from a rifle if such weapon as modified has an overall length of less than 26 inches or a barrel or barrels of less than 16 inches in length; (e) any other weapon, as defined in this subpart; (f) a machine gun; (g) a muffler or a silencer for any firearm whether or not such firearm is included within this definition; and (h) a destructive device. The term shall not include an antique firearm or any device (other than a machine gun or destructive device) which, although designed as a weapon, the Director finds by reason of the date of its manufacture, value, design, and other characteristics is primarily a collector's item and is not likely to be used as a weapon. For purposes of this definition, the length of the barrel having an integral chamber(s) on a shotgun or rifle shall be determined by measuring the distance between the muzzle and the face of the bolt, breech, or breech block when closed and when the shotgun or rifle is cocked. The overall length of a weapon made from a shotgun or rifle is the distance between the extreme ends of the weapon measured along a line parallel to the center line of the bore.

Fixed ammunition. That self-contained unit consisting of the case, primer, propellant charge, and projectile or projectiles.

Frame or receiver. That part of a firearm which provides housing for the hammer, bolt or breechblock and firing mechanism, and which is usually threaded at its forward portion to receive the barrel.

Importation. The bringing of a firearm within the limits of the United States or any territory under its control or jurisdiction, from a place outside thereof (whether such place be a foreign country or territory subject to the jurisdiction of the United States), with intent to unlade. Except that, bringing a firearm from a foreign country or a territory subject to the jurisdiction of the United States into a foreign trade zone for storage pending shipment to a foreign country or subsequent importation into this country, under Title 26 of the United States Code, and this part, shall not be deemed importation.

Importer. Any person who is engaged in the business of importing or bringing firearms into the United States.

Machine gun. Any weapon which shoots, is designed to shoot, or can be readily restored to shoot, automatically more than one shot, without manual reloading, by a single function of the trigger. The term shall also include the frame or receiver of any such weapon, any part designed and intended solely and exclusively, or combination of parts designed and intended, for use in converting a weapon into a machine gun, and any combination of parts from which a machine gun can be assembled if such parts are in the possession or under the control of a person.

Make. This term and the various derivatives thereof shall include manufacturing (other than by one qualified to engage in such business under this part), putting together, altering, any combination of these, or otherwise producing a firearm.

Manual reloading. The inserting of a cartridge or shell into the chamber of a firearm either with the hands or by means of a mechanical device controlled and energized by the hands.

Manufacturer. Any person who is engaged in the business of manufacturing firearms.

Muffler or silencer. Any device for silencing, muffling, or diminishing the report of a portable firearm, including any combination of parts, designed or redesigned, and intended for the use in assembling or fabricating a firearm silencer or firearm muffler, and any part intended only for use in such assembly or fabrication.

Person. A partnership, company, association, trust, estate, or corporation, as well as a natural person.

Pistol. A weapon originally designed, made, and intended to fire a projectile (bullet) from one or more barrels when held in one hand, and having (a) a chamber(s) as an integral part(s) of, or permanently aligned with, the bore(s); and (b) a short stock designed to be gripped by one hand and at an angle to and extending below the line of the bore(s).

Regional director (compliance). The principal ATF regional official responsible for administering regulations in this part.

Revolver. A projectile weapon, of the pistol type, having a breechloading chambered cylinder so arranged that the cocking of the hammer or movement of the trigger rotates it and brings the next cartridge in line with the barrel for firing.

Rifle. A weapon designed or redesigned, made or remade, and intended to be fired from the shoulder and designed or redesigned and made or remade to use the energy of the explosive in a fixed cartridge to fire only a single projectile through a rifled bore for each single pull of the trigger, and shall include any such weapon which may be readily restored to fire a fixed cartridge.

Shotgun. A weapon designed or redesigned, made or remade, and intended to be fired from the shoulder and designed or redesigned and made or remade to use the energy of the explosive in a fixed shotgun shell to fire through a smooth bore either a number of projectiles (ball shot) or a single projectile for each pull of the trigger, and shall include any such weapon which may be readily restored to fire a fixed shotgun shell.

Transfer. This term and the various derivatives thereof shall include selling, assigning, pledging, leasing, loaning, giving away, or otherwise disposing of.

United States. The States and the District of Columbia.

U.S.C. The United States Code.

Unserviceable firearm. A firearm which is incapable of discharging a shot by means of an explosive and incapable of being readily restored to a firing condition.

Subpart C-Administrative and Miscellaneous Provisions

§ 479.21 Forms prescribed.

(a) The Director is authorized to prescribe all forms required by this part. All of the information called for in each form shall be furnished as indicated by the headings on the form and the instructions on or pertaining to the form. In addition, information called for in each form shall be furnished as required by this part. Each form requiring that it be executed under penalties of perjury shall be executed under penalties of perjury.

(b) Requests for forms should be mailed to the ATF Distribution Center, 7943 Angus Court, Springfield, Virginia 22153.

§ 479.22 Right of entry and examination.

Any ATF officer or employee of the Bureau of Alcohol, Tobacco and Firearms duly authorized to perform any function relating to the administration or enforcement of this part may enter during business hours the premises (including places of storage) of any importer or manufacturer of or dealer in firearms, to examine any books, papers, or records required to be kept pursuant to this part, and any firearms kept by such importer, manufacturer or dealer on such premises, and may require the production of any books, papers, or records necessary to determine any liability for tax under 26 U.S.C. Chapter 53, or the observance of 26 U.S.C. Chapter 53, and this part.

§ 479.23 Restrictive use of required information.

No information or evidence obtained from an application, registration, or record required to be submitted or retained by a natural person in order to comply with any provision of 26 U.S.C. Chapter 53, or this part or section 207 of the Gun Control Act of 1968 shall be used, directly or indirectly, as evidence against that person in a criminal proceeding with respect to a violation of law occurring prior to or concurrently with the filing of the application or registration, or the compiling of the record containing the information or evidence: Provided, however, that the provisions of this section shall not preclude the use of any such information or evidence in a prosecution or other action under any applicable provision of law with respect to the furnishing of false information.

§ 479.24 Destructive device determination.

The Director shall determine in accordance with 26 U.S.C. 5845(f) whether a device is excluded from the definition of a destructive device. A person who desires to obtain a determination under that provision of law for any device which he believes is not likely to be used as a weapon shall submit a written request, in triplicate, for a ruling thereon to the Director. Each such request shall be executed under the penalties of perjury and contain a complete and accurate description of the device, the name and address of the manufacturer or importer thereof, the purpose of and use for which it is intended, and such photographs, diagrams, or drawings as may be necessary to enable the Director to make his determination. The Director may require the submission to him, of a sample of such device for examination and evaluation. If the submission of such device is impracticable, the person requesting the ruling shall so advise the Director and designate the place where the device will be available for examination and evaluation.

§ 479.25 Collector's items.

The Director shall determine in accordance with 26 U.S.C. 5845(a) whether a firearm or device, which although originally designed as a weapon, is by reason of the date of its manufacture, value, design, and other characteristics primarily a collector's item and is not likely to be used as a weapon. A person who desires to obtain a determination under that provision of law shall follow the procedures prescribed in § 479.24 relating to destructive device determinations, and shall include information as to date of manufacture, value, design and other characteristics which would sustain a finding that the firearm or device is primarily a collector's item and is not likely to be used as a weapon.

§ 479.26 Alternate methods or procedures; emergency variations from requirements.

(a) Alternate methods or procedures. Any person subject to the provisions of this part, on specific approval by the Director as provided in this paragraph, may use an alternate method or procedure in lieu of a method or procedure specifically prescribed in this part. The Director may approve an alternate method or procedure, subject to stated conditions, when it is found that:

(1) Good cause is shown for the use of the alternate method or procedure;

(2) The alternate method or procedure is within the purpose of, and consistent with the effect intended by, the specifically prescribed method or procedure and that the alternate method or procedure is substantially equivalent to that specifically prescribed method or procedure; and

(3) The alternate method or procedure will not be contrary to any provision of law and will not result in an increase in cost to the Government or hinder the effective administration of this part. Where such person desires to employ an alternate method or procedure, a written application shall be submitted to the appropriate regional director (compliance), for transmittal to the Director. The application shall specifically describe the proposed alternate method or procedure and shall set forth the reasons for it. Alternate methods or procedures may not be employed until the application is approved by the Director. Such person shall, during the period of authorization of an alternate method or procedure, comply with the terms of the approved application. Authorization of any alternate method or procedure may be withdrawn whenever, in the judgment of the Director, the effective administration of this part is hindered by the continuation of the authorization.

(b) Emergency variations from requirements. The Director may approve a method of operation other than as specified in this part, where it is found that an emergency exists and the proposed variation from the specified requirements are necessary and the proposed variations (1) will not hinder the effective administration of this part, and (2) will not be contrary to any provisions of law. Variations from requirements granted under this paragraph are conditioned on compliance with the procedures, conditions, and limitations set forth in the approval of the application. Failure to comply in good faith with the procedures, conditions, and limitations shall automatically terminate the authority for the variations, and the person granted the variance shall fully comply with the prescribed requirements of regulations from which the variations were authorized. Authority for any variation may be withdrawn whenever, in the judgment of the Director, the effective administration of this part is hindered by the continuation of the variation. Where a person desires to employ an emergency variation, a written application shall be submitted to the appropriate regional director (compliance) for transmittal to the Director. The application shall describe the proposed variation and set forth the reasons for it. Variations may not be employed until the application is approved.

(c) Retention of approved variations. The person granted the variance shall retain and make available for examination by ATF officers any application approved by the Director under this section.

Subpart D-Special (Occupational) Taxes

§ 479.31 Liability for tax.

(a) General. Every person who engages in the business of importing, manufacturing, or dealing in (including pawnbrokers) firearms in the United States shall pay a special (occupational) tax at a rate specified by § 479.32. The tax shall be paid on or before the date of commencing the taxable business, and thereafter every year on or before July 1. Special (occupational) tax shall not be prorated. The tax shall be computed for the entire tax year (July 1 through June 30), regardless of the portion of the year during which the taxpayer engages in business. Persons commencing business at any time after July 1 in any year are liable for the special (occupational) tax for the entire tax year.

(b) Each place of business taxable. An importer, manufacturer, or dealer in firearms incurs special tax liability at each place of business where an occupation subject to special tax is conducted. A place of business means the entire office, plant or area of the business in any one location under the same proprietorship. Passageways, streets, highways, rail crossings, waterways, or partitions dividing the premises are not sufficient separation to require additional special tax, if the divisions of the premises are otherwise contiguous. See also §§ 479.38-479.39.

§ 479.32 Special (occupational) tax rates.

(a) Prior to January 1, 1988, the special (occupational) tax rates were as follows:

	Per year or fraction thereof
Class 1 Importer of firearms	$500.
Class 2 Manufacturer of firearms	$500.
Class 3 Dealer in firearms	$200
Class 4 Importer only of weapons classified as "any other weapon"	$25.
Class 5 Manufacturer only of weapons classified as "any other weapon"	$25.

Class 6
Dealer only in weapons classified as "any other weapon" $10.

(b) Except as provided in § 479.32a, the special (occupational) tax rates effective January 1, 1988, are as follows:

	Per year or fraction Thereof
Class 1 Importer of firearms (including an importer only of weapons classified as "any other weapon")	$1000.
Class 2 Manufacturer of firearms (including a manufacturer only of weapons classified as "any other weapon")	$1000.
Class 3 Dealer in firearms (including a dealer only of weapons classified as "any other weapon")	$500.

(c) A taxpayer who was engaged in a business on January 1, 1988, for which a special (occupational) tax was paid for a taxable period which began before January 1, 1988, and included that date, shall pay an increased special tax for the period January 1, 1988, through June 30, 1988. The increased tax shall not exceed one half the excess (if any) of (1) the rate of special tax in effect on January 1, 1988, over (2) the rate of such tax in effect on December 31, 1987. The increased special tax shall be paid on or before April 1, 1988.

§ 479.32a Reduced rate of tax for small importers and manufacturers.

(a) General. Effective January 1, 1988, 26 U.S.C. 5801(b) provides for a reduced rate of special tax with respect to any importer or manufacturer whose gross receipts (for the most recent taxable year ending before the first day of the taxable period to which the special tax imposed by § 479.32 relates) are less than $500,000. The rate of tax for such an importer or manufacturer is $500 per year or fraction thereof. The "taxable year" to be used for determining gross receipts is the taxpayer's income tax year. All gross receipts of the taxpayer shall be included, not just the gross receipts of the business subject to special tax. Proprietors of new businesses that have not yet begun a taxable year, as well as proprietors of existing businesses that have not yet ended a taxable year, who commence a new activity subject to special tax, quality for the reduced special (occupational) tax rate, unless the business is a member of a "controlled group;" in that case, the rules of paragraph (b) of this section shall apply.

(b) Controlled group. All persons treated as one taxpayer under 26 U.S.C. 5061 (e)(3) shall be treated as one taxpayer for the purpose of determining gross receipts under paragraph (a) of this section. "Controlled group" means a controlled group of corporations, as defined in 26 U.S.C. 1563 and implementing regulations in 26 CFR 1.1563-1 through 1.1563-4, except that the words "at least 80 percent" shall be replaced by the words "more than 50 percent" in each place they appear in subsection (a) of 26 U.S.C. 1563, as well as in the implementing regulations. Also, the rules for a "controlled group of corporations" apply in a similar fashion to groups which include partnerships and/or sole proprietorships. If one entity maintains more than 50% control over a group consisting of corporations and one, or more, partnerships and/or sole proprietorships, all of the members of the controlled group are one taxpayer for the purpose of this section.

(c) Short taxable year. Gross receipts for any taxable year of less than 12 months shall be annualized by multiplying the gross receipts for the short period by 12 and dividing the result by the number of months in the short period, as required by 26 U.S.C. 448(c)(3).

(d) Returns and allowances. Gross receipts for any taxable year shall be reduced by returns and allowances made during that year under 26 U.S.C. 448(c)(3).

§ 479.33 Special exemption.

(a) Any person required to pay special (occupational) tax under this part shall be relieved from payment of that tax if he establishes to the satisfaction of the Director that his business is conducted exclusively with, or on behalf of, the United States or any department, independent establishment, or agency thereof. The Director may relieve any person manufacturing firearms for or on behalf of the United States from compliance with any provision of this part in the conduct of the business with respect to such firearms.

(b) The exemption in this section may be obtained by filing with the Director an application, in letter form, setting out the manner in which the applicant conducts his business, the type of firearm to be manufactured, and proof satisfactory to the Director of the existence of the contract with the United States, department, independent establishment, or agency thereof, under which the applicant intends to operate.

§ 479.34 Special tax registration and return.

(a) General. Special tax shall be paid by return. The prescribed return is ATF Form 5630.7, Special Tax

Registration and Return. Special tax returns, with payment of tax, shall be filed with A TF in accordance with instructions on the form. Properly completing, signing, and timely filing of a return (Form 5630.7) constitutes compliance with 26 U.S.C. 5802.

(b) Preparation of ATF Form 5630.7. All of the information called for on Form 5630.7 shall be provided, including:

(1) The true name of the taxpayer.

(2) The trade name(s) (if any) of the business(es) subject to special tax.

(3) The employer identification number (see § 479.35).

(4) The exact location of the place of business, by name and number of building or street, or if these do not exist, by some description in addition to the post office address. In the case of one return for two or more locations, the address to be shown shall be the taxpayer's principal place of business (or principal office, in the case of a corporate taxpayer).

(5) The class(es) of special tax to which the taxpayer is subject.

(6) Ownership and control information: That is, the name, position, and residence address of every owner of the business and of every person having power to control its management and policies with respect to the activity subject to special tax. "Owner of the business" shall include every partner, if the taxpayer is a partnership, and every person owning 10% or more of its stock, if the taxpayer is a corporation. However, the ownership and control information required by this paragraph need not be stated if the same information has been previously provided to ATF in connection with a license application under Part 478 of this chapter, and if the information previously provided is still current.

(c) Multiple locations and/or classes of tax. A taxpayer subject to special tax for the same period at more than one location or for more than one class of tax shall

(1) File one special tax return,

ATF Form 5630.7, with payment of tax, to cover all such locations and classes of tax; and

(2) Prepare, in duplicate, a list identified with the taxpayer's name, address (as shown on ATF Form 5630.7), employer identification number, and period covered by the return. The list shall show, by States, the name, address, and tax class of each location for which special tax is being paid. The original of the list shall be filed with A TF in accordance with instructions on the return, and the copy shall be retained at the taxpayer's principal place of business (or principal office, in the case of a corporate taxpayer) for not less than 3 years.

(d) Signing of ATF Forms 5630.7- (1) Ordinary returns. The return of an individual proprietor shall be signed by the individual. The return of a partnership shall be signed by a general partner. The return of a corporation shall be signed by any officer. In each case, the person signing the return shall designate his or her capacity as "individual owner," "member of firm," or, in the case of a corporation, the title of the officer.

(2) Fiduciaries. Receivers, trustees, assignees, executors, administrators, and other legal representatives who continue the business of a bankrupt, insolvent, deceased person, etc., shall indicate the fiduciary capacity in which they act.

(3) Agent or attorney in fact. If a return is signed by an agent or attorney in fact, the signature shall be preceded by the name of the principal and followed by the title of the agent or attorney in fact. A return signed by a person as agent will not be accepted unless there is filed, with the ATF office with which the return is required to be filed, a power of attorney authorizing the agent to perform the act.

(4) Perjury statement. ATF Forms 5630.7 shall contain or be verified by a written declaration that the

return has been executed under the penalties of perjury.

(e) Identification of taxpayer. If the taxpayer is an individual, with the initial return such person shall securely attach to Form 5630.7 a photograph of the individual 2 x 2 inches in size, clearly showing a full front view of the features of the individual with head bare, with the distance from the top of the head to the point of the chin approximately 1 1/4 inches, and which shall have been taken within 6 months prior to the date of completion of the return. The individual shall also attach to the return a properly completed FBI Form FD-258 (Fingerprint Card). The fingerprints must be clear for accurate classification and should be taken by someone properly equipped to take them: Provided, That the provisions of this paragraph shall not apply to individuals who have filed with A TF a properly executed Application for License under 18 U.S.C. Chapter 44, Firearms, ATF Form 7 (5310.12) (12-93 edition), as specified in § 478.44(a).

§ 479.35 Employer identification number.

(a) Requirement. The employer identification number (defined in 26 CFR 301.7701-12) of the taxpayer who has been assigned such a number shall be shown on each special tax return, including amended returns, filed under this subpart. Failure of the taxpayer to include the employer identification number may result in the imposition of the penalty specified in § 70.113 of this chapter.

(b) Application for employer identification number. Each taxpayer who files a special tax return, who has not already been assigned an employer identification number, shall file IRS Form SS-4 to apply for one. The taxpayer shall apply for and be assigned only one employer identification number, regardless of the number of places of business for which the taxpayer is required to file a special tax return. The employer identification number shall be applied for no later than 7 days after the filing of the taxpayer's first special tax return. IRS Form SS-4 may be obtained from the director of an IRS service center or from any IRS district director.

(c) Preparation and filing of IRS Form SS-4. The taxpayer shall prepare and file IRS Form SS-4, together with any supplementary statement, in accordance with the instructions on the form or issued in respect to it.

§ 479.36 The special tax stamp, receipt for special (occupational) taxes.

Upon filing a properly completed and executed return (Form 5630.7) accompanied by remittance of the full amount due, the taxpayer will be issued a special tax stamp as evidence of payment of the special (occupational) tax.

§ 479.37 Certificates in lieu of stamps lost or destroyed.

When a special tax stamp has been lost or destroyed, such fact should be reported immediately to the regional director (compliance) who issued the stamp. A certificate in lieu of the lost or destroyed stamp will be issued to the taxpayer upon the submission of an affidavit showing to the satisfaction of the regional director (compliance) that the stamp was lost or destroyed.

§ 479.38 Engaging in business at more than one location.

A person shall pay the special (occupational) tax for each location where he engages in any business taxable under 26 U.S.C. 5801. However, a person paying a special (occupational) tax covering his principal place of business may utilize other locations solely for storage of firearms without incurring special (occupational) tax liability at such locations. A manufacturer, upon the single payment of the appropriate special (occupational) tax, may sell firearms, if such firearms are of his own manufacture, at the place of manufacture and at his principal office or place of business if no such firearms, except samples, are kept at such office or place of business. When a person changes the location of a business for which he has paid the special (occupational) tax, he will be liable for another such tax unless the change is properly registered with the regional director (compliance) for the region in which the special tax stamp was issued, as provided in § 479.46.

§ 479.39 Engaging in more than one business at the same location.

If more than one business taxable under 26 U.S.C. 5801 is carried on at the same location during a taxable year, the special (occupational) tax imposed on each such business must be paid. This section does not require a qualified manufacturer or importer to qualify as a dealer if such manufacturer or importer also engages in business on his qualified premises as a dealer. However, a qualified manufacturer who engages in business as an importer must also qualify as an importer. Further, a qualified dealer is not entitled to engage in business as a manufacturer or importer.

§ 479.40 Partnership liability.

Any number of persons doing business in partnership at anyone location shall be required to pay but one special (occupational) tax.

§ 479.41 Single sale.

A single sale, unattended by circumstances showing the one making the sale to be engaged in business, does not create special (occupational) tax liability.

Change of ownership

§ 479.42 Changes through death of owner.

Whenever any person who has paid special (occupational) tax dies, the surviving spouse or child, or executors or administrators, or other legal representatives, may carry on this business for the remainder of the term for which tax has been paid and at the place (or places) for which the tax was paid, without any additional payment, subject to the following conditions. If the surviving spouse or child, or executor or administrator, or other legal representative of the deceased taxpayer continues the business, such person shall, within 30 days after the date on which the successor begins to carry on the business, file a new return, Form 5630.7, with ATF in accordance with the instructions on the form. The return thus executed shall show the name of the original taxpayer, together with the basis of the succession. (As to liability in case of failure to register, see § 479.49.)

§ 479.43 Changes through bankruptcy of owner.

A receiver or referee in bankruptcy may continue the business under the stamp issued to the taxpayer at the place and for the period for which the tax was paid. An assignee for the benefit of creditors may continue business under his assignor's special tax stamp without incurring additional special (occupational) tax liability. In such cases, the change shall be registered with A TF in a manner similar to that required by § 479.42.

§ 479.44 Change in partnership or unincorporated association.

When one or more members withdraw from a partnership or an unincorporated association, the remaining member, or members, may, without incurring additional special (occupational) tax liability, carry on the same business at the same location for the balance of the taxable period for which special (occupational) tax was paid, provided any such change shall be registered in the same manner as required by § 479.42. Where new member(s) are taken into a partnership or an unincorporated association, the new firm so constituted may not carry on business under the special tax stamp of the old firm. The new firm must file a return, pay the special (occupational) tax and register in the same manner as a person who first engages in business is required to do under § 479.34 even though the name of the new firm may be the same as that of the old. Where the members of a partnership or an unincorporated association, which has paid special (occupational) tax, form a corporation to continue the business, a new special tax stamp must be taken out in the name of the corporation.

§ 479.45 Changes in corporation.

Additional special (occupational) tax is not required by reason of a mere change of name or increase in the capital stock of a corporation if the laws of the State of incorporation provide for such change or increase without the formation of a new corporation. A stockholder in a corporation, who after its dissolution continues the business, incurs new special (occupational) tax liability.

Change of Business Location

§ 479.46 Notice by taxpayer.

Whenever during the taxable year a taxpayer intends to remove his business to a location other than specified in his last special (occupational) tax return (see § 479.34), he shall file with ATF (a) a return, Form 5630.7, bearing the notation "Removal Registry," and showing the new address intended to be used, (b) his current special tax stamp, and (c) a letter application requesting the amendment of his registration. The regional director (compliance), upon approval of the application, shall return the special tax stamp, amended to show the new business location. Firearms operations shall not be commenced at the new business location by the taxpayer prior to the required approval of his application to so change his business location.

Change of Trade Name

§ 479.47 Notice by taxpayer.

Whenever during the taxable year a taxpayer intends to change the name of his business, he shall file with ATF (a) a return, Form 5630.7, bearing the notation "Amended," and showing the trade name intended to be used, (b) his current special tax stamp, and (c) a letter application requesting the amendment of his registration. The regional director (compliance), upon approval of the application, shall return the special tax stamp, amended to show the new trade name. Firearms operations shall not be commenced under the new trade name by the taxpayer prior to the required approval of his application to so change the trade name.

Penalties and Interest

§ 479.48 Failure to pay special (occupational) tax.

Any person who engages in a business taxable under 26 U.S.C. 5801, without timely payment of the tax imposed with respect to such business (see § 479.34) shall be liable for such tax, plus the interest and penalties thereon (see 26 U.S.C. 6601 and 6651). In addition, such person may be liable for criminal penalties under 26 U.S.C. 5871.

§ 479.49 Failure to register change or removal.

Any person succeeding to and carrying on a business for which special (occupational) tax has been paid without registering such change within 30 days thereafter, and any taxpayer removing his business with respect to which special (occupational) tax has been paid to a place other than that for which tax was paid without obtaining approval therefor (see § 479.46), will incur liability to an additional payment of the tax, addition to tax and interest, as provided in sections 5801, 6651, and 6601, respectively, LRC., for failure to make return (see § 479.50) or pay tax, as well as criminal penalties for carrying on business without payment of special (occupational) tax (see section 5871 LRC.)

§ 479.50 Delinquency.

Any person liable for special (occupational) tax under section 5801, LR.C., who fails to file a return (Form 5630.7), as prescribed, will be liable for a delinquency penalty computed on the amount of tax due unless a return (Form 5630.7) is later filed and failure to file the return timely is shown to the satisfaction of the regional director (compliance), to be due to reasonable cause. The delinquency penalty to be added to the tax is 5 percent if the failure is for not more than 1 month, with an additional 5 percent for each additional month or fraction thereof during which failure continues, not to exceed 25 percent in the aggregate (section 6651, LRC.). However, no delinquency penalty is assessed where the 50 percent addition to tax is assessed for fraud (see § 479.51).

§ 479.51 Fraudulent return.

If any part of any underpayment of tax required to be shown on a return is due to fraud, there shall be added to the tax an amount equal to 50 percent of the underpayment, but no delinquency penalty shall be assessed with respect to the same underpayment (section 6653, I.R.C.).

Application of State Laws

§ 479.52 State regulations.

Special tax stamps are merely receipts for the tax. Payment of tax under Federal law confers no privilege to act contrary to State law. One to whom a special tax stamp has been issued may still be punishable under a State law prohibiting or controlling the manufacture, possession or transfer of firearms. On the other hand, compliance with State law confers no immunity under Federal law. Persons who engage in the business of importing, manufacturing or dealing in firearms, in violation of the law of a State, are nevertheless required to pay special (occupational) tax as imposed under the internal revenue laws of the United States. For provisions relating to restrictive use of information furnished to comply with the provisions of this part see § 479.23.

Subpart E- Tax on Making Firearms

§ 479.61 Rate of tax.

Except as provided in this subpart, there shall be levied, collected, and paid upon the making of a firearm a tax at the rate of $200 for each firearm made. This tax shall be paid by the person making the firearm. Payment of the tax on the making of a firearm shall be represented by a $200 adhesive stamp bearing the words "National Firearms Act: The stamps are maintained by the Director.

Application to Make a Firearm

§ 479.62 Application to make.

No person shall make a firearm unless the person has filed with the Director a written application on Form 1 (Firearms), Application to Make and Register a Firearm, in duplicate, executed under the penalties of perjury, to make and register the firearm and has received the approval of the Director to make the firearm which approval shall effectuate registration of the weapon to the applicant. The application shall identify the firearm to be made by serial number, type, model, caliber or gauge, length of barrel, other marks of identification, and the name and address of original manufacturer (if the applicant is not the original manufacturer). The applicant must be identified on the Form 1 (Firearms) by name and address and, if other than a natural person, the name and address of the principal officer or authorized representative and the employer identification number and, if an individual, the identification must include the date and place of birth and the information prescribed in § 479.63. Each applicant shall identify the Federal firearms license and special (occupational) tax stamp issued to the applicant, if any. The applicant shall also show required information evidencing that making or possession of the firearm would not be in violation of law. If the making is taxable, a remittance in the amount of $200 shall be submitted with the application in accordance with the instructions on the form. If the making is taxable and the application is approved, the Director will affix a National Firearms Act stamp to the original application in the space provided therefor and properly cancel the stamp (see § 479.67). The approved application will be returned to the applicant. If the making of the firearm is tax exempt under this part, an explanation of the basis of the exemption shall be attached to the Form 1 (Firearms).

§ 479.63 Identification of applicant..

If the applicant is an individual, the applicant shall securely attach to each copy of the Form 1 (Firearms), in the space provided on the form, a photograph of the applicant 2 x 2 inches in size, clearly showing a full front view of the features of the applicant with head bare, with the distance from the top of the head to the point of the chin approximately 1 1/4 inches, and which shall have been taken within 1 year prior to the date of the application. The applicant shall attach two properly completed FBI Forms FD-258 (Fingerprint Card) to the application. The fingerprints must be clear for accurate classification and should be taken by someone properly equipped to take them. A certificate of the local chief of police, sheriff of the county, head of the State police, State or local district attorney or prosecutor, or such other person whose certificate may in a particular case be acceptable to the Director, shall be completed on each copy of the Form 1 (Firearms). The certificate shall state that the certifying official is satisfied that the fingerprints and photograph accompanying the application are those of the applicant and that the certifying official has no information indicating that possession of the firearm by the maker would be in violation of State or local law or that the maker will use the firearm for other than lawful purposes.

§ 479.64 Procedure for approval of application.

The application to make a firearm, Form 1 (Firearms), must be forwarded directly, in duplicate, by the maker of the firearm to the Director in accordance with the instructions on the form. The Director will consider the application for approval or disapproval. If the application is approved, the Director will return the original thereof to the maker of the firearm and retain the duplicate. Upon receipt of the approved application, the maker is authorized to make the firearm described therein. The maker of the firearm shall not, under any circumstances, make the firearm until the application, satisfactorily executed, has been forwarded to the Director and has been approved and returned by the Director with the National Firearms Act stamp affixed. If the application is disapproved, the original Form 1(Firearms) and the remittance submitted by the applicant for the purchase of the stamp will be returned to the applicant with the reason for disapproval stated on the form.

§ 479.65 Denial of application.

An application to make a firearm shall not be approved by the Director if the making or possession of the firearm would place the person making the firearm in violation of law.

§ 479.66 Subsequent transfer of firearms.

Where a firearm which has been made in compliance with 26 U.S.C. 5821, and the regulations contained in this part, is to be transferred subsequently, the transfer provisions of the firearms laws and regulations must be complied with. (See subpart F of this part).

§ 479.67 Cancellation of stamp.

The person affixing to a Form 1(Firearms) a "National Firearms Act stamp shall cancel it by writing or stamping thereon, in ink, his initials, and the day, month and year, in such manner as to render it unfit for reuse. The cancellation shall not so deface the stamp as to prevent its denomination and genuineness from being readily determined.

Exceptions to Tax on Making Firearms

§ 479.68 Qualified manufacturer.

A manufacturer qualified under this part to engage in such business may make firearms without payment of the making tax. However, such manufacturer shall report and register each firearm made in the manner prescribed by this part.

§ 479.69 Making a firearm for the United States.

A firearm may be made by, or on behalf of, the United States or any department, independent establishment, or agency thereof without payment of the making tax. However, if a firearm is to be made on behalf of the United States, the maker must file an application, in duplicate, on Form 1 (Firearms) and obtain the approval of the Director in the manner prescribed in § 479.62.

§ 479.70 Certain government entities.

A firearm may be made without payment of the making tax by, or on behalf of, any State, or possession of the United States, any political subdivision thereof, or any official police organization of such a government entity engaged in criminal investigations. Any person making a firearm under this exemption shall first file an application, in duplicate, on Form 1 (Firearms) and obtain the approval of the Director as prescribed in § 479.62.

Registration

§ 479.71 Proof of registration.

The approval by the Director of an application, Form 1 (Firearms), to make a firearm under this subpart shall effectuate registration of the firearm described in the Form 1 (Firearms) to the person making the firearm. The original Form 1 (Firearms) showing approval by the Director shall be retained by the maker to establish proof of his registration of the firearm described therein, and shall be made available to any ATF officer on request.

Subpart F-Transfer Tax § 479.81 Scope of tax.

Except as otherwise provided in this part, each transfer of a firearm in the United States is subject to a tax to be represented by an adhesive stamp of the proper denomination bearing the words "National Firearms Act" to be affixed to the Form 4 (Firearms), Application for Transfer and Registration of Firearm, as provided in this subpart.

§ 479.82 Rate of tax.

The transfer tax imposed with respect to firearms transferred within the United States is at the rate of $200 for each firearm transferred, except that the transfer tax on any firearm classified as "any other weapon" shall be at the rate of $5 for each such firearm transferred. The tax imposed on the transfer of the firearm shall be paid by the transferor.

§ 479.83 Transfer tax in addition to import duty.

The transfer tax imposed by section 5811, !.R.C., is in addition to any import duty.

Application and Order for Transfer of Firearm

§ 479.84 Application to transfer.

Except as otherwise provided in this subpart, no firearm may be transferred in the United States unless an application, Form 4 (Firearms), Application for Transfer and Registration of Firearm, in duplicate, executed under the penalties of perjury to transfer the firearm and register it to the transferee has been filed with and approved by the Director. The application, Form 4 (Firearms), shall be filed by the transferor and shall identify the firearm to be transferred by type; serial number; name and address of the manufacturer and importer, if known; model; caliber, gauge or size; in the case of a short-barreled shotgun or a short-barreled rifle, the length of the barrel; in the case of a weapon made from a rifle or shotgun, the overall length of the weapon and the length of the barrel; and any other identifying marks on the firearm. In the event the firearm does not bear a serial number, the applicant shall obtain a serial number from the Regional director (compliance) and shall stamp (impress) or otherwise conspicuously place such serial number on the firearm in a manner not susceptible of being readily obliterated, altered or removed. The application, Form 4 (Firearms), shall identify the transferor by name and address; shall identify the transferor's Federal firearms license and special (occupational) Chapter tax stamp, if any; and if the transferor is other than a natural person, shall show the title or status of the person executing the application. The application also shall identify the transferee by name and address, and, if the transferee is a natural person not qualified as a manufacturer, importer or dealer under this part, he shall be further identified in the manner prescribed in § 479.85. The application also shall identify the special (occupational) tax stamp and Federal firearms license of the transferee, if any. Any tax payable on the transfer must be represented by an adhesive stamp of proper denomination being affixed to the application, Form 4 (Firearms), properly cancelled.

§ 479.85 Identification of transferee.

If the transferee is an individual, such person shall securely attach to each copy of the application, Form 4 (Firearms), in the space provided on the form, a photograph of the applicant 2)(2 inches in size, clearly showing a full front view of the features of the applicant with head bare, with the distance from the top of the head to the point of the chin approximately 1 1/4 inches, and which shall have been taken within 1 year prior to the date of the application. The transferee shall attach two properly completed FBI Forms FD258 (Fingerprint Card) to the application. The fingerprints must be clear for accurate classification and should be taken by someone properly equipped to take them. A certificate of the local chief of police, sheriff of the county, head of the State police, State or local district attorney or prosecutor, or such other person whose certificate may in a particular case be acceptable to the Director, shall be completed on each copy of the Form 4 (Firearms). The certificate shall state that the certifying official is satisfied that the fingerprints and photograph accompanying the application are those of the applicant and that the certifying official has no information indicating that the receipt or possession of the firearm would place the transferee in violation of State or local law or that the transferee will use the firearm for other than lawful purposes.

§ 479.86 Action on application.

The Director will consider a completed and properly executed application, Form 4 (Firearms), to transfer a firearm. If the application is approved, the Director will affix the appropriate National Firearms Act stamp, cancel it, and return the original application showing approval to the transferor who may then transfer the firearm to the transferee along with the approved application. The approval of an application, Form 4 (Firearms), by the Director will effectuate registration of the firearm to the transferee. The transferee shall not take possession of a firearm until the application, Form 4 (Firearms), for the transfer filed by the transferor has been approved by the Director and registration of the firearm is effectuated to the transferee. The transferee shall retain the approved application as proof that the firearm described therein is registered to the transferee, and shall make the approved Form 4 (Firearms) available to any ATF officer on request. If the application, Form 4 (Firearms), to transfer a firearm is disapproved by the Director, the original application and the remittance for purchase of the stamp will be returned to the transferor with reasons for the disapproval stated on the application. An application, Form 4 (Firearms), to transfer a firearm shall be denied if the transfer, receipt, or possession of a firearm would place the transferee in violation of law. In addition to any other records checks that may be conducted to determine whether the transfer, receipt, or possession of a firearm would place the transferee in violation of law, the Director shall contact the National Instant Criminal Background Check System.

§ 479.87 Cancellation of stamp.

The method of cancellation of the stamp required by this subpart as prescribed in § 479.67 shall be used.

Exemptions Relating to Transfers of Firearms

§ 479.88 Special (occupational) taxpayers.

(a) A firearm registered to a person qualified under this part to engage in business as an importer, manufacturer, or dealer may be transferred by that person without payment of the transfer tax to any other person qualified under this part to manufacture, import, or deal in firearms.

(b) The exemption provided in paragraph (a) of this section shall be obtained by the transferor of the firearm filing with the Director an application, Form 3 (Firearms), Application for Tax-exempt Transfer of Firearm and Registration to Special (Occupational) Taxpayer, in duplicate, executed under the penalties of perjury. The application, Form 3 (Firearms), shall (1) show the name and address of the transferor and of the transferee, (2) identify the Federal firearms license and special (occupational) tax stamp of the transferor and of the transferee, (3) show the name and address of the manufacturer and the importer of the firearm, if known, (4) show the type, model, overall length (if applicable), length of barrel, caliber, gauge or size, serial number, and other marks of identification of the firearm, and (5) contain a statement by the transferor that he is entitled to the exemption because the transferee is a person qualified under this part to manufacture, import, or deal in firearms. If the Director approves an application, Form 3 (Firearms), he shall return the original Form 3 (Firearms) to the transferor with the approval noted thereon. Approval of an application, Form 3 (Firearms), by the Director shall remove registration of the firearm reported thereon from the transferor and shall effectuate the registration of that firearm to the transferee. Upon receipt of the approved Form 3 (Firearms), the transferor shall deliver same with the firearm to the transferee. The transferor shall not transfer the firearm to the transferee until his application, Form 3 (Firearms), has been approved by the Director and the original thereof has been returned to the transferor. If the Director disapproves the application, Form 3 (Firearms), he shall return the original Form 3 (Firearms) to the transferor with the reasons for the disapproval stated thereon.

(c) The transferor shall be responsible for establishing the exempt status of the transferee before making a transfer under the provisions of this section. Therefore, before engaging in transfer negotiations with the transferee, the transferor should satisfy himself as to the claimed exempt status of the transferee and the bona fides of the transaction. If not fully satisfied, the transferor should communicate with the Director, report all circumstances regarding the proposed transfer, and await the Director's advice before making application for the transfer. An unapproved transfer or a transfer to an unauthorized person may subject the transferor to civil and criminal liabilities. (See 26 U.S.C. 5852, 5861, and 5871.)

§ 479.89 Transfers to the United States.

A firearm may be transferred to the United States or any department, independent establishment or agency thereof without payment of the transfer tax. However, the procedures for the transfer of a firearm as provided in § 479.90 shall be followed in a tax-exempt transfer of a firearm under this section, unless the transferor is relieved of such requirement under other provisions of this part.

§ 479.90 Certain government entities.

(a) A firearm may be transferred without payment of the transfer tax to or from any State, possession of the United States, any political subdivision thereof, or any official police organization of such a governmental entity engaged in criminal investigations.

(b) The exemption provided in paragraph (a) of this section shall be obtained by the transferor of the firearm filing with the Director an application, Form 5 (Firearms), Application for Tax-exempt Transfer and Registration of Firearm, in duplicate, executed under the penalties of perjury. The application shall (1) show the name and address of the transferor and of the transferee, (2) identify the Federal firearms license and special (occupational) tax stamp, if any, of the transferor and of the transferee, (3) show the name and address of the manufacturer and the importer of the firearm, if known, (4) show the type, model, overall length (if applicable), length of barrel, caliber, gauge or size, serial number, and other marks of identification of the firearm, and (5) contain a statement by the transferor that the transferor is entitled to the exemption because either the transferor or the transferee is a governmental entity coming within the purview of paragraph (a) of this section. In the case of a transfer of a firearm by a governmental entity to a transferee who is a natural person not qualified as a manufacturer, importer, or dealer under this part, the transferee shall be further identified in the manner prescribed in § 479.85. If the Director approves an application, Form 5 (Firearms), the original Form 5 (Firearms) shall be returned to the transferor with the approval noted thereon. Approval of an application, Form 5 (Firearms), by the Director shall effectuate the registration of that firearm to the transferee. Upon receipt of the approved Form 5 (Firearms), the transferor shall deliver same with the firearm to the transferee. The transferor shall not transfer the firearm to the transferee until the application, Form 5 (Firearms), has been approved by the Director and the original thereof has been returned to the transferor. If the Director disapproves the application, Form 5 (Firearms), the original Form 5 (Firearms) shall be returned to the transferor with the reasons for the disapproval stated thereon. An application by a governmental entity to transfer a firearm shall be denied if the transfer, receipt, or possession of a firearm would place the transferee in violation of law.

(c) The transferor shall be responsible for establishing the exempt status of the transferee before making a transfer under the provisions of this section. Therefore, before engaging in transfer negotiations with the transferee, the transferor should satisfy himself of the claimed exempt status of the transferee and the bona fides of the transaction. If not fully satisfied, the transferor should communicate with the Director, report all circumstances regarding the proposed transfer, and await the Director's advice before making application for transfer. An unapproved transfer or a transfer to an unauthorized person may subject the transferor to civil and criminal liabilities. (See 26 U.S.C. 5852, 5861, and 5871.)

§ 479.91 Unserviceable firearms.

An unserviceable firearm may be transferred as a curio or ornament without payment of the transfer tax. However, the procedures for the transfer of a firearm as provided in § 479.90 shall be followed in a tax exempt transfer of a firearm under this section, except a statement shall be entered on the transfer application, Form 5 (Firearms), by the transferor that he is entitled to the exemption because the firearm to be transferred is unserviceable and is being transferred as a curio or ornament. An unapproved transfer, the transfer of a firearm under the provisions of this section which is in fact not an unserviceable firearm, or the transfer of an unserviceable firearm as something other than a curio or ornament, may subject the transferor to civil and criminal liabilities. (See 26 U.S.C. 5811, 5852, 5861, and 5871.)

§ 479.92 Transportation of firearms to effect transfer.

Notwithstanding any provision of § 478.28 of this chapter, it shall not be required that authorization be obtained from the Director for the transportation in interstate or foreign commerce of a firearm in order to effect the transfer of a firearm authorized under the provisions of this subpart.

Other Provisions

§ 479.93 Transfers of firearms to certain persons.

Where the transfer of a destructive device, machine gun, shortbarreled shotgun, or short-barreled rifle is to be made by a person licensed under the provisions of Title I of the Gun Control Act of 1968 (82 Stat. 1213) to a person not so licensed, the sworn statement required by § 478.98 of this chapter shall be attached to and accompany the transfer application required by this subpart.

Subpart G-Registration and Identification of Firearms

§ 479.101 Registration of Firearms.

(a) The Director shall maintain a central registry of all firearms in the United States which are not in the possession of or under the control of the United States. This registry shall be known as the National Firearms Registration and Transfer Record and shall include:

(1) Identification of the firearm as required by this part;

(2) Date of registration; and

(3) Identification and address of person entitled to possession of the firearm as required by this part.

(b) Each manufacturer, importer, and maker shall register each firearm he manufactures, imports, or makes in the manner prescribed by this part. Each firearm transferred shall be registered to the transferee by the transferor in the manner prescribed by this part. No firearm may be registered by a person unlawfully in possession of the firearm except during an amnesty period established under section 207 of the Gun Control Act of 1968 (82 Stat. 1235).

(c) A person shown as possessing firearms by the records maintained by the Director pursuant to the National Firearms Act (26 U.S.C. Chapter 53) in force on October 31, 1968, shall be considered to have registered the firearms in his possession which are disclosed by that record as being in his possession on October 31, 1968.

(d) The National Firearms Registration and Transfer Record shall include firearms registered to the possessors thereof under the provisions of section 207 of the Gun Control Act of 1968.

(e) A person possessing a firearm registered to him shall retain proof of registration which shall be made available to any ATF officer upon request.

(f) A firearm not identified as required by this part shall not be registered.

§ 479.102 How must firearms be identified?

(a) You, as a manufacturer, importer, or maker of a firearm, must legibly identify the firearm as follows:

(1) By engraving, casting, stamping (impressing), or otherwise conspicuously placing or causing to be engraved, cast, stamped (impressed) or placed on the frame or receiver thereof an individual serial number. The serial number must be placed in a manner not susceptible of being readily obliterated, altered, or removed, and must not duplicate any serial number placed by you on any other firearm. For firearms manufactured, imported, or made on and after January 30, 2002, the engraving, casting, or stamping (impressing) of the serial number must be to a minimum depth of .003 inch and in a print size no smaller than 1/16 inch; and

(2) By engraving, casting, stamping (impressing), or otherwise conspicuously placing or causing to be engraved, cast, stamped (impressed), or placed on the frame, receiver, or barrel thereof certain additional information. This information must be placed in a manner not susceptible of being readily obliterated, altered or removed. For firearms manufactured, imported, or made on and after January 30, 2002, the engraving, casting, or stamping (impressing) of this information must be to a minimum depth of .003

inch. The additional information includes:

(i) The model, if such designation has been made;

(U) The caliber or gauge;

(iii) Your name (or recognized abbreviation) and also, when applicable, the name of the foreign manufacturer or maker;

(iv) In the case of a domestically made firearm, the city and State (or recognized abbreviation thereof) where you as the manufacturer maintain your place of business, or where you, as the maker, made the firearm; and

(v) In the case of an imported firearm, the name of the country in which it was manufactured and the city and State (or recognized abbreviation thereof) where you as the importer maintain your place of business. For additional requirements relating to imported firearms, see Customs regulations at 19 CFR part 134.

(b) The depth of all markings required by this section will be measured from the flat surface of the metal and not the peaks or ridges. The height of serial numbers required by paragraph (a)(1) of this section will be measured as the distance between the latitudinal ends of the character impression bottoms (bases).

(c) The Director may authorize other means of identification upon receipt of a letter application from you, submitted in duplicate, showing that such other identification is reasonable and will not hinder the effective administration of this part.

(d) In the case of a destructive device, the Director may authorize other means of identifying that weapon upon receipt of a letter application from you, submitted in duplicate, showing that engraving, casting, or stamping (impressing) such a weapon would be dangerous or impracticable.

(e) A firearm frame or receiver that is not a component part of a complete weapon at the time it is sold, shipped, or otherwise disposed of by you must be identified as required by this section.

(f)(1) Any part defined as a machine gun, muffler, or silencer for the purposes of this part that is not a component part of a complete firearm at the time it is sold, shipped, or otherwise disposed of by you must be identified as required by this section.

(2) The Director may authorize other means of identification of parts defined as machine guns other than frames or receivers and parts defined as mufflers or silencers upon receipt of a letter application from you, submitted in duplicate, showing that such other identification is reasonable and will not hinder the effective administration of this part.

(Approved by the Office of Management and Budget under control number 1512--D550)

§ 419.103 Registration of firearms manufactured.

Each manufacturer qualified under this part shall file with the Director an accurate notice on Form 2 (Firearms), Notice of Firearms Manufactured or Imported, executed under the penalties of perjury, to show his manufacture of firearms. The notice shall set forth the name and address of the manufacturer, identify his special (occupational) tax stamp and Federal firearms license, and show the date of manufacture, the type, model, length of barrel, overall length, caliber, gauge or size, serial numbers, and other marks of identification of the firearms he manufactures, and the place where the manufactured firearms will be kept. All firearms manufactured by him during a single day shall be included on one notice, Form 2 (Firearms), filed by the manufacturer no later than the close of the next business day. The manufacturer shall prepare the notice, Form 2 (Firearms), in duplicate, file the original notice as prescribed herein and keep the copy with the records required by subpart I of this part at the premises covered by his special (occupational) tax stamp. Receipt of the notice, Form 2 (Firearms), by the Director shall effectuate the registration of the firearms listed on that notice. The requirements of this part relating to the transfer of a firearm are applicable to transfers by qualified manufacturers.

§ 419.104 Registration of firearms by certain governmental entities.

Any State, any political subdivision thereof, or any official police organization of such a government entity engaged in criminal investigations, which acquires for official use a firearm not registered to it, such as by abandonment or by forfeiture, will register such firearm with the Director by filing Form 10 (Firearms), Registration of Firearms Acquired by Certain Governmental Entities, and such registration shall become a part of the National Firearms Registration and Transfer Record. The application shall identify the applicant, describe each firearm covered by the application, show the location where each firearm usually will be kept, and, if the firearm is unserviceable, the application shall show how the firearm was made unserviceable. This section shall not apply to a firearm merely being held for use as evidence in a criminal proceeding. The Form 10 (Firearms) shall be executed in duplicate in accordance with the instructions thereon. Upon registering the firearm, the Director shall return the original Form 10 (Firearms) to be returned to the applicant showing such approval and he will present the approved application, Form 6 (Firearms), to the Customs officer at the port of importation. The approval of an application to import a firearm shall be automatically terminated at the expiration of one year from the date of approval unless, upon request, it is further extended by the Director. If the firearm described in the approved application is not imported prior to the expiration of the approval, the Director shall be so notified. Customs officers will not permit release of a firearm from Customs custody, except for exportation, unless covered by an application which has been approved by the Director and which is currently effective. The importation or bringing in of a firearm not covered by an approved application may subject the person responsible to civil and criminal liabilities. (26 U.S.C. 5861, 5871, and 5872.)

(b) Part 478 of this chapter also contains requirements and procedures for the importation of firearms into the United States. A firearm may not be imported into the United States under this part unless those requirements and procedures are also complied with by the person importing the firearm.

(c) The provisions of this subpart shall not be construed as prohibiting the return to the United States or any territory under its control or jurisdiction of a firearm by a person who can establish to the satisfaction of Customs that (1) the firearm was taken out of the United States or any territory under its control or jurisdiction by such person, (2) the firearm is registered to that person, and (3) if appropriate, the authorization required by Part 478 of this chapter for the transportation of such a firearm in interstate or foreign commerce has been obtained by such person.

§ 479.112 Registration of imported firearms.

(a) Each importer shall file with the Director an accurate notice on Form 2 (Firearms), Notice of Firearms Manufactured or Imported, executed under the penalties of perjury, showing the importation of a firearm. The notice shall set forth the name and address of the importer, identify the importer's special (occupational) tax stamp and Federal firearms license, and show the import permit number, the date of release from Customs custody, the type, model, length of barrel, overall length, caliber, gauge or size, serial number, and other marks of identification of the firearm imported, and the place where the imported firearm will be kept. The Form 2 (Firearms) covering an imported firearm shall be filed by the importer no later than fifteen (15) days from the date the firearm was released from Customs custody. The importer shall prepare the notice, Form 2 (Firearms), in duplicate, file the original return as prescribed herein, and keep the copy with the records required by subpart I of this part at the premises covered by the special (occupational) tax stamp. The timely receipt by the Director of the notice, Form 2 (Firearms), and the timely receipt by the Director of the copy of Form 6A (Firearms), Release and Receipt of Imported Firearms, Ammunition and Implements of War, required by § 478.112 of this chapter, covering the weapon reported on the Form 2 (Firearms) by the qualified importer, shall effectuate the registration of the firearm to the importer.

(b) The requirements of this part relating to the transfer of a firearm are applicable to the transfer of imported firearms by a qualified importer or any other person.

(c) Subject to compliance with the provisions of this part, an application, Form 6 (Firearms), to import a firearm by an importer or dealer qualified under this part, for use as a sample in connection with sales of such firearms to Federal, State or local governmental entities, will be approved if it is established by specific information attached to the application that the firearm is suitable or potentially suitable for use by such entities. Such information must show why a sales sample of a particular firearm is suitable for such use and the expected governmental customers who would require a demonstration of the firearm. Information as to the availability of the firearm to fill subsequent orders and letters from governmental entities expressing a need for a particular model or interest in seeing a demonstration. of a particular firearm would establish suitability for governmental use. Applications to import more than one firearm of a particular model for use as a sample by an importer or dealer must also establish the importer's or dealer's need for the quantity of samples sought to be imported.

(d) Subject to compliance with the provisions of this part, an application, Form 6 (Firearms), to import a firearm by an importer or dealer qualified under this part, for use as a sample in connection with sales of such firearms to Federal, State or local governmental entities, will be approved if it is established by specific information attached to the application that the firearm is particularly suitable for use by such entities. Such information must show why a sales sample of a particular firearm is suitable for such use and the expected governmental customers who would require a demonstration of the firearm. Information as to the availability of the firearm to fill subsequent orders and letters from governmental entities expressing a need for a particular model or interest in seeing a demonstration of a particular firearm would establish suitability for governmental use. Applications to import more than one firearm of a particular model for use as a sample by an importer or dealer must also establish the importer's or dealer's need for the quantity of samples sought to be imported.

§ 479.113 Conditional importation.

The Director shall permit the conditional importation or bringing into the United States of any firearm for the purpose of examining and testing the firearm in connection with making a determination as to whether the importation or bringing in of such firearm will be authorized under this subpart. An application under this section shall be filed on Form 6 (Firearms), in triplicate, with the Director. The Director may impose conditions upon any importation under this section including a requirement that the firearm be shipped directly from Customs custody to the Director and that the person importing or bringing in the firearm must agree to either export the weapon or destroy it if a final determination is made that it may not be imported or brought in under this subpart. A firearm so imported or brought into the United States may be released from Customs custody in the manner prescribed by the conditional authorization of the registrant with notification thereon that registration of the firearm has been made. The registration of any firearm under this section is for official use only and a subsequent transfer will be approved only to other governmental entities for official use.

Machine Guns

§ 479.105 Transfer and possession of machine guns.

(a) General. As provided by 26 U.S.C. 5812 and 26 U.S.C. 5822, an application to make or transfer a firearm shall be denied if the making, transfer, receipt, or possession of the firearm would place the maker or transferee in violation of law. Section 922(0), Title 18, U.S.C., makes it unlawful for any person to transfer or possess a machine gun, except a transfer to or by, or possession by or under the authority of, the United States or any department or agency thereof or a State, or a department, agency, or political subdivision thereof; or any lawful transfer or lawful possession of a machine gun that was lawfully possessed before May 19, 1986. Therefore, notwithstanding any other provision of this part, no application to make, transfer, or import a machine gun will be approved except as provided by this section.

(b) Machine guns lawfully possessed prior to May 19, 1986. A machine gun possessed in compliance with the provisions of this part prior to May 19, 1986, may continue to be lawfully possessed by the person to whom the machine gun is registered and may, upon compliance with the provisions of this part, be lawfully transferred to and possessed by the transferee.

(c) Importation and manufacture. Subject to compliance with the provisions of this part, importers and manufacturers qualified under this part may import and manufacture machine guns on or after May 19, 1986, for sale or distribution to any department or agency of the United States or any State or political subdivision thereof, or for use by dealers qualified under this part as sales samples as provided in paragraph (d) of this section. The registration of such machine guns under this part and their subsequent transfer shall be conditioned upon and restricted to the sale or distribution of such weapons for the official use of Federal, State or local governmental entities. Subject to compliance with the provisions of this part, manufacturers qualified under this part may manufacture machine guns on or after May 19, 1986, for exportation in compliance with the Arms Export Control Act (22 U.S.C. 2778) and regulations prescribed thereunder by the Department of State.

(d) Dealer sales samples. Subject to compliance with the provisions of this part, applications to transfer and register a machine gun manufactured or imported on or after May 19, 1986, to dealers qualified under this part will be approved if it is established by specific information the expected governmental customers who would require a demonstration of the weapon, information as to the availability of the machine gun to fill subsequent orders, and letters from governmental entities expressing a need for a particular model or interest in seeing a demonstration of a particular weapon. Applications to transfer more than one machine gun of a particular model to a dealer must also establish the dealer's need for the quantity of samples sought to be transferred.

(e) The making of machine guns on or after May 19, 1986. Subject to compliance with the provisions of this part, applications to make and register machine guns on or after May 19, 1986, for the benefit of a Federal, State or local governmental entity (e.g., an invention for possible Mure use of a governmental entity or the making of a weapon in connection with research and development on behalf of such an entity) will be approved if it is established by specific information that the machine gun is particularly suitable for use by Federal, State or local governmental entities and that the making of the weapon is at the request and on behalf of such an entity.

(f) Discontinuance of business. Since section 922(0), Title 18, U.S.C., makes it unlawful to transfer or possess a machine gun except as provided in the law, any qualified manufacturer, importer, or dealer intending to discontinue business shall, prior to going out of business, transfer in compliance with the provisions of this part any machine gun manufactured or imported after May 19, 1986, to a Federal, State or local governmental entity, qualified manufacturer, qualified importer, or, subject to the provisions of paragraph (d) of this section, dealer qualified to possess such, machine gun.

Subpart H-Importation and Exportation

Importation

§479.111 Procedure.

(a) No firearm shall be imported or brought into the United States or any territory under its control or jurisdiction unless the person importing or bringing in the firearm establishes to the satisfaction of the Director that the firearm to be imported or brought in is being imported or brought in for:

(1) The use of the United States or any department, independent establishment, or agency thereof or any State or possession or any political subdivision thereof; or

(2) Scientific or research purposes; or

(3) Testing or use as a model by a registered manufacturer or solely for use as a sample by a registered importer or registered dealer.

The burden of proof is affirmatively on any person importing or bringing the firearm into the United States or any territory under its control or jurisdiction to show that the firearm is being imported or

brought in under one of the above paragraphs. Any person desiring to import or bring a firearm into the United States under this paragraph shall file with the Director an application on Form 6 (Firearms), Application and Permit for Importation of Firearms, Ammunition and Implements of War, in triplicate, executed under the penalties of perjury. The application shall show the information required by subpart G of Part 478 of this chapter. A detailed explanation of why the importation of the firearm falls within the standards set out in this paragraph shall be attached to the application. The person seeking to import or bring in the firearm will be notified of the approval or disapproval of his application. If the application is approved, the original Form 6 (Firearms) will be returned to the applicant showing such approval and he will present the approved application, Form 6 (Firearms), to the Customs officer at the port of importation. The approval of an application to import a firearm shall be automatically terminated at the expiration of one year from the date of approval unless, upon request, it is further extended by the Director. If the firearm described in the approved application is not imported prior to the expiration of the approval, the Director shall be so notified. Customs officers will not permit release of a firearm from Customs custody, except for exportation, unless covered by an application which has been approved by the Director and which is currently effective. The importation or bringing in of a firearm not covered by an approved application may subject the person responsible to civil and
criminal liabilities. (26 U.S.C. 5861, 5871, and 5872.)

(b) Part 478 of this chapter also contains requirements and procedures for the importation of firearms into the United States. A firearm may not be imported into the United States under this part unless those requirements and procedures are also complied with by the person importing the firearm.

(c) The provisions of this subpart shall not be construed as prohibiting the return to the United States or any territory under its control or jurisdiction of a firearm by a person who can establish to the satisfaction of Customs that **(1)** the firearm was taken out of the United States or any territory under its control or jurisdiction by such person, **(2)** the firearm is registered to that person, and **(3)** if appropriate, the authorization required by Part 478 of this chapter for the transportation of such a firearm in interstate or foreign commerce has been obtained by such person.

§ 479.112 Registration of imported firearms.

(a) Each importer shall file with the Director an accurate notice on Form 2 (Firearms), Notice of Firearms Manufactured or Imported, executed under the penalties of perjury, showing the importation of a firearm. The notice shall set forth the name and address of the importer, identify the importer's special (occupational) tax stamp and Federal firearms license, and show the import permit number, the date of release from Customs custody, the type, model, length of barrel, overall length, caliber, gauge or size, serial number, and other marks of identification of the firearm imported, and the place where the imported firearm will be kept. The Form 2 (Firearms) covering an imported firearm shall be filed by the importer no later than fifteen (15) days from the date the firearm was released from Customs custody. The importer shall prepare the notice, Form 2 (Firearms), in duplicate, file the original return as prescribed herein, and keep the copy with the records require by subpart I of this part at the premises covered by the special (occupational) tax stamp. The timely receipt by the Director of the notice, Form 2 (Firearms), and the timely receipt by the Director of the copy of Form 6A (Firearms), Release and Receipt of Imported Firearms, Ammunition and Implements of War, required by § 478.112 of this chapter, covering the weapon reported on the Form 2 (Firearms) by the qualified importer, shall effectuate the registration of the firearm to the importer.

(b) The requirements of this part relating to the transfer of a firearm are applicable to the transfer of imported firearms by a qualified importer or any other person.

(c) Subject to compliance with the provisions of this part, an application, Form 6 (Firearms), to import a firearm by an importer or dealer qualified under this part, for use as a sample in connection with sales of such firearms to Federal, State or local governmental entities, will be approved if it is established by specific information attached to the application that the firearm is suitable or potentially suitable for use by such entities. Such information must show why a sales sample of a particular firearm is suitable for such use and the expected governmental customers who would require a demonstration of the firearm. Information as to the availability of the firearm to fill subsequent orders and letters from governmental entities expressing a need for a particular model or interest in seeing a demonstration of a particular firearm would establish suitability for governmental use. Applications to import more than one firearm of a particular model for use as a sample by an importer or dealer must also establish the importer's or dealer's need for the quantity of samples sought to be imported.

(d) Subject to compliance with the provisions of this part, an application, Form 6 (Firearms), to import a firearm by an importer or dealer qualified under this part, for use as a sample in connection with sales of such firearms to Federal, State or local governmental entities, will be approved if it is established by specific information attached to the application that the firearm is particularly suitable for use by such entities. Such information must show why a sales sample of a particular firearm is suitable for such use and the expected governmental customers who would require a demonstration of the firearm. Information as to the availability of the firearm to fill subsequent orders and letters from governmental entities expressing a need for a particular model or interest in seeing a demonstration of a particular firearm would establish suitability for governmental use. Applications to import more than one firearm of a particular model for use as a sample by an importer or dealer must also establish the importer's or dealer's need for the quantity of samples sought to be imported.

§ 479.113 Conditional importation.

The Director shall permit the conditional importation or bringing into the United States of any firearm for the purpose of examining and testing the firearm in connection with making a determination as to whether the importation or bringing in of such firearm will be authorized under this subpart. An application under this section shall be filed on Form 6 (Firearms), in triplicate, with the Director. The Director may impose conditions upon any importation under this section including a requirement that the firearm be shipped directly from Customs custody to the Director and that the person importing or bringing in the firearm must agree to either export the weapon or destroy it if a final determination is made that it may not be imported or brought in under this subpart. A firearm so imported or brought into the United States may be released from Customs custody in the manner prescribed by the conditional authorization of the Director.

Exportation

§ 479.114 Application and permit for exportation of firearms.

Any person desiring to export a firearm without payment of the transfer tax must file with the Director an application on Form 9 (Firearms), Application and Permit for Exportation of Firearms, in quadruplicate, for a permit providing for deferment of tax liability. Part 1 of the application shall show the name and address of the foreign consignee, number of firearms covered by the application, the intended port of exportation, a complete description of each firearm to be exported, the name, address, State Department license number (or date of application if not issued), and identification of the special (occupational) tax stamp of the transferor. Part 1 of the application shall be executed under the penalties of perjury by the transferor and shall be supported by a certified copy of a written order or contract of sale or other evidence showing that the firearm is to be shipped to a foreign designation. Where it is desired to make a transfer free of tax to another person who in turn will export the firearm, the transferor shall likewise file an application supported by evidence that the transfer will start the firearm in course of exportation, except, however, that where such transferor and exporter are registered special taxpayers the transferor will not be required to file an application on Form 9 (Firearms).

§ 479.115 Action by Director.

If the application is acceptable, the Director will execute the permit, Part 2 of Form 9 (Firearms), to export the firearm described on the form and return three copies thereof to the applicant. Issuance of the permit by the Director will suspend assertion of tax liability for a period of six (6) months from the date of issuance. If the application is disapproved, the Director will indicate thereon the reason for such action and return the forms to the applicant.

§ 479.116 Procedure by exporter.

Shipment may not be made until the permit, Form 9 (Firearms), is received from the Director. If exportation is to be made by means other than by parcel post, two copies of the form must be addressed to the District Director of Customs at the port of exportation, and must precede or accompany the shipment in order to permit appropriate inspection prior to lading. If exportation is to be made by parcel post, one copy of the form must be presented to the postmaster at the office receiving the parcel who will execute Part 4 of such form and return the form to the exporter for transmittal to the Director. In the event exportation is not effected, all copies of the form must be immediately returned to the Director for cancellation.

§ 479.117 Action by Customs.

Upon receipt of a permit, Form 9 (Firearms), in duplicate, authorizing the exportation of firearms, the District Director of Customs may order such inspection as deemed necessary prior to lading of the merchandise. If satisfied that the shipment is proper and the information contained in the permit to export is in agreement with information shown in the shipper's export declaration, the District Director of Customs will, after the merchandise has been duly exported, execute the certificate of exportation (Part 3 of Form 9 (Firearms»). One copy of the form will be retained with the shipper's export declaration and the remaining copy thereof win be transmitted to the Director.

§ 479.118 Proof of exportation.

Within a six-month's period from date of issuance of the permit to export firearms, the exporter shall furnish or cause to be furnished to the Director (a) the certificate of exportation (Part 3 of Form 9

(Firearms» executed by the District Director of Customs as provided in § 479.117, or (b) the certificate of mailing by parcel post (Part 4 of Form 9 (Firearms» executed by the postmaster of the post office receiving the parcel containing the firearm, or (c) a certificate of lading executed by a Customs officer of the foreign country to which the firearm is exported, or Cd) a sworn statement of the foreign consignee covering the receipt of the firearm, or (e) the return receipt, or a reproduced copy thereof, signed by the addressee or his agent, where the shipment of a firearm was made by insured or registered parcel post. Issuance of a permit to export a firearm and furnishing of evidence establishing such exportation under this section will relieve the actual exporter and the person selling to the exporter for exportation from transfer tax liability. Where satisfactory evidence of exportation of a firearm is not furnished within the stated period, the transfer tax will be assessed.

§ 479.119 Transportation of firearms to effect exportation.

Notwithstanding any provision of § 478.28 of this chapter, it shall not be required that authorization be obtained from the Director for the transportation in interstate or foreign commerce of a firearm in order to effect the exportation of a firearm authorized under the provisions of this subpart.

§479.120 Refunds.

Where, after payment of tax by the manufacturer, a firearm is exported, and satisfactory proof of exportation (see § 479.118) is furnished, a claim for refund may be submitted on Form 843 (see § 479.172). If the manufacturer waives all claim for the amount to be refunded, the refund shall be made to the exporter. A claim for refund by an exporter of tax paid by a manufacturer should be accompanied by waiver of the manufacturer and proof of tax payment by the latter.

§ 479.121 Insular possessions.

Transfers of firearms to persons in the insular possessions of the United States are exempt from transfer tax, provided title in cases involving change of title (and custody or control, in cases not involving change of title), does not pass to the transferee or his agent in the United States. However, such exempt transactions must be covered by approved permits and supporting documents corresponding to those required in the case of firearms exported to foreign countries (see §§ 479.114 and 479.115), except that the Director may vary the requirements herein set forth in accordance with the requirements of the governing authority of the insular possession. Shipments to the insular possessions will not be authorized without compliance with the requirements of the governing authorities thereof. In the case of a nontaxable transfer to a person in such insular possession, the exemption extends only to such transfer and not to prior transfers.

Arms Export Control Act

§ 479.122 Requirements.

(a) Persons engaged in the business of importing firearms are required by the Arms Export Control Act (22 U.S.C. 2778) to register with the Director. (See Part 447 of this chapter.)

(b) Persons engaged in the business of exporting firearms caliber .22 or larger are subject to the requirements of a license issued by the Secretary of State. Application for such license should be made to the Office of Munitions Control, Department of State, Washington, DC 20502, prior to exporting firearms.

Subpart I-Records and Returns

§ 479.131 Records.

For the purposes of this part, each manufacturer, importer, and dealer in firearms shall keep and maintain such records regarding the manufacture, importation, acquisition (whether by making, transfer, or otherwise), receipt, and disposition of firearms as are prescribed, and in the manner and place required, by part 478 of this chapter. In addition, each manufacturer, importer, and dealer shall maintain, in chronological order, at his place of business a separate record consisting of the documents required by this part showing the registration of any firearm to him. If firearms owned or possessed by a manufacturer, importer, or dealer are stored or kept on premises other than the place of business shown on his special (occupational) tax stamp, the record establishing registration shall show where such firearms are stored or kept. The records required by this part shall be readily accessible for inspection at all reasonable times by ATF officers.

(Approved by the Office of Management and Budget under control number *1512-0387)*

Subpart J-Stolen or Lost Firearms or Documents

§ 479.141 Stolen or lost firearms.

Whenever any registered firearm is stolen or lost, the person losing possession thereof will, immediately upon discovery of such theft or loss, make a report to the Director showing the following: (a) Name and address of the person in whose name the firearm is registered, (b) kind of firearm, (c) serial number, (d) model, (e) caliber, (I) manufacturer of the firearm, (g) date and place of theft or loss, and (h) complete statement of facts and circumstances surrounding such theft or loss.

§ 479.142 Stolen or lost documents.

When any Form 1,2,3,4,5, 6A, or 10 (Firearms) evidencing possession of a firearm is stolen, lost, or destroyed, the person losing possession will immediately upon discovery of the theft, loss, or destruction report the matter to the Director. The report will show in detail the circumstances of the theft, loss, or destruction and will include all known facts which may serve to identify the document. Upon receipt of the report, the Director will make such investigation as appears appropriate and may issue a duplicate document upon such conditions as the circumstances warrant.

Subpart K-Examination of Books and Records

§ 479.151 Failure to make returns: Substitute returns.

If any person required by this part to make returns shall fail or refuse to make any such return within the time prescribed by this part or designated by the Director, then the return shall be made by an ATF officer upon inspection of the books, but the making of such return by an ATF officer shall not relieve the person from any default or penalty incurred by reason of failure to make such return.

§ 479.152 Penalties (records and returns).

Any person failing to keep records or make returns, or making, or causing the making of, a false entry on any application, return or record, knowing such entry to be false, is liable to fine and imprisonment as provided in section 5871, I.R.C.

Subpart L-Distribution and Sale of Stamps

§ 479.161 stamps.

National Firearms Act

"National Firearms Act" stamps evidencing payment of the transfer tax or tax on the making of a firearm are maintained by the Director. The remittance for purchase of the appropriate tax stamp shall be submitted with the application. Upon approval of the application, the Director will cause the appropriate tax to be paid by affixing the appropriate stamp to the application.

§ 479.162 Stamps authorized.

Adhesive stamps of the $5 and $200 denomination, bearing the words "National Firearms Act," have been prepared and only such stamps shall be used for the payment of the transfer tax and for the tax on the making of a firearm.

§ 479.163 Reuse of stamps prohibited.

A stamp once affixed to one document cannot lawfully be removed and affixed to another. Any person willfully reusing such a stamp shall be subject to the penalty prescribed by 26 U.S.C. 7208.

Subpart M-Redemption of or Allowance for Stamps or Refunds

§ 479.171 Redemption of or allowance for stamps.

Where a National Firearms Act stamp is destroyed, mutilated or rendered useless after purchase, and before liability has been incurred, such stamp may be redeemed by giving another stamp in lieu thereof. Claim for redemption of the stamp should be filed on ATF Form 2635 (5620.8) with the Director. Such claim shall be accompanied by the stamp or by a satisfactory explanation of the reasons why the stamp cannot be returned, and shall be filed within 3 years after the purchase of the stamp.

§ 479.172 Refunds.

As indicated in this part, the transfer tax or tax on the making of a firearm is ordinarily paid by the purchase and affixing of stamps, while special tax stamps are issued in payment of special (occupational) taxes. However, in exceptional cases, transfer tax, tax on the making of firearms, and/or special (occupational) tax may be paid pursuant to assessment. Claims for refunds of such taxes, paid pursuant to assessment, shall be filed on ATF Form 2635 (5620.8) within 3 years next after payment of the taxes. Such claims shall be filed with the regional director (compliance) serving the region in which the tax was paid. (For provisions relating to hand-carried documents and manner of filing, see 26 CFR 301.60911 (b) and 301.6402-2(a).) When an applicant to make or transfer a firearm wishes a refund of the tax paid on an approved application where the firearm was not made pursuant to an approved Form 1 (Firearms) or transfer of the firearm did not take place pursuant to an approved Form 4 (Firearms), the applicant shall file a claim for refund of the tax on ATF Form 2635 (5620.8) with the Director. The claim shall be accompanied by the approved application bearing the stamp and an explanation why the tax liability was not incurred. Such claim shall be filed within 3 years next after payment of the tax.

Subpart N-Penalties and Forfeitures

§ 479.181 Penalties.

Any person who violates or fails to comply with the requirements of 26 U.S.C. Chapter 53 shall, upon conviction, be subject to the penalties imposed under 26 U.S.C. 5871.

§ 479.182 Forfeitures.

Any firearm involved in any violation of the provisions of 26 U.S.C. Chapter 53, shall be subject to seizure, and forfeiture under the internal revenue laws: Provided, however, That the disposition of forfeited firearms shall be in conformance with the requirements of 26 U.S.C. 5872. In addition, any vessel, vehicle or aircraft used to transport, carry, conveyor conceal or possess any firearm with respect to which there has been committed any violation of any provision of 26 U.S.C. Chapter 53, or the regulations in this part issued pursuant thereto, shall be subject to seizure and forfeiture under the Customs laws, as provided by the act of August 9, 1939 (49 U.S.C. App., Chapter 11).

Subpart O-Other Laws Applicable

§ 479.191 Applicability of other provisions of internal revenue laws.

All of the provisions of the internal revenue laws not inconsistent with the provisions of 26 U.S.C. Chapter 53 shall be applicable with respect to the taxes imposed by 26 U.S.C. 5801, 5811, and 5821 (see 26 U.S.C.5846).

§ 479.192 Commerce in firearms and ammunition.

For provisions relating to commerce in firearms and ammunition, including the movement of destructive devices, machine guns, short-barreled shotguns, or short-barreled rifles, see 18 U.S.C. Chapter 44, and Part 478 of this chapter issued pursuant thereto.

§ 479.193 Arms Export Control

For provisions relating to the registration and licensing of persons engaged in the business of manufacturing, importing or exporting arms, ammunition, or implements of war, see the Arms Export Control Act (22 U.S.C. 2778), and the regulations issued pursuant thereto. (See also Part 447 of this chapter.)

APPENDIX B

RULINGS AND ATF ARTICLES

27 CFR 479.11[232]: MEANING OF TERMS

The AR15 auto sear is a machine gun as defined by 26 U.S.C. 5845(b)

ATF Rul. 81-4

The Bureau of Alcohol, Tobacco and Firearms has examined an auto sear known by the various trade names including "AR15 Auto Sear," "Drop In Auto Sear," and "Auto Sear II," which consists of a sear mounting body, sear, return spring, and pivot pin. The Bureau finds that the single addition of this auto sear to certain AR15 type semiautomatic rifles, manufactured with M16 internal components already installed, will convert such rifles into machine guns.

The National Firearms Act, 26 U.S.C. 5845(b) defines "machine gun" to include any combination of parts designed and intended for use in converting a weapon to shoot automatically more than one shot, without manual reloading, by a single function of the trigger.

Held: The auto sear known by various trade names including "AR15 Auto Sear," "Drop In Auto Sear," and "Auto Sear II," is a combination of parts designed and intended for use in converting a weapon to shoot automatically more than one shot, without manual reloading, by a single function of the trigger. Consequently, the auto sear is a machine gun as defined by 26 U.S.C. 5845(b).

With respect to the machine gun classification of the auto sear under the National Firearms Act, pursuant to 26 U.S.C. 7805(b), this ruling will not be applied to auto sears manufactured before November 1, 1981. Accordingly, auto sears manufactured on or after November 1, 1981, will be subject to all of the provisions of the National Firearms Act and 27 C.F.R. Part 479.

Editor's Note: Regardless of the date of manufacture of a drop in auto sear, possession of such a sear and certain M16 fire control parts is possession of a machine gun as defined by the NFA. Specifically, these parts are a combination of parts designed and intended for use in converting a weapon into a machine gun as defined in the NFA. (See "Important Information Concerning AR15-Type rifles" which follows)

IMPORTANT INFORMATION CONCERNING AR-15 TYPE RIFLES

ATF has encountered various AR-15 type rifles such as those manufactured by Colt, E.A. Company, SGW, Sendra and others which have been assembled with fire control components designed for use in M16 machine guns.

---

[232] The citations to 27 CFR part 179 have been rewritten as 27 CFR part 479 in conformance with the reorganization of title 27 CFR which became effective on January 24, 2003.

The vast majority of these rifles which have been assembled with an M16 bolt carrier, hammer, trigger, disconnector and selector will fire automatically merely by manipulation of the selector or removal of the disconnector. Many of these rifles using less than the 5 M16 parts listed above will also shoot automatically by manipulation of the selector or removal of the disconnector.

Any weapon which shoots automatically, more than 1 shot, without manual reloading, by a single function of the trigger, is a machine gun as defined in 26 U.S.C. 5845(b), the National Firearms Act (NFA). In addition, the definition of machine gun also includes any combination of parts from which a machine gun may be assembled, if such parts are in possession or under the control of a person. An AR-15 type assault rifle which fires more than one shot by a single function o the trigger is a machine gun under the NFA. Any machine gun is subject to the NFA and the possession of an unregistered machine gun could the possessor to criminal prosecution.

Additionally, these rifles could pose a safety hazard in that they may fire automatically without the user being aware that the weapon will fire more than 1 shot with a single pull of the trigger.

In order to avoid violations of the NFA, M16, hammers, triggers, disconnectors, selectors and bolt carriers must not be used in assembly of AR-15 type semiautomatic rifles, unless the M16 parts have been modified to AR-15 Model SP1 configuration. Any AR-15 type rifles which have been assembled with M16 internal components should have those parts removed and replaced with AR-15 Model SP1 type parts which are available commercially. The M16 components also may be modified to AR-15 Model SP1 configuration.

It is important to note that any modification of the M16 parts should be attempted by fully qualified personnel only.

Should you have any questions concerning AR-15 type rifles with M16 parts, please contact your nearest ATF office. Our telephone numbers are listed in the **"United States Government"** section of your telephone directory under the **"United States Department of Justice."**

27 CFR 479.11: MEANING OF TERMS

The KG-9 pistol is a machinegun as defined in the National Firearms Act.

ATF Rul. 82-2

The Bureau of Alcohol, Tobacco and Firearms has examined a firearm identified as the KG-9 pistol. The KG-9 is a 9 millimeter caliber, semiautomatic firearm which is blowback operated and which fires from the open bolt position with the bolt incorporating a fixed firing pin. In addition, a component part of the weapon is a disconnector which prevents more than one shot being fired with a single function of the trigger.

The disconnector is designed in the KG-9 pistol in such a way that a simple modification to it, such as cutting, filing, or grinding, allows the pistol to operate automatically. Thus, this simple modification to the disconnector together with the configuration of the above design features (blowback operation, firing from the open bolt position, and fixed firing pin) in the KG-9 permits the firearm to shoot automatically, more than one shot, without manual reloading, by a single function of the trigger. The above combination of design features as employed in the KG-9 is normally not found in the typical sporting firearm.

The National Firearms Act, 26 U.S.C. 5845(b), defines a machine gun to include any weapon which shoots, is designed to shoot, or can be readily restored to shoot, automatically more than one shot, without manual reloading, by a single function of the trigger.

The "shoots automatically" definition covers weapons that will function automatically. The "readily restorable" definition defines weapons which previously could shoot automatically but will not in their present condition. The "designed" definition includes those weapons which have not previously functioned as machine guns but possess design features which facilitate full automatic fire by simple modification or elimination of existing component parts.

Held: The KG-9 pistol is designed to shoot automatically more than one shot, without manual reloading, by a single function of the trigger. Consequently, the KG-9 pistol is a machine gun as defined in section 5845(b) of the Act.

With respect to the machine gun classification of the KG-9 pistol under the National Firearms Act, pursuant to 26 U.S.C. § 7805(b), this ruling will not be applied to KG-9 pistols manufactured before January 19, 1982. Accordingly, KG-9 pistols manufactured on or after January 19, 1982, will be subject to all the provisions of the National Firearms Act and 27 C.F.R., Part 479.

27 CFR 479.11: MEANING OF TERMS

The SM10 and SM11A1 pistols and SAC carbines are machineguns as defined in the National Firearms Act.

ATF Rul. 82-8

The Bureau of Alcohol, Tobacco and Firearms has reexamined firearms identified as SM10 pistols, SM11A1 pistols, and SAC carbines .The SM10 is a 9 millimeter or .45ACP caliber, semiautomatic firearm; the SM11A1 is a .380ACP caliber, semiautomatic firearm. And the SAC carbine is a 9 millimeter or .45ACP caliber, semiautomatic firearm. The weapons are blowback operated, fire from the open bolt position with the bolt incorporating a fixed firing pin, and the barrels of the pistols are threaded to accept a silencer. In addition, component parts of the weapons are a disconnector and a trip which prevent more than one shot being fired with a single function of the trigger.

The disconnector and trip are designed in the SM10 and SM11A1 pistols and in the SAC carbine (firearms) in such a way that a simple modification to them, such as cutting, filing, or grinding, allows the firearms to operate automatically. Thus, this simple modification to the disconnector or trip together with the configuration of the above design features (blowback operation, firing from the open bolt position, and fixed firing pin) in the SM10 and SM11A1pistols and in the SAC carbine, permits the firearms to shoot automatically, more than one shot, without manual reloading, by a single function of the trigger. The above combination of design features as employed in the SM10 and SM11A1 pistols and the SAC carbine are normally not found in the typical sporting firearm.

The National Firearms Act, 26 U.S.C. § 5845(b), defines a machine gun to include any weapon which shoots, is designed to shoot, or can be readily restored to shoot, automatically more than one shot, without manual reloading, by a single function of the trigger.

The "shoots automatically" definition covers weapons that will function automatically. The "readily restorable" definition defines weapons which previously could shoot automatically but will not in their present condition. The "designed" definition includes those weapons which have not previously functioned as machine guns but possess design features which facilitate full automatic fire by simple modification or elimination of existing component parts.

Held: The SM10 and SM11A1 pistols and the SAC carbine are designed to shoot automatically more than one shot, without manual reloading, by a single function of the trigger. Consequently, the SM10 and SM11A1 pistols and SAC carbines are machine guns as defined in Section 5845(b) of the Act.

With respect to the machine gun classification of the SM10 and SM11A1 pistols and SAC carbines, under the National Firearms Act, pursuant to 26 U.S.C. 7805(b), this ruling will not be applied to SM10 and SM11A1 pistols and SAC carbines manufactured or assembled before June, 21, 1982. Accordingly, SM10 and SM11A1 pistols and SAC carbines, manufactured or assembled on or after June 21, 1982, will be subject to all the provisions of the National Firearms Act and 27 C.F.R., Part 479.

27 CFR 479.11: MEANING OF TERMS

The YAC STEN MK II carbine is a machine gun as defined in the National Firearms Act.

ATF Rul. 83-5

The Bureau of Alcohol, Tobacco and Firearms has examined a firearm identified as YAC STEN MK II carbine. The YAC STEN MKII carbine is a 9 millimeter caliber, semiautomatic firearm which has identical design characteristics to the original selective fire STEN submachine gun designed by Reginald Vernon Shepherd and Harold John Turpin. The weapon is blowback operated and fires from the open bolt position with the bolt incorporating a fixed firing pin. In addition, a component part of the weapon is a trip lever (disconnector) which has been modified to prevent more than one shot being fired with a single function of the trigger.

The trip lever (disconnector) is designed in such a way that a simple modification to it, such as bending, breaking or cutting, allows the weapon to operate automatically. Thus, this simple modification to the trip lever (disconnector) or trip together with STEN submachine gun design features and components in the YAC STEN MK II carbine, permits the firearm to shoot automatically, more than one shot, without manual reloading, by a single function of the trigger. The above combination of machine gun design features as employed in the YAC STEN MK II carbine are normally not found in the typical sporting firearm.

The National Firearms Act, 26 U.S.C. 5845(b), defines a machine gun to include any weapon which shoots, is designed to shoot, or can be readily restored to shoot, automatically more than one shot, without manual reloading, by a single function of the trigger.

The "shoots automatically" definition covers weapons that will function automatically. The "readily restorable" definition defines weapons which previously could shoot automatically but will not in their present condition. The "designed" definition includes those weapons which have not previously functioned as machine guns but possess specific machine gun design features which facilitate full automatic fire by simple modification or elimination of existing component parts.

Held: The YAC STEN MK II carbine is designed to shoot automatically more than one shot, without manual reloading, by a single function of the trigger. Consequently, the YAC STEN MK II semiautomatic carbine is a machine gun as defined in Section 5845(b) of the Act.

27 CFR 479.111: IMPORTATION PROCEDURE

A National Firearms Act (NFA) firearm may not be imported for use as a sample for sales to law enforcement agencies if the firearm is a curio or relic unless it is established that the firearm is particularly suitable for use as a law enforcement weapon.

ATF Rul. 85-2

The Bureau of Alcohol, Tobacco and Firearms has approved a number of applications to import National Firearms Act (NFA) firearms for the use of registered importers to generate orders for such firearms from law enforcement agencies.

A review of the characteristics of the NFA firearms approved for importation as sales samples indicates that some of the firearms are not being imported for the purposes contemplated by the statute. Some of the NFA firearms imported are, in fact, curios or relics and are more suitable for use as collector's items than law enforcement weapons.

Importations of NFA firearms are permitted by 26 U.S.C. 5844, which provides in pertinent part:

"No firearms shall be imported or brought into the United States or any territory under its control or jurisdiction unless the importer establishes, under regulations as may be prescribed by the Secretary, that the firearm to be imported or brought in is:

(1) being imported or brought in for the use of the United States or any department., independent establishment, or agency thereof or any State or possession or any political subdivision thereof; or
(2) ***
(3) being imported or brought in solely for ... use as a sample by a registered importer or registered dealer;

except that, the Secretary may permit the conditional importation or bringing in of a firearm for examination and testing in connection with classifying the firearm."

The sole purpose of the statute permitting the importation of NFA firearms as sales samples is to permit registered importers to generate orders for firearms from government agencies, on the basis of the sample.

The implementing regulation, 27 CFR Section 479.111, provides that the person importing or bringing a firearm into the United States or any territory under its control or jurisdiction has the burden of proof to affirmatively establish that the firearm is being imported or brought in for one of the authorized purposes. In addition, a detailed explanation of why the importation falls within one of the authorized purposes must be attached to the application to import. The mere statement that an NFA firearm is being imported as a sales sample for demonstration to law enforcement agencies does not meet the required burden of proof and is not a detailed explanation of why the importation falls within the import standards.

Held, an application to import a National Firearms Act firearm as a sample in connection with sales of such firearms to law enforcement agencies will not be approved if the firearm is determined to be a curio or relic unless it is established by specific information that the firearm is particularly suitable for use as a law enforcement weapon. For example, the importer must provide detailed information as to why a sales sample of a particular weapon is suitable for law enforcement purposes and the expected customers who would require a demonstration of the weapon. Information as to the availability of firearms to fill subsequent orders would help meet the burden of establishing use as a sales sample. Also, letters from law enforcement agencies expressing a need for a particular model or interest in seeing a demonstration of a particular firearm would be relevant.

Editor's Note:

The importation of machine guns for use as sales samples must also meet the requirements of 27 CFR 479.105(d).

26 U.S.C. § 5845(f)(2): DESTRUCTIVE DEVICE (Nonsporting shotgun having a bore of more than one-half inch in diameter)

The USAS-12 shotgun has a bore of more than one-half inch in diameter and is not generally recognized as particularly suitable for sporting purposes. Therefore, it is classified as a destructive device for purposes of the National Firearms Act, 26 U.S.C. Chapter 53.

ATF Rul. 94-1

The Bureau of Alcohol, Tobacco and Firearms (ATF) has examined a firearm identified as the USAS-12 shotgun to determine whether it is a destructive device as that term is used in the National Firearms Act (NFA), 26 U.S.C. Chapter 53.

The USAS-12 is a 12 gauge, gas-operated, autoloading semiautomatic shotgun which is chambered for 12 gauge 2 ¾-inch ammunition. It has an 18 ¼-inch barrel, is approximately 38 inches long, and weighs 12.4 pounds unloaded and approximately 15 pounds with a loaded magazine, depending on the capacity of the magazine. The USAS-12 is equipped with a 12 round detachable box magazine, but a 28 round detachable drum magazine is also available. The shotgun is approximately 11 inches deep with a box magazine. There is an integral carrying handle on top of the receiver which houses a rifle –type aperture rear and adjustable post-type front sight. The USAS-12 has a separate combat-style pistol grip located on the bottom of the receiver, forward of the buttstock. An optional telescopic sight may be attached to the carrying handle. The barrel is located below the operating mechanism in such fashion that the barrel is in a straight line with the center of the buttstock.

Section 5845(f), Title 26 U.S.C., classifies certain weapons as "destructive devices" which are subject to the registration and tax provisions of the NFA. Section 5845(f)(2) provides the following:

(f) **Destructive Device** – The term "destructive device" means* * *

(2) any type of weapon by whatever name known which will, or which may be readily converted to, expel a projectile by the action of an explosive or other propellant, the barrel or barrels of which have a bore of more than one-half inch in diameter, except a shotgun or shotgun shell the Secretary or his delegate finds is generally recognized as particularly suitable for sporting purposes.

A "sporting purpose" test which is almost identical to that in section 5845(f)(2) appears in 18 U.S.C. § 925(d)(3). This provision of the Gun Control Act of 21968 (GCA) provides that the Secretary shall authorize a firearm to be imported into the United States if the firearm is "generally recognized as particularly suitable for or readily adaptable to sporting purposes." With the exception of the "readily adaptable" language, this provision is identical to the sporting shotgun exception to the destructive device definition. The definition of "destructive device" in the GCA (18 U.S.C. § 921(a)(4)) is identical to that in the NFA.

In determining whether shotguns with a bore diameter of more than one-half inch in diameter are "generally recognized as particularly suitable for sporting purposes" and thus are not destructive devices under the NFA, we believe it is appropriate to use the same criteria used for evaluating shotguns under the "sporting purposes" test of section 925(d)(3). Congress used virtually identical language in describing the weapons subject to the two statutory schemes, and the language was added to the GCA and the NFA at the same time.

In connection with the determination of importability, ATF determined that the USAS-12 shotgun was not eligible for importation under the sporting purposes test in section 925(d)(3). In reaching this determination, ATF evaluated the weight, size, bulk, designed magazine capacity, configuration, and other characteristics of the USAS-12. It was determined that the weight of the USAS-12, 12.4 pounds, made it much heavier than traditional 12 gauge sporting shotguns, which made it awkward to carry for extended periods, as in hunting, and cumbersome to fire at multiple small moving targets, as in skeet and trap shooting. The width of the USAS-12 with drum magazine, approximately 6 inches, and the depth with box magazine, in excess of 11 inches, far exceed that of traditional sporting shotguns, which do not exceed 3 inches in width and 4 inches in depth. The large size and bulk of the USAS-12 made it extremely difficult to maneuver quickly enough to engage moving targets as is necessary in hunting, skeet, and trap shooting. The detachable box magazine with 12 cartridge capacity and the detachable drum magazine with 28 cartridge capacity were or a larger capacity than traditional repeating sporting shotguns, which generally contain tubular magazines with a capacity of 3 – 5 cartridges. Additionally, detachable magazines permit more rapid reloading than do tubular magazines. Finally, the combat-style pistol grip, the barrel-to-buttstock configuration, the bayonet lug, and the overall appearance and general shape of the weapon were radically different from traditional sporting shotguns and strikingly similar to shotguns designed specifically for or modified for combat and law enforcement use.

Section 7805(b), title 26 U.S.C., provides that the Secretary may prescribe the extent, if any, to which any ruling relating to the internal revenue laws shall be applied without retroactive effect. Accordingly, all rulings issued under the Internal Revenue Code are applied retroactively unless they specifically provide otherwise. Pursuant to section 7805(b), the Director, as the delegate of the Secretary, may prescribe the extent to which any ruling will apply without retroactive effect.

Held: TheUSAS-12 is a shotgun with a bore of more than one-half inch in diameter which is not particularly suitable for sporting purposes. The weight, size, bulk, designed magazine capacity, configuration, and other factors indicate that the USAS-12 is a semiautomatic version of a military type assault shotgun. Accordingly, the USAS-12 is a destructive device as that term is used in 26 U.S.C. § 5845(f)(2). Pursuant to section 7805(b), this ruling is applied prospectively effective March 1, 1994, with respect to the making, transfer, and special (occupational) taxes imposed by the NFA. All other provisions of the NFA apply retroactively effective March 1, 1994.

26 U.S.C. § 5845(f)(2): DESTRUCTIVE DEVICE (Non-sporting shotgun having a bore of more than one-half inch in diameter)

The Striker-12/Streetsweeper shotgun has a bore of more than one-half inch in diameter and is not generally recognized as particularly suitable for sporting purposes. Therefore, it is classified as a destructive device for purposes of the National Firearms Act, 26 U.S.C. Chapter 53.

ATF Rul. 94-2

The Bureau of Alcohol, Tobacco and Firearms (ATF) has examined a firearm identified as the Striker-12/Streetsweeper shotgun to determine whether it is a destructive device as that term is used in the National Firearms Act (NFA), 26 U.S.C. Chapter 53.

The Striker-12 and Streetsweeper shotguns are virtually identical 12 - gauge shotguns with a spring-driven revolving magazine. The magazine has a 12 round capacity, The shotgun has a fixed stock or folding stock and may be fired with the folding stock collapsed. The shotgun with 18-inch barrel is 37 inches in length with the stock extended, and 26 .5 inches in length with the stock folded. The shotgun is 5.7 inches in width and weighs 9.24 pounds unloaded. The Striker/Streetsweeper has two pistol grips, one in the center of the firearm below the buttstock, and one on the forearm. The Striker/Streetsweeper was designed and developed in South Africa as a military, security, and anti-terrorist weapon. Various types of 12-gauge cartridges can be fired from the shotgun, and a rapid indexing procedure allows various types of ammunition to be loaded into the cylinder and selected for firing. All 12 rounds can be fired from the shotgun in 3 seconds or less.

Section 5845(f), Title 26 U.S.C., classifies certain weapons as "destructive devices" which are subject to the registration and tax provisions of the NFA. Section 5845(f)(2) provides as follows:

(f) **Destructive Device** – The term "destructive device" means* * *

(2) any type of weapon by whatever name known which will, or which may be readily converted to, expel a projectile by the action of an explosive or other propellant, the barrel or barrels of which have a bore of more than one-half inch in diameter, except a shotgun or shotgun shell the Secretary or his delegate finds is generally recognized as particularly suitable for sporting purposes.

A "sporting purpose" test which is almost identical to that in section 5845(f)(2) appears in 18 U.S.C. § 925(d)(3). This provision of the Gun Control Act of 21968 (GCA) provides that the Secretary shall authorize a firearm to be imported into the United States if the firearm is "generally recognized as particularly suitable for or readily adaptable to sporting purposes." With the exception of the "readily adaptable" language, this provision is identical to the sporting shotgun exception to the destructive device definition. The definition of "destructive device" in the GCA (18 U.S.C. § 921(a)(4)) is identical to that in the NFA.

In determining whether shotguns with a bore diameter of more than one-half inch in diameter are "generally recognized as particularly suitable for sporting purposes" and thus are not destructive devices under the NFA, we believe it is appropriate to use the same criteria used for evaluating shotguns under the "sporting purposes" test of section 925(d)(3). Congress used virtually identical language in describing the weapons subject to the two statutory schemes, and the language was added to the GCA and the NFA at the same time.

1n 1984, ATF ruled that the Striker – 12 was not eligible for importation under section 925(d)(3) since it is not particularly suitable for or readily adaptable to sporting purposes. In making this determination, the 1984 letter-ruling notes that the Striker was being used in a number of "combat" shooting events. In a letter dated June 30, 1986, ATF again denied importation of the Striker – 12, on the basis that it did not meet the "sporting purposes" test of section 925(d)(3). This letter states that, "We believe the weapon to have been specifically designed for military and law enforcement uses."

In evaluating the physical characteristics of the Striker – 12 /Streetsweeper, ATF concludes that the weight, bulk, designed magazine capacity, configuration, and other features indicate that it was designed primarily for military and law enforcement use and is not particularly suitable for sporting purposes.

The weight of the Striker – 12/Streetsweeper, 9.24 pounds unloaded, is on the high end for traditional 12-gauge sporting shotguns, which generally weigh between 7 and 10 pounds. Thus, the weight of the Striker – 12/Streetsweepe, makes it awkward to carry for extended periods, as in hunting, and cumbersome to fire at multiple small moving targets, as in skeet and trap shooting. The width of the Striker – 12/Streetsweeper, 5.7 inches, far exceeds that of traditional sporting shotguns, which do not exceed three inches in width or four inches in depth. The large size and bulk of the Striker – 12/Streetsweeper make it extremely difficult to maneuver quickly enough to engage moving targets as is necessary in hunting, skeet and trap shooting. The spring driven revolving magazine with 12 –cartridge capacity is a much larger capacity than traditional repeating shotguns, which generally contain tubular magazines with a capacity of 3 – 5 cartridges. The folding shoulder stock and the two pistol grips are not typical of sporting-type shotguns. Finally, the overall appearance and general shape of the weapon are radically different from traditional sporting shotguns and strikingly similar to shotguns designed specifically for or modified for combat and law enforcement use.

Section 7805(b), title 26 U.S.C., provides that the Secretary may prescribe the extent, if any, to which any ruling relating to the internal revenue laws shall be applied without retroactive effect. Accordingly, all rulings issued under the Internal Revenue Code are applied retroactively unless they specifically provide otherwise. Pursuant to section 7805(b), the Director, as the delegate of the Secretary, may prescribe the extent to which any ruling will apply without retroactive effect.

Held: The Striker – 12/Streetsweeper is a shotgun with a bore of more than one-half inch in diameter which is not particularly suitable for sporting purposes. The weight, size, bulk, designed magazine capacity, configuration, and other factors indicate that the Striker – 12/Streetsweeper is a military-type shotgun, as opposed to a shotgun particularly suitable for sporting purposes. Accordingly, the Striker – 12/Streetsweeper is a destructive device as that term is used in 26 U.S.C. § 5845(f)(2). Pursuant to section 7805(b), this ruling is applied prospectively effective March 1, 1994, with respect to the making, transfer, and special (occupational) taxes imposed by the NFA. All other provisions of the NFA apply retroactively effective March 1, 1994.

18 U.S.C. § 921(a)(4)
DESTRUCTIVE DEVICE

26 U.S.C. § 5845(f)(2):
DESTRUCTIVE DEVICE

(Firearm having a bore of more than one-half inch in diameter)

37/38 mm gas/flare guns possessed with cartridges containing wood pellets, rubber pellets or balls, or bean bags are classified as destructive devices for purposes of the Gun Control Act, 18 U.S.C. Chapter 44, and the National Firearms Act, 26 U.S.C. Chapter 53.

ATF Rul. 95-3

The Bureau of Alcohol, Tobacco and Firearms (ATF) has examined various 37/38 mm gas/flare guns in combination with certain types of ammunition to determine whether these are destructive devices as defined in the Gun Control Act (GCA), 18 U.S.C. Chapter 44, and the National Firearms Act (NFA), 26 U.S.C. Chapter 53.

Section 5845(f), Title 26 U.S.C., classifies certain weapons as "destructive devices" which are subject to the registration and tax provisions of the NFA. Section 5845(f)(2) provides the following:

(f) **Destructive Device** – The term "destructive device" means* * *

(2) any type of weapon by whatever name known which will, or which may be readily converted to, expel a projectile by the action of an explosive or other propellant, the barrel or barrels of which have a bore of more than one-half inch in diameter, except a shotgun or shotgun shell the Secretary or his delegate finds is generally recognized as particularly suitable for sporting purposes: . ."

Section 5845(f)(3) excludes from the term "destructive device" any device which is neither designed or redesigned for use as a weapon and any device, although originally designed for use as a weapon, which is redesigned for use as a signaling, pyrotechnic,Line throwing, safety, or similar device.

The definition of "destructive device" in the GCA (18 U.S.C. § 921(a)(4)) is identical to that in the NFA.

ATF has previously held that devices designed for expelling tear gas or pyrotechnic signals are not weapons and are exempt from the destructive device definition. However, ammunition designed to be used against individuals is available for these 37/38 mm devices. This "anti-personnel" ammunition consists of cartridges containing wood pellets, rubber pellets or balls, and bean bags.

When a gas/flare gun is possessed with "anti-personnel" type ammunition, it clearly becomes an instrument of offensive or defensive combat and is capable of use as a weapon. Since these gas/flare guns have a bore diameter greater than one-half inch, fire a projectile by means or an explosive, and, when possessed with "anti-personnel" ammunition, are capable of use as weapons, the combination of the gas/flare gun and "anti-personnel" ammunition is a destructive as defined in the GCA and the NFA. As a result, registration as a destructive device is required. Any person possessing a gas/flare gun with which "anti-personnel" ammunition will be used must register the making of a destructive device prior to the acquisition of any "anti-personnel" ammunition. In addition, the gas/flare guns are classified as firearms as defined by the GCA when possessed with "anti-personnel" type ammunition.

Each gas/flare gun possessed with ant–personnel ammunition will be required to be identified as required by law and regulations (27 C.F.R. §§ 478.92and 479.102), including a serial number. Any person manufacturing the gas/flare gun and "anti-personnel" ammunition must, if selling them in combination, have the appropriate Federal firearms license as a manufacturer of destructive devices and must have paid the special (occupational) tax as a manufacturer of National Firearms Act firearms. Any person importing the gas/flare gun and the "anti-personnel" type ammunition must, if importing them in combination, have the appropriate Federal firearms license as an importer of destructive devices and must have paid the special (occupational) tax as an importer of National Firearms Act firearms.

Further, the "anti-personnel" ammunition to be used in the gas/flare launchers is ammunition for destructive devices for purposes of the GCA. Any person manufacturing the "anti-personnel" ammunition ,must have the appropriate Federal firearms license as a manufacturer of ammunition for destructive devices. Any person importing the "anti-personnel" ammunition must have the appropriate Federal firearms license as an importer of ammunition for destructive devices.

HELD: 37/38 mm gas/flare guns possessed with "anti-personnel" ammunition, consisting of cartridges containing wood pellets, rubber pellets or balls, or bean bags, are destructive devices as that term is used in 18 U.S.C. § 921(a)(4) and 26 U.S.C. 5845(f)(2).

26 USC 5844, 18 USC 922(o), 22 USC 2778: IMPORTATION OF BROWNING M1919 TYPE RECEIVERS FOR UNRESTRICTED COMMERCIAL SALE.

An ATF – approved method of destruction for the Browning M 1919 type machinegun will result in the severed portions of the receiver being importable for unrestricted commercial sale.

ATF Rul. 2003-1

The Bureau of Alcohol, Tobacco and Firearms (ATF) has received inquiries about modifications necessary to the receiver of a Browning M1919 type machinegun to make it importable under 26 U.S.C. 5844 and 18 U.S.C. 922(o) for unrestricted commercial sale.

The Browning M1919 is a machinegun as defined in 26 U.S.C. 5845(b). The receiver of a Browning M1919 is also a machinegun as defined. Various manufacturers made Browning M1919 style machineguns in caliber .30-06 and 7.62x51mm (.308). The M1919 is a recoil operated, belt-fed machinegun designed to be fired from a mount.

Section 5844 of title 26, United States Code, makes it unlawful to import any firearm into the United States, unless the firearm to be imported or brought in is: (1) being imported for use by the United States or any department, independent establishment, or agency thereof or any State or possession or any political subdivision thereof; or (2) the firearm is being imported for scientific or research purposes; or (3) it is being imported solely for testing or use as a model by a registered or dealer. Additionally, the Secretary may permit the conditional importation of a firearm for examination and testing in connection with classifying the firearm.

Section 922(o) of Title 18, United States Code, makes it unlawful for any person to transfer or possess a machinegun, except a transfer to or by the United States or any department or agency thereof or a State or department, agency or political subdivision thereof; or any lawful transfer or lawful possession of a machinegun lawfully possessed before May 19, 1986.

A review of the statutes above indicates that machinegun and machinegun receivers cannot be lawfully imported for unrestricted commercial sale. Accordingly. Machinegun receivers may be imported for commercial sale only if they are destroyed in a manner that will prevent their function and future use as a firearm. The resulting severed receiver portions would not be subject to the provisions of 26 U.S.C. 5844 or 18 U.S.C. 922(o); however, these articles would be subject the provisions of the Arms Export Control Act, 18 U.S.C. 925, 22 U.S.C. 2778, and implementing regulation at 27 CFR Part 47. It is important to note that these machinegun receivers must be destroyed and cannot be imported whether they are serviceable or unserviceable.

An ATF-approved method of destruction for a Browning M1919 type machinegun receiver requires three diagonal torch cuts that sever or pass through the following areas: (1) the trunion or barrel mounting block (corner to corner), (2) the center area of the bolt handle slot, and (3) the cover catch and back plate spline. All cutting must be done with a cutting torch having a tip of sufficient size to displace at least ¼ inch of material at each location. Each cut must completely sever the receiver in the designated areas and must be done with a diagonal torch cut. Using a bandsaw or a cut-off wheel to destroy the receiver does not ensure destruction of the weapon.

This method of destruction is illustrated in the diagram below.

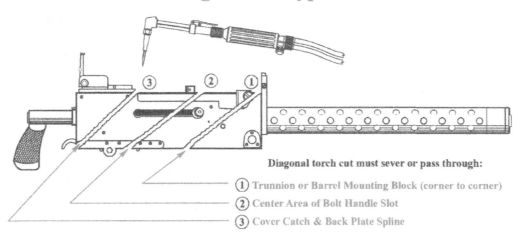

Alternative methods of destruction may also be acceptable. These alternative methods must be equivalent in degree to the approved method of destruction. Receivers that are not sufficiently modified cannot be approved for importation. To ensure compliance with the law, it is recommended that the importer submit in writing the alternative method of destruction to the ATF Firearms Technology Branch (FTB) for review and approval prior to importation.

Held, an ATF-approved method of destruction for a Browning M1919 type machinegun receiver will result in the severed portions of the receiver being importable for unrestricted commercial sale. The severed articles would not be subject to the provisions of 26 U.S.C. 5844 or 18 U.S.C. 922(o), but would continue to be subject to the provisions of the Arms Export Control Act, 22 U.S.C. 2778. Alternative methods of destruction may also be acceptable. It is recommended that such methods be reviewed and approved by the ATF Firearms Technology Branch prior to the weapon's importation.

Date signed: January 24, 2003

26 USC 5844, 18 USC 922(o), 22 USC 2778: IMPORTATION OF FN FAL TYPE RECEIVERS FOR UNRESTRICTED COMMERCIAL SALE.

<u>An ATF – approved method of destruction for the FN FAL type machinegun will result in the severed portions of the receiver being importable for unrestricted commercial sale.</u>

ATF Rul. 2003-2

The Bureau of Alcohol, Tobacco and Firearms (ATF) has received inquiries about modifications necessary to the receiver of an FN FAL type machinegun to make it importable under 26 U.S.C. 5844 and 18 U.S.C. 922(o) for unrestricted commercial sale.

The FN FAL is a machinegun as defined in 26 U.S.C. 5845(b). The receiver of an FAL is also a machinegun as defined. Various manufacturers made FAL style machineguns in caliber 7.62x51mm (.308). The FAL is a gas operated, shoulder fired, magazine fed, selective fire machinegun.

Section 5844 of title 26, United States Code, makes it unlawful to import any firearm into the United States, unless the firearm to be imported or brought in is: (1) being imported for use by the United States or any department, independent establishment, or agency thereof or any State or possession or any political subdivision thereof; or (2) the firearm is being imported for scientific or research purposes; or (3) it is being imported solely for testing or use as a model by a registered or dealer. Additionally, the Secretary may permit the conditional importation of a firearm for examination and testing in connection with classifying the firearm.

Section 922(o) of Title 18, United States Code, makes it unlawful for any person to transfer or possess a machinegun, except a transfer to or by the United States or any department or agency thereof or a State or department, agency or political subdivision thereof; or any lawful transfer or lawful possession of a machinegun lawfully possessed before May 19, 1986.

A review of the statutes above indicates that machinegun and machinegun receivers cannot be lawfully imported for unrestricted commercial sale. Accordingly. Machinegun receivers may be imported for commercial sale only if they are destroyed in a manner that will prevent their function and future use as a firearm. The resulting severed receiver portions would not be subject to the provisions of 26 U.S.C. 5844 or 18 U.S.C. 922(o); however, these articles would be subject the provisions of the Arms Export Control Act, 18 U.S.C. 925, 22 U.S.C. 2778, and implementing regulation at 27 CFR Part 47. It is important to note that these machinegun receivers must be destroyed and cannot be imported whether they are serviceable or unserviceable.

An ATF-approved method of destruction for an FN FAL type machinegun receiver requires three diagonal torch cuts that sever or pass through the following areas: (1) the threaded portion of the receiver ring and magazine well opening at bottom, (2) the hinge pin, ejector block and bolt guide rails, and (3) the body locking lug and bolt guide rails. All cutting must be done with a cutting torch having a tip of sufficient size to displace at least ¼ inch of material at each location. Each cut must completely sever the receiver in the designated areas and must be done with a diagonal torch cut. Using a bandsaw or a cut-off wheel to destroy the receiver does not ensure destruction of the weapon.

This method of destruction is illustrated in the diagram below.

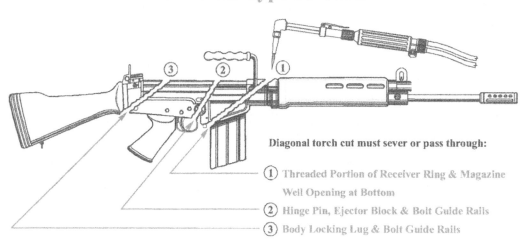

Alternative methods of destruction may also be acceptable. These alternative methods must be equivalent in degree to the approved method of destruction. Receivers that are not sufficiently modified cannot be approved for importation. To ensure compliance with the law, it is recommended that the importer submit in writing the alternative method of destruction to the ATF Firearms Technology Branch (FTB) for review and approval prior to importation.

Held, an ATF-approved method of destruction for an FN FAL type machinegun receiver will result in the severed portions of the receiver being importable for unrestricted commercial sale. The severed articles would not be subject to the provisions of 26 U.S.C. 5844 or 18 U.S.C. 922(o), but would continue to be subject to the provisions of the Arms Export Control Act, 22 U.S.C. 2778. Alternative methods of destruction may also be acceptable. It is recommended that such methods be reviewed and approved by the ATF Firearms Technology Branch prior to the weapon's importation.

Date signed: January 24, 2003

26 USC 5844, 18 USC 922(o), 22 USC 2778: IMPORTATION OF HECKLER & KOCH G3 TYPE RECEIVERS FOR UNRESTRICTED COMMERCIAL SALE.

<u>An ATF – approved method of destruction for the Heckler & Koch G3 type machinegun will result in the severed portions of the receiver being importable for unrestricted commercial sale.</u>

ATF Rul. 2003-3

The Bureau of Alcohol, Tobacco and Firearms (ATF) has received inquiries about modifications necessary to the receiver of a Heckler & Koch G3 machinegun to make it importable under 26 U.S.C. 5844 and 18 U.S.C. 922(o) for unrestricted commercial sale.

The G3 is a machinegun as defined in 26 U.S.C. 5845(b). The receiver of a G3 is also a machinegun as defined. Various manufacturers made G3 style machineguns in caliber 7.62x51mm (.308). The G3 is a delayed blowback, shoulder fired, magazine fed, selective fire machinegun.

Section 5844 of title 26, United States Code, makes it unlawful to import any firearm into the United States, unless the firearm to be imported or brought in is: (1) being imported for use by the United States or any department, independent establishment, or agency thereof or any State or possession or any political subdivision thereof; or (2) the firearm is being imported for scientific or research purposes; or (3) it is being imported solely for testing or use as a model by a registered or dealer. Additionally, the Secretary may permit the conditional importation of a firearm for examination and testing in connection with classifying the firearm.

Section 922(o) of Title 18, United States Code, makes it unlawful for any person to transfer or possess a machinegun, except a transfer to or by the United States or any department or agency thereof or a State or department, agency or political subdivision thereof; or any lawful transfer or lawful possession of a machinegun lawfully possessed before May 19, 1986.

A review of the statutes above indicates that machinegun and machinegun receivers cannot be lawfully imported for unrestricted commercial sale. Accordingly. Machinegun receivers may be imported for commercial sale only if they are destroyed in a manner that will prevent their function and future use as a firearm. The resulting severed receiver portions would not be subject to the provisions of 26 U.S.C. 5844 or 18 U.S.C. 922(o); however, these articles would be subject the provisions of the Arms Export Control Act, 18 U.S.C. 925, 22 U.S.C. 2778, and implementing regulation at 27 CFR Part 47. It is important to note that these machinegun receivers must be destroyed and cannot be imported whether they are serviceable or unserviceable.

An ATF-approved method of destruction for a Heckler & Koch G3 type machinegun receiver requires four diagonal torch cuts that sever or pass through the following areas: (1) the chamber area, (2) the grip assembly locking pin hole, (3) the ejection port, and (4) the buttstock locking pin hole. All cutting must be done with a cutting torch having a tip of sufficient size to displace at least ¼ inch of material at each location. Each cut must completely sever the receiver in the designated areas and must be done with a diagonal torch cut. Using a bandsaw or a cut-off wheel to destroy the receiver does not ensure destruction of the weapon.

This method of destruction is illustrated in the diagram below.

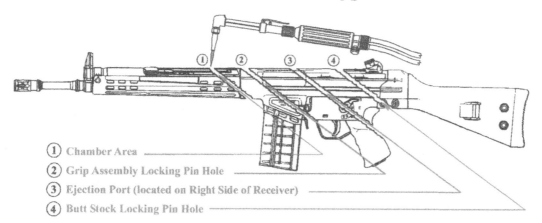

Heckler & Koch G3 Type Firearm

① Chamber Area
② Grip Assembly Locking Pin Hole
③ Ejection Port (located on Right Side of Receiver)
④ Butt Stock Locking Pin Hole

Alternative methods of destruction may also be acceptable. These alternative methods must be equivalent in degree to the approved method of destruction. Receivers that are not sufficiently modified cannot be approved for importation. To ensure compliance with the law, it is recommended that the importer submit in writing the alternative method of destruction to the ATF Firearms Technology Branch (FTB) for review and approval prior to importation.

Held, an ATF-approved method of destruction for a Heckler & Koch G3 type machinegun receiver will result in the severed portions of the receiver being importable for unrestricted commercial sale. The severed articles would not be subject to the provisions of 26 U.S.C. 5844 or 18 U.S.C. 922(o), but would continue to be subject to the provisions of the Arms Export Control Act, 22 U.S.C. 2778. Alternative methods of destruction may also be acceptable. It is recommended that such methods be reviewed and approved by the ATF Firearms Technology Branch prior to the weapon's importation.

Date signed: January 24, 2003

26 USC 5844, 18 USC 922(o), 22 USC 2778: IMPORTATION OF STEN TYPE RECEIVERS FOR UNRESTRICTED COMMERCIAL SALE.

<u>An ATF – approved method of destruction for the Sten type machinegun will result in the severed portions of the receiver being importable for unrestricted commercial sale.</u>

ATF Rul. 2003-4

The Bureau of Alcohol, Tobacco and Firearms (ATF) has received inquiries about modifications necessary to the receiver of a Sten type machinegun to make it importable under 26 U.S.C. 5844 and 18 U.S.C. 922(o) for unrestricted commercial sale.

The Sten is a machinegun as defined in 26 U.S.C. 5845(b). The receiver of a Sten is also a machinegun as defined. Various manufacturers made Sten style machineguns in caliber 9x19mm (9mm Luger). The Sten is a blowback-operated, shoulder fired, magazine fed, selective-fire submachinegun.

Section 5844 of title 26, United States Code, makes it unlawful to import any firearm into the United States, unless the firearm to be imported or brought in is: (1) being imported for use by the United States or any department, independent establishment, or agency thereof or any State or possession or any political subdivision thereof; or (2) the firearm is being imported for scientific or research purposes; or (3) it is being imported solely for testing or use as a model by a registered or dealer. Additionally, the Secretary may permit the conditional importation of a firearm for examination and testing in connection with classifying the firearm.

Section 922(o) of Title 18, United States Code, makes it unlawful for any person to transfer or possess a machinegun, except a transfer to or by the United States or any department or agency thereof or a State or department, agency or political subdivision thereof; or any lawful transfer or lawful possession of a machinegun lawfully possessed before May 19, 1986.

A review of the statutes above indicates that machinegun and machinegun receivers cannot be lawfully imported for unrestricted commercial sale. Accordingly. Machinegun receivers may be imported for commercial sale only if they are destroyed in a manner that will prevent their function and future use as a firearm. The resulting severed receiver portions would not be subject to the provisions of 26 U.S.C. 5844 or 18 U.S.C. 922(o); however, these articles would be subject the provisions of the Arms Export Control Act, 18 U.S.C. 925, 22 U.S.C. 2778, and implementing regulation at 27 CFR Part 47. It is important to note that these machinegun receivers must be destroyed and cannot be imported whether they are serviceable or unserviceable.

An ATF-approved method of destruction for a Sten type machinegun receiver requires three diagonal torch cuts that sever or pass through the following areas: (1) the threaded portion of the receiver/chamber area, (2) the return spring cap socket, and (3) the sear slot in the lower side of the receiver. All cutting must be done with a cutting torch having a tip of sufficient size to displace at least ¼ inch of material at each location. Each cut must completely sever the receiver in the designated areas and must be done with a diagonal torch cut. Using a bandsaw or a cut-off wheel to destroy the receiver does not ensure destruction of the weapon.

This method of destruction is illustrated in the diagram below.

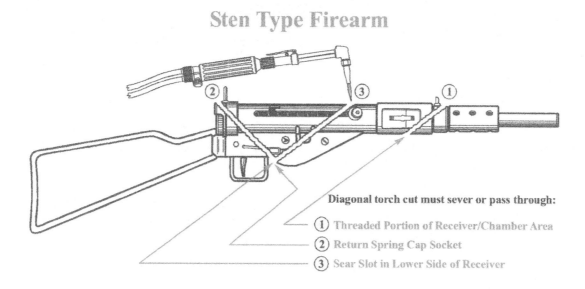

Alternative methods of destruction may also be acceptable. These alternative methods must be equivalent in degree to the approved method of destruction. Receivers that are not sufficiently modified cannot be approved for importation. To ensure compliance with the law, it is recommended that the importer submit in writing the alternative method of destruction to the ATF Firearms Technology Branch (FTB) for review and approval prior to importation.

Held, an ATF-approved method of destruction for a Sten type machinegun receiver will result in the severed portions of the receiver being importable for unrestricted commercial sale. The severed articles would not be subject to the provisions of 26 U.S.C. 5844 or 18 U.S.C. 922(o), but would continue to be subject to the provisions of the Arms Export Control Act, 22 U.S.C. 2778. Alternative methods of destruction may also be acceptable. It is recommended that such methods be reviewed and approved by the ATF Firearms Technology Branch prior to the weapon's importation.

Date signed: January 24, 2003

26 U.S.C. 5812, 5841, 5844, 5861, 5872
27 CFR 479.11, 479.26, 479.105, 479.111, 479.112, 479.114 – 479.119: **IMPORTATION OF FIREARMS SUBJECT TO THE NATIONAL FIREARMS ACT.**

18 U.S.C. 921(a)(3), 922(i), 922(o), 923(e), 924(d), 925(d)(3)
27 CFR 478.11, 478.22, 478.111 – 478.113: **IMPORTATION OF MACHINEGUNS, DESTRUCTIVE DEVICES, SHORT –BARREL SHOTGUNS, SHORT-BARREL RIFLES, FIREARMS SILENCERS, AND OTHER FIREARMS SUBJECT TO THE NATIONAL FIREARMS ACT.**

22 U.S.C. 2778
27 CFR 447.11, 447.21: **TEMPORARY IMPORTATION OF DEFENSE ARTICLES**

The Bureau of Alcohol, Tobacco, Firearms and Explosives (ATF) has approved an alternate method or procedure for importers to use when temporarily importing firearms subject to the National Firearms Act, the Gun Control Act and the Arms Export Control Act for inspection, testing, calibration, repair, or incorporation into another defense article.

ATF Rul. 2004-2

The Bureau of Alcohol, Tobacco, Firearms and Explosives (ATF) has received numerous inquiries from importers who wish to temporarily import firearms subject to the Gun Control Act of 1968 (GCA), 18 U.S.C. Chapter 44, and the National Firearms Act (NFA), 26 U.S.C. Chapter 53, for inspection, testing, calibration, repair, or incorporation into another defense article. Importers advise ATF that they generally obtain a temporary import license, DSP-61, from the Department of State authorizing the importation or comply with one of the regulatory exemptions from licensing in 22 CFR 123.4. They ask whether such a license or exemption is sufficient to satisfy the requirements of the GCA and NFA.

Statutory Background

1. *The National Firearms Act*

The NFA imposes restrictions on certain firearms, including registration requirements, transfer approval requirements, and import restrictions. 26 U.S.C. 5812, 5841, 5844. The term "firearm" is defined in 26 U.S.C. 5845(a) to include machineguns, short-barrel shotguns, short-barrel rifles, silencers, destructive devices, and "any other weapons." Section 5844 of the NFA provides that no firearm may be imported into the United States unless the importer establishes that the firearm to be imported is –

> (1) Being imported or brought in for the use of the United States or any department, independent establishment, or agency thereof or any State or possession or any political subdivision thereof; or

> (2) Being imported or brought in for scientific or research purposes; or

(3) Being imported or brought in solely for testing or use as a model by a registered manufacturer or solely for use as a sample by a registered importer or registered dealer.

Regulations implementing the NFA in 27 CFR Part 479 require importers to obtain an ATF Form 6, Application and Permit for Importation of Firearms, Ammunition and Implements of War, prior to importing NFA firearms into the United States. 27 CFR 479.111. In addition, the regulations require importers to register the firearms they import by filing with the Director an accurate notice on Form 2, Notice of Firearms Manufactured or Imported, executed under the penalties of perjury, showing the importation of the firearm. 27 CFR 479.112. When an NFA firearm is to be exported from the United States, the exporter must file with the Director an application on form 9, Application and Permit for Exportation of Firearms, to obtain authorization to export the firearm. 27 CFR 479.114-119.

Regulations in 27 CFR Part 479 indicate that NFA firearms may be imported for scientific or research purposes or for testing or use as a model by a registered manufacturer or as a sample by a registered importer or a registered dealer. 27 CFR 479.111(a). However, section 479.105(c), implementing section 922(o) of the GCA, clarifies that machineguns manufactured on or after May 19, 1986, may be imported only with a purchase order for transfer to a governmental entity, or as a dealer's sales sample pursuant to section 479.105(d).

The regulations in Part 479 give the Director the authority to approve an alternate method or procedure in lieu of a method or procedure specifically prescribed in the regulations when it is found that:

(1) The alternate method or procedure is within the purpose of, and consistent with the effect intended by, the specifically prescribed method or procedure and that the alternate method or procedure is substantially equivalent to that specifically prescribed method or procedure; and

(2) Good cause is shown for the use of the alternate method or procedure.

(3) The alternate method or procedure will not be contrary to any provision of law and will not result in an increase in cost to the Government or hinder the effective administration of the GCA or regulations issued thereunder.

27 CFR 479.26

2. The Gun Control Act

Import provisions of the GCA, 18 U.S.C. 922(i) and 925(d)(3), generally prohibit the importation of firearms subject to the NFA, except for the use of governmental entities. 18 U.S.C. 925(a)(1). The term "firearm" is defined in section 921(a)(3) to include any weapon which will or is designed to or may be readily converted to expel a projectile by the action of an explosive; the frame or receiver of any such weapon; any firearm silencer; and any destructive device. In addition, section 922(o) of the GCA prohibits the transfer or possession of a machinegun manufactured on or after May 19, 1986, except for the official use of governmental entities.

Regulations implementing the GCA in 27 CFR part 478 require that persons importing firearms into the United States obtain an approved ATF Form 6, Application and Permit for Importation of Firearms, Ammunition and Implements of War, prior to bringing the firearm into the United States. 27 CFR 478.111-114. Regulations in Part 478 provide that the Director may approve an alternate method or procedure in lieu of a method or procedure specifically prescribed by the GCA and regulations when it is found that:

(1) The alternate method or procedure is within the purpose of, and consistent with the effect intended by, the specifically prescribed method or procedure and that the alternate method or procedure is substantially equivalent to that specifically prescribed method or procedure; and

(2) Good cause is shown for the use of the alternate method or procedure.

(2) The alternate method or procedure will not be contrary to any provision of law and will not result in an increase in cost to the Government or hinder the effective administration of the GCA or regulations issued thereunder.

27 CFR 478.22

3. *The Arms Export Control Act*

The Arms Export Control Act (AECA), 22 U.S.C. 2778, gives the President the authority to control the export and import of defense articles and defense services in furtherance of world peace and the security and foreign policy of the United States. Authority to administer the permanent import provisions of the AECA was delegated to Attorney General, while the authority to administer the export and temporary import provisions of the AECA was delegated to the Secretary of State, Executive Order 11958 of January 18, 1977, as amended by Executive Order 13333 of January 23, 2003, 3 CFR Executive Order 13284.

The term "defense article" is defined in 27 CFR 447.11 as any item designated in sections 447.21 or 447.22. Section 447.21, the U.S. Munitions Import List, includes a number of defense articles that are also subject to the GCA and NFA. Category I, "Firearms," includes nonautomatic and semiautomatic firearms to caliber .50 inclusive, combat shotguns, shotguns with barrels less than 18 inches in length, and firearms silencers and suppressors. All Category I firearms are subject to the GCA. "Combat shotguns" include the USAS-12 shotgun and the Striker-12/Streetsweeper shotgun, which have been classified as destructive devices under the GCA and NFA. In addition, all shotguns with barrels of less than 18 inches in length are subject to both the GCA and NFA. All rifles with barrels of less than 16 inches in length are subject to both the GCA and NFA, and silencers are subject to both the GCA and NFA.

Category II, "Artillery Projectors," includes guns over .50, howitzers, mortars, and recoilless rifles. Firearms over .50 caliber have a bore of more than one-half inch in diameter and are "destructive devices" as defined in the GCA and NFA.

Category IV, "launch Vehicles, Guided Missiles, Ballistic Missiles, Rockets, torpedoes, Bombs and Mines," includes rockets, bombs, grenades, torpedoes, and land and naval mines. All these articles are "destructive devices" as defined in the GCA and NFA.

Regulations of the Department of State implementing the AECA generally require a temporary import license, DSP-61, for the temporary import and subsequent export of unclassified defense articles, unless otherwise exempted. 22 CFR 123.3. Regulations in 22 CFR 123.4 provide an exemption from licensing if the item temporarily imported:

> (1) Is serviced (e.g., inspection, testing, calibration or repair, including overhaul, reconditioning and one-to-one replacement of any defective items, parts or components, but excluding any modification, enhancement, upgrade or other form of alteration or improvement that changes the basic performance of the item), and is subsequently returned to the country from which it was imported. Shipment may be made by the U.S. importer or a foreign government representative of the country from which the goods were imported; or

> (2) Is to be enhanced, upgraded or incorporated into another item whish has already been authorized by the Office of Defense Trade Controls for permanent export; or

> (3) Is imported for the purpose of exhibition, demonstration or marketing in the United States and is subsequently returned to the country from which it was imported; or

> (4) Has been rejected for permanent import by the Department of the Treasury [after January 24, 2003, the Department of Justice] and is being returned to the country from which it was shipped; or

> (5) Is approved for such import under the U.S. Foreign Military Sales (FMS) program pursuant to an executed U.S. Department of Defense Letter of Offer and Acceptance (LOA).

Willful violations of the AECA are punishable by imprisonment for not more than 10 years, a fine of not more than $1,000,000, or both. 22 U.S.C. 2778©. Articles imported in violation of the AECA are also subject to seizure and forfeiture. 18 U.S.C. 545.

Discussion

A temporary import license authorizing the temporary importation and subsequent export of a defense article by the Department of State satisfies all legal requirements under the AECA. Importers may also comply with AECA requirements if the importation meets one of the exemptions in 22 CFR 123.4. However, if the defense article is subject to the GCA and NFA, the importer must also comply with the requirements of those statutes. Neither the GCA nor NFA make a distinction between temporary importation and permanent importation, as is the case under the AECA. Regulations implementing the GCA and NFA make it clear that an "importation" occurs when firearms are brought into the territory of the United States. 27 CFR 478.11 and 479.11. Accordingly, any bringing of firearms into the territory of the United States is subject to the import provisions of the GCA and NFA. Issuance of a temporary import license by the Department of State, or exemption from licensing under regulations in 22 CFR Part 123, will not excuse compliance with the GCA and NFA.

The statutes and regulations outlined above do not address the importation of machineguns manufactured after May 19, 1986, for scientific or research purposes or for testing, repair, or for use as a model by a manufacturer or importer. Nor do the regulations address the importation of post-86 machineguns for repair, inspection, calibration, or incorporation into another defense article.

For other" defense articles" that are subject to the requirements of the GCA and NFA, such as silencers, destructive devices, and short-barrel weapons, ATF has the authority to approve the importation of such firearms for scientific or research purposes or for testing or use as a model or sample by a registered importer or a registered dealer. However, such importation must comply with all applicable provisions of the NFA, including filing of a Form2, Notice of Firearms Manufactured or Imported, to effect registration. If such articles are subsequently exported, a Form 9, Application and Permit for Permanent Exportation of Firearms, must also be approved prior to exportation.

As with post-86 machineguns, neither the law nor regulation specifically address the importation of firearms subject to the NFA for purposes of repair, inspection, calibration, or for incorporation into another defense article.

ATF recognizes that inspection, repair, calibration, incorporation into another defense article, and reconditioning of machineguns, destructive devices, and other NFA firearms is often necessary for National defense. These defense articles are frequently sold to allies of the United States for their legitimate defense needs. Accordingly, ATF believes it is appropriate to recognize an alternate method that allows importers to temporarily import these firearms, subject to requirements to ensure the security of these defense articles while they are in the United States and accountability of the persons who import them.

Pursuant to 27 CFR 478.22 and 479.26, ATF hereby authorizes an alternate method or procedure for importers of defense articles to use for temporary importation of such articles for inspection, calibration, repair, or incorporation into another defense article when such articles are subject to the requirements of the NFA and GCA. The procedure requires that importers-

(1) Be qualified under the GCA and NFA to import the type of firearms sought for importation;

(2) Obtain a temporary import license, DSP-61, from the Department of State in accordance with 22CFR 123.3 OR qualify for a temporary import license exemption pursuant to 22 CFR 123.4;

(3) Within 15 days of the release of the firearms from Customs custody, file an ATF Form2, Notice of Firearms Manufactured or Imported, showing the importation of the firearms. The DSP-61 must be attached to the Form 2. If the importation is subject to a licensing exemption under 22 VFR 123.4, the importer must submit with the ATF Form 2 a statement, under penalty of perjury, attesting to the exemption and stating that the article will be exported within four years of its importation into the United States;

(4) Maintain the defense articles in a secure place and manner to ensure that the articles are not diverted to criminal or terrorist use; and

(5) Export the articles within 4 years of importation into the United States.

Importers who follow the procedures outlined above will be in compliance with the provisions of the GCA, NFA, and AECA administered and enforced by ATF. All other provisions of the law must be followed.

ATF finds that the procedure outlined above meets the legal requirements for an alternate method or procedure because there is a good cause to authorize the importation of defense articles for repair, inspection, calibration, or incorporation into another defense article. Because such defense articles are often provided to allies of the United States, it is imperative that the original manufacturers have a lawful method of importing such articles for repair and routing maintenance. The alternate method or procedure is consistent with the effect intended by the procedure set forth in the GCA and NFA, because the firearms must be registered and stored securely. Finally, the alternate method is consistent with the requirements of the GCA and NFA and will not result in any additional costs to ATF or the Department of State.

"Transfers" of NFA Weapons After Importation

ATF recognizes that temporarily imported NFA firearms are sometimes "transferred" from the importer to a contractor within the United States for inspection, testing, calibration, repair, or incorporation into another defense article. ATF has approved a procedure for authorizing the transportation or delivery of temporarily imported NFA firearms to licensed contractors for repair or manipulation, as noted above.

Conveyance of an NFA weapon to a licensee for purposes of inspection, testing, calibration, repair, or incorporation into another defense article is generally not considered to be a "transfer" under 26 U.S.C. 5845(j). ATF has taken the position that temporary custody by a licensee is not a transfer for purposes of the NFA since no sale, lease, or other disposal is intended by the owner. However, in order to document the transaction as a temporary conveyance and make clear that an actual "transfer" of a firearm has not taken place, ATF strongly recommends that the importer submit a Form 5, Application for Tax Exempt Transfer and Registration of Firearm, for approval prior to conveying a firearm for repair or manipulation. In the alternative, the importer should convey the weapon with a letter to the contractor, stating: (1) the weapon is being temporarily conveyed for inspection, testing, calibration, repair, or incorporation into another defense article; and (2) the approximate time period the weapon is to be in the contractor's possession. The transferee must be properly licensed to engage in an NFA firearms business.

Held, pursuant to 27 CFR 478.22 and 479.26, the Bureau of Alcohol, Tobacco, Firearms and Explosives has approved an alternate method or procedure for importers to use when temporarily importing firearms subject to the Gun Control Act, National Firearms Act, and the Arms Export Control Act for inspection, testing, calibration, repair, or incorporation into another defense article. This procedure applies to all defense articles that are also subject to the NFA and GCA. The procedure requires that importers-

>(1) Be qualified under the GCA and NFA to import the type of firearms sought for importation;

>(2) Obtain a temporary import license, DSP-61, from the Department of State in accordance with 22CFR 123.3 OR qualify for a temporary import license exemption pursuant to 22 CFR 123.4;

>(3) Within 15 days of the release of the firearms from Customs custody, file an ATF Form2, Notice of Firearms Manufactured or Imported, showing the importation of the firearms. The DSP-61 must be attached to the Form 2. If the importation is subject to a licensing exemption under 22 VFR 123.4, the importer must submit with the ATF Form 2 a statement, under penalty of perjury, attesting to the exemption and stating that the article will be exported within four years of its importation into the United States;

(4) Maintain the defense articles in a secure place and manner to ensure that the articles are not diverted to criminal or terrorist use; and

(5) Export the articles within 4 years of importation into the United States.

Held further, temporary conveyance of NFA weapons from the importer to a contractor within the United States for purposes of inspection, testing, calibration, repair, or incorporation into another defense article may be accomplished through advance approval of ATF Form 5, Application for Tax Exempt Transfer and Registration of Firearm, or with a letter from the importer to the contractor stating: (1) the weapon is being temporarily conveyed for inspection, testing, calibration, repair, or incorporation into another defense article; and (2) the approximate time period the weapon is to be in the contractor's possession. The transferee must be properly licensed to engage in an NFA firearms business.

Date signed: April 7, 2004

26 U.S.C. 5845(B): DEFINITIONS (MACHINEGUN)
27 CFR 479.11: MEANING OF TERMS

The 7.62mm Aircraft Machine Gun, identified in the U.S. military inventory as the "m-134" (Army), "GAU-2B/A" (Air Force), and "GAU-17/A" (Navy), is a machinegun as defined by 26 U.S.C. 5845(b), Rev. Rul. 55-528 modified.

ATF Rul. 2004-5

The Bureau of Alcohol, Tobacco, firearms and Explosives (ATF) has examined the 7.62mm Aircraft Machine Gun, commonly referred to as a "Minigun." The Minigun is a 36 pound, six barrel, electrically powered machinegun. It is in the U.S. military inventory and identified as the "M-134" (Army), "GAU 2B/A" (Air force), and "GAU 17/A" (Navy). It is a lightweight and extremely reliable weapon, capable of discharging up to 6,000 rounds per minute. It has been used on helicopters, fixed-wing aircraft, and wheeled vehicles. It is highly adaptable, being used with pintle mounts, turrets, pods, and internal installations.

The Minigun has six barrels and bolts which are mounted on a rotor. The firing sequence begins with the manual operation of a trigger. On an aircraft, the trigger is commonly found on the control column, or joy stick. Operation of the trigger causes an electric motor to turn the rotor. As the rotor turns, a stud on each bolt travels along an elliptical groove on the inside of the housing, which causes the bolts to move forward and rearward on tracks n the rotor. A triggering cam, or sear shoulder, trips the firing pin when the bolt has traveled forward through the full length of the bolt track. One complete revolution of the rotor discharges cartridges from all six barrels. The housing that surrounds the rotor, bolts and firing mechanism constitutes the frame or receiver of the firearm.

The National Firearms Act defines "machinegun" as "any weapon which shoots, is designed to shoot, or can be readily restored to shoot, automatically more than one shot, without manual reloading, by a single function of the trigger." 26 U.S.C. 5845(b). The term also includes "the frame or receiver of any such weapon, any part designed and intended solely and exclusively, or combination of parts designed and intended, for use in converting a weapon into a machinegun, and any combination of parts from which a machinegun can be assembled if such parts are in the possession or under the control of a person." Id; see 18 U.S.C. 921(a)(23); 27 CFR 478.11, 479.11.

ATF and its predecessor agency, the Internal Revenue Service (IRS), have historically held that the original, crank-operated Gatling Gun, and replicas thereof, are not automatic firearms or machineguns as defined. See Rev. Rul. 55-528, 1955-2 C.B. 482. The original Gatling gun is a rapid-firing, hand-operated weapon. The rate of fire is regulated by the rapidity of the hand cranking movement, manually controlled by the operator. It is not a "machinegun" as that term is defined in 26 U.S.C. 5845(b) because it is not a weapon that fires automatically.

The Minigun is not a Gatling Gun. It was not produced under the 1862 – 1893 patents of the original Gatling Gun. While using a basic design concept of the Gatling Gun, the Minigun does not incorporate any of Gatling's original components and its fed mechanisms are entirely different. Critically, the Minigun shoots more than one shot, without manual reloading, by a single function of the trigger, as prescribed by 26 U.S.C> 5845(b). See United States v. Fleischli, 305 F. 3d 643, 655-656 (7th Cir. 2002). See also Staples v. United States, 511 U.S. 600, 603 (1994) (automatic refers to a weapon that "once its trigger is depressed, the weapon will automatically continue to fire until its trigger is released or the ammunition is exhausted"); GEORGE C. NONTE, JR., FIREARMS ENCYCLOPEDIA 13 (Harper &

Rowe 1973) (the term "automatic" is defined to include "any firearm in which a single pull and continuous pressure upon the trigger (or other firing device) will produce rapid discharge of successive shots so long as ammunition remains in the magazine or feed device in other words, a machinegun"); WEBSTER'S II NEW RIVERSIDE-UNIVERSITY DICTIONARY (1988) (defining automatically as "acting or operating in a manner essentially independent of external influence or control"); JOHN B. QUICK, PH.D., DICTIONARY OF WEAPONS AND MILITARY TERMS 40 (McGraw-hill 1973) (defining automatic fire as "continuous fire from an automatic gun, lasting until pressure on the trigger is released").

The term "trigger" is generally held to be the part of a firearm that is used to initiate the firing sequence. See United States v. Fleischli, 305 F.3d at 655-56 (and cases cited therein); see also ASSOCIATION OF FIREARMS AND TOOLMARK EXAMINERS (ATFE) GLOSSARY 185 (1st ed. 1980) ("that part of a firearm mechanism which is moved manually to cause the firearm to discharge"); WEBSTER'S II NEW RIVERSIDE-UNIVERSITY DICTIONARY (1988) ("lever pressed by the finger in discharging a firearm").

Held, the 7.62mm Minigun is designed to shoot automatically more than one shot, without manual reloading, by a single function of the trigger. Consequently, the 7.62mm Minigun is a machinegun as defined in section 5845(b) of the National Firearms Act. See United States v. Fleischli, 305 F. 3d at 655-56. Similarly, the housing that surrounds the rotor is the frame or receiver of the Minigun, and thus is also a machinegun. Id .; see 18 U.S.C. 921(a)(23); 27 CFR 478.11, 479.11.

To the extent this ruling is inconsistent with Revenue Ruling 55-528 issued by the IRS, Revenue Ruling 55-528, 1955-2 C.B. 482 is hereby modified.

Date signed: August 18, 2004

Carl J. Truscott

Director

U.S. Department of Justice

Bureau of Alcohol, Tobacco,
Firearms and Explosives

January 31, 2006

www.atf.gov

901040:GS
5320

Federal Firearms Licensees and National Firearms Act
Special (Occupational) Taxpayers

SUBJECT: Filing National Firearms Act Transaction Forms by Facsimile Transmission

This is to update information regarding the filing of certain National Firearms Act (NFA) forms by facsimile transmission as the functions of the NFA Branch have been relocated to Martinsburg, West Virginia from Washington, DC. Please note that the contact information for the NFA Branch is:

Bureau of Alcohol, Tobacco, Firearms and Explosives
NFA Branch
244 Needy Road
Martinsburg, WV 25401
Telephone: (304) 616-4500
Facsimile: (304) 616-4501

The Bureau of Alcohol, Tobacco, Firearms and Explosives (ATF) held in ATF Ruling 89-1, that certain forms required by ATF may be filed by facsimile transmission. This ruling and ATF Industry Circular 89-6 set forth the requirements and procedures.

The NFA Branch had determined that for forms filed under the NFA, the procedure would be available for ATF Form 2, Form 3, Form 9, and for Form 5 in situations where the application is not accompanied by fingerprint cards. The submission of NFA forms may only be done by Federal firearms licensees who have paid the special (occupational) tax to import, manufacture, or deal in NFA firearms.

If you choose to utilize the procedure, each person who will be filing forms on behalf of the licensee must first submit to us (in original) an affidavit declaring, under penalties of perjury, that certain conditions will be met. These conditions are detailed in the attached sample affidavit. The affidavit needs only to be submitted once. If you have previously filed an affidavit with us, there is no need to file another.

**AFFIDAVIT FOR FACSIMILE TRANSMITTAL OF
NFA NOTICE OR TRANSFER APPLICATION FORMS**

TO: Bureau of ATF
    NFA Branch
    244 Needy Road, Martinsburg, WV 25401

AFFIDAVIT

I, _____, doing business as _____

_____ hereby state:

1. In addition to those applications sent via U.S. mail, I will be filing ATF Forms (2, 3, 5 and/or 9) by facsimile transmission;
2. The signature appearing on the facsimile copies will be mine and is intended as the original signature;
3. I will be submitting the facsimile copies as originals for purposes of approval under the provisions of Title 27, Code of Federal Regulations, Part 479, and that the facsimile copies are to be treated as originals; and
4. I will personally transmit the copies via facsimile machine.

I declare under penalty of perjury under the laws of the United States that the above information is true and correct.

_____   _____
Signature   Date

Name _____

Title _____

Trade name _____

Address _____

Telephone _____

FFL number _____

EIN _____

ATF Ruling 89-1

The Bureau of Alcohol, Tobacco and Firearms has been asked whether certain forms and other documents could optionally be transmitted to the Bureau by means of facsimile machines. These include various application forms, comments on notices of proposed rulemaking, reports, and other documents submitted to the Bureau.

Recent technology advances have made transmitting documents by facsimile machine practical and the use of facsimile machines has become widespread. The Bureau has acquired several facsimile machines and found them to be acceptable for transmitting many types of documents.

The statutes administered by the Bureau (including the Internal Revenue Code, the Federal Alcohol Administration Act, the Gun Control Act, Title XI of the Organized Crime Control Act of 1970, and the Arms Export Control Act) generally specify the information to be included on documents that are submitted to the Bureau. However, the form of the documents and the manner of filing are generally left to the Secretary of the Treasury to prescribe by regulation. The regulations issued pursuant to these statutes generally require that forms and other documents be submitted in original and signed by the applicant, licensee, or permittee.

The Bureau has concluded that if the person transmitting the form or document intends that it be treated as an original and it is filed via a facsimile machine at the person's direction, then the facsimile copy received by the Bureau would be for all intents and purposes the original.

In order to verify the authenticity of a signature on forms and other documents required to be signed under penalties of perjury, the Bureau will require that an affidavit executed by the person signing the facsimile documents be submitted to the Bureau prior to acceptance of any facsimile transmitted copies of such forms or documents.

The affidavit should declare, under penalties of perjury, that the affiant will be filing the appropriate forms or documents by facsimile machine, that the signature appearing on the facsimile copies will be that of the affiant, and is intended as the original signature.

The affidavit should also state that the affiant will be submitting the facsimile copies as originals for approval or other purposes under the appropriate regulations and that the affiant intends that the facsimile copies be treated as originals.

Finally, the affidavit should also state that the person signing the form or other document will personally transmit the copy via facsimile machine, or, if a designated agent is to do the transmittal, the name of the agent who will do the actual transmittal.

The affidavit would only have to be submitted one time to each Bureau office to which facsimile transmitted copies are to be sent, and would not have to be resubmitted unless a different official would be signing or transmitting the copies.

The Bureau concludes that only documents that are legible and of suitable size (8 1/2" X 11") may be submitted by facsimile transmission. The Bureau also concludes that facsimile transmitted copies would not be acceptable with respect to documents which are accompanied by such articles as samples, fingerprint cards, photographs, checks, and labels for alcoholic beverage containers.

The acceptance of facsimile transmitted copies at some Bureau offices may be restricted due to limited availability of facsimile machines, telephone lines or other reasons. If an ATF form may be submitted by facsimile transmission, the instructions on the form will so specify, and will also indicate the locations and telephone numbers where the transmissions may be sent. Instructions for facsimile transmitted copies of comments on a notice of proposed rulemaking will be provided in the notice itself.

Accordingly, the Bureau has determined that facsimile transmitted copies of forms and other documents may be accepted under certain conditions.

Held, forms and other documents submitted to the Bureau may be accepted when transmitted by facsimile machines under the following conditions:

1. The Bureau office to where the forms or other documents are to be submitted is suitably equipped with facsimile machines and telephone lines to receive the facsimile transmitted copies.

2. The forms or other documents are legible and of suitable size (8 1/2" X 11") for facsimile transmission.

3. The forms or other documents are transmitted in accordance with instructions provided on the form, notice of proposed rulemaking, or by other competent authority.

4. The forms or other documents are not accompanied by other articles such as samples, fingerprint cards, photographs, checks, and labels for alcoholic beverage containers.

5. Prior to accepting any facsimile transmitted copies of forms and other documents required to be signed under penalties of perjury, the Bureau must have received an acceptable affidavit executed by the person whose signature appears on the forms or documents. The affidavit must declare, under penalties of perjury, that

a. the affiant will be filing the appropriate forms or other documents by facsimile machine,

b. that the signature appearing on the facsimile copies will be that of the affiant, and is intended as the original signature,

c. the affiant will be submitting the facsimile copies as originals for purposes of approval or other purpose under the appropriate regulations and that the affiant intends that the facsimile copies be treated as originals, and

d. the person signing the forms or other documents will personally transmit the copies via facsimile machine, or, if a designated agent is to do the transmittal, the name of the agent who will do the actual transmittal.

6. The affidavit is required to be submitted only one time to each Bureau office to which facsimile transmitted copies are to be sent, and need not be resubmitted unless a different official will be signing or transmitting the forms.

http://www.ttb.gov/rulings/89-1.htm					4/9/2007

Industry Circular
Number: 89-6
Date: September 27, 1989

Department of the Treasury
Bureau of Alcohol, Tobacco and Firearms
Washington, DC 20226

FACSIMILE TRANSMITTED COPIES OF FORMS AND OTHER DOCUMENTS

All Alcohol, Tobacco, Firearms and Explosives Licensees, Permittees, and Others Concerned:

PURPOSE. The purpose of this circular is to advise industry members that an ATF ruling will be published in a future issue of the Alcohol, Tobacco and Firearms Quarterly Bulletin. The ruling will read substantially as follows:

The Bureau of Alcohol, Tobacco and Firearms has been asked whether certain forms and other documents could optionally be transmitted to the Bureau by means of facsimile machines. These include various application forms, comments on notices of proposed rulemaking, reports, and other documents submitted to the Bureau.

Recent technological advances have made transmitting documents by facsimile machine practical and the use of facsimile machines has become widespread. The Bureau has acquired several facsimile machines and found them to be acceptable for transmitting many types of documents.

The statutes administered by the Bureau (including the Internal Revenue Code of 1986, the Federal Alcohol Administration Act, the Gun Control Act of 1968, Title XI of the Organized Crime Control Act of 1970, and the Arms Export Control Act) generally specify the information to be included on documents that are submitted to the Bureau. However, the form of the documents and the manner of filing are generally left to the Secretary of the Treasury to prescribe by regulation. The regulations issued pursuant to these statutes generally require that forms and other documents be submitted in original and signed by the applicant, licensee, or permittee.

The Bureau has concluded that if the person transmitting the form or document intends that it be treated as an original and it is filed via a facsimile machine at the person's direction, then the facsimile copy received by the Bureau would be for all intents and purposes the original.

In order to verify the authenticity of a signature on forms and other documents required to be signed under penalties of perjury, the Bureau will require that an affidavit executed by the person signing the forms or documents be submitted to the Bureau prior to acceptance of any facsimile transmitted copies of such forms or documents.

The affidavit should declare, under penalties of perjury, that the affiant will be filing the appropriate forms or documents by facsimile machine, that the signature appearing on the facsimile copies will be that of the affiant, and that the signature on the facsimile is intended as the original signature.

The affidavit should also state that the affiant will be submitting the facsimile copies as originals for approval or other purposes under the appropriate regulations and that the affiant intends that the facsimile copies be treated as originals.

Finally, the affidavit should also state that the person signing the form or other document will personally transmit the copy via facsimile machine, or, if a designated agent is to do the transmittal, the name of the agent who will do the actual transmittal will be stated.

The affidavit would only have to be submitted one time to each Bureau office to which facsimile transmitted copies are to be sent, and would not have to be resubmitted unless a different official would be signing or transmitting the copies.

The Bureau concludes that only documents that are legible and of suitable size (8 1/2" X 11" or as specifically authorized by the receiving office) may be submitted by facsimile transmission. The Bureau also concludes that facsimile transmitted copies would not be acceptable with respect to fingerprint cards, bonds, photographs, checks, or labels for alcoholic beverage containers or the forms or documents required to be submitted with such items.

The acceptance of facsimile transmitted copies at some Bureau offices may be restricted due to limited availability of facsimile machines, telephone lines or other reasons. Instructions on the form or instructions otherwise provided will state whether a facsimile transmitted copy of a form or other document may be used.

The instructions will also indicate the locations and telephone numbers where the transmissions may be sent. Instructions for facsimile transmitted copies of comments on a notice of proposed rulemaking will be provided in the notice itself.

Accordingly, the Bureau has determined that facsimile transmitted copies of forms and other documents may be accepted under certain conditions.

Held: Forms and other documents submitted to the Bureau may be accepted when transmitted by facsimile machines under the following conditions:

1. The Bureau office to which the forms or other documents are to be submitted is suitably equipped with facsimile machines and telephone lines to receive the facsimile transmitted copies.
2. The forms or other documents are legible and of suitable size (8 1/2" X 11" or as specifically authorized by the receiving office) for facsimile transmission.
3. The forms or other documents are transmitted in accordance with instructions on the form, notice of proposed rulemaking, or otherwise provided.
4. The forms or other documents are not fingerprint cards, bonds, photographs, checks, or labels for alcoholic beverage containers and are not the forms or documents required to be submitted with such items.
5. Prior to accepting any facsimile transmitted copies of forms and other documents required to be signed under penalties of perjury, the Bureau must have received an affidavit executed by the person whose signature appears on the forms or documents. The affidavit must declare, under penalties of perjury, that:

    a. the affiant will be filing the appropriate forms or other documents by facsimile machine,
    b. the signature appearing on the facsimile copies will be that of the affiant, and is intended as the original signature,
    c. the affiant will be submitting the facsimile copies as originals for purposes of approval or other purpose under the appropriate regulations and that the affiant intends that the facsimile copies be treated as originals, and
    d. the person signing the forms or other documents will personally transmit the copies via facsimile machine, or, if a designated agent is to do the transmittal, the name of the agent who will do the actual transmittal.

6. The affidavit is required to be submitted only one time to each Bureau office to which facsimile transmitted copies are to be sent, and need not be resubmitted unless a different official will be

signing or transmitting the forms.

INQUIRIES. Inquiries concerning this circular should refer to its number and be addressed to the Associate Director (Compliance Operations), Bureau of Alcohol, Tobacco and Firearms, 1200 Pennsylvania Avenue, NW, Washington, DC 20226.

Acting Director

Frequently Asked Questions - Silencers

Q1: What part of a silencer must be marked?

A: The silencer must be marked in accordance with 27 C.F.R. §§ 478.92 and 479.102. The regulations require that the markings be conspicuous and legible, meaning that the markings may be placed on any external part, such as the outer tube or end cap.

ATF strongly recommends that manufacturers place all required markings on the outer tube of the silencer, as this is the accepted industry standard. Moreover, this practice eliminates the need to remark in the event an end cap bearing the markings is damaged and requires replacement.

Q2: May a Federal firearms licensee repair a silencer by replacing worn or damaged components?

A: A person who is licensed under the Gun Control Act (GCA) to manufacture firearms and who has paid the special (occupational) tax to manufacture National Firearms Act (NFA) firearms may replace a component part or parts of a silencer. Repairs may not be done if they result in removal, obliteration, or alteration of the serial number, as this would violate 18 U.S.C. § 922(k). If a silencer part bearing the serial number, other than the outer tube, must be replaced, the new part must be marked with the same serial number as the replacement part.

The term "repair" does not include replacement of the outer tube of the silencer. The outer tube is the largest single part of the silencer, the main structural component of the silencer, and is the part to which all other component parts are attached. The replacement of the outer tube is so significant an event that it amounts to the "making" of a new silencer. As such, the new silencer must be marked, registered and transferred in accordance with the NFA and GCA.

In the event that identical replacement parts for a silencer are not available, new and different component parts may be used as long as the silencer retains the same dimensions and caliber. In addition, the repair may result in a minimal reduction in the length of the outer tube due to rethreading, but repair may not increase the length of the outer tube. Increasing the length of the outer tube significantly affects the performance of the silencer and results in the "making" of a new silencer. As stated above, a new silencer must be marked, registered and transferred in accordance with the NFA and GCA. Reducing the length of the tube by a minimal amount in order to repair a silencer is often necessary to replace damaged end caps, as the tube must be rethreaded. Such minimal reduction of the length of the tube uses all of the original parts, does not significantly affect performance of the silencer, and may be done as part of a repair process without making a new silencer.

Persons other than qualified manufacturers may repair silencers, but replacement parts are "silencers" as defined in 18 U.S.C. § 921(a)(24) that must be registered and transferred in accordance with the NFA and GCA.

Q3: May the outer tube of a registered silencer be repaired due to damage? If so, may the repair be done by someone other than the original manufacturer?

A damaged outer tube may be repaired by any Federal firearms licensee qualified to perform gunsmithing or by the registered owner. The repair may not alter the dimensions or caliber of the silencer, except that the length of the outer tube may be reduced, as set forth above. The repair may not be performed if it results in the removal, obliteration, or alteration of the serial number, as this would violate 18 U.S.C. § 922(k). In that case, the silencer may be returned to the registered owner in its original, damaged condition or destroyed. A replacement silencer must be registered and transferred to the registrant of the damaged silencer in the same manner as a new silencer, subject to the registration and transfer procedures of the NFA and GCA.

Q4: If the outer tube is destroyed or damaged beyond repair, may it be replaced?

A: Unless the outer tube is replaced by the manufacturer prior to its removal from the manufacturing premises for purposes of sale or distribution (see **Q6**), the replacement of the outer tube amounts to the making of a new silencer. For the registered owner to fabricate a new outer tube, he or she must submit an ATF Form 1, Application to Make and Register a Firearm, pay the making tax of $200, and receive ATF approval. The application to make should indicate that the new tube is being fabricated for use in replacing a damaged outer tube on a registered silencer, and the application should indicate the make, model and serial number of the registered silencer. It would be helpful for the applicant to include a copy of the approved registration for the silencer. Assembly of the newly fabricated tube with the other parts of the registered silencer does not require an additional application to make nor payment of another making tax, as the one Form 1 will provide permission to fabricate the new tube and to assemble it with the old silencer parts. The replacement tube must be marked in accordance with 27 C.F.R. § 479.102. The registrant may use the same serial number that appeared on the damaged tube.

If the registered owner wishes to acquire a replacement tube from a person other than a qualified manufacturer, the replacement tube must be registered as a new silencer by the other person and transferred to the registered owner in accordance with the NFA and GCA. The other person must submit an ATF Form 1, pay the $200 making tax, and receive ATF approval to make the replacement tube. The replacement tube must be marked in accordance with 27 C.F.R. §§ 478.92 and 479.102. The other person would then transfer the replacement tube to the owner of the damaged silencer, subject to the transfer tax, in accordance with the NFA and GCA. The new tube may be then be assembled with the other parts. The original damaged silencer should be reported to the NFA Branch as destroyed.

Alternatively, a qualified manufacturer may replace the tube, report the manufacture on ATF Form 2, Notice of Firearms Manufactured or Imported, and transfer the replacement tube to the owner in accordance with the NFA and GCA. The transfer must comply with the $200 transfer tax and all other provisions of the NFA, as it would be a new silencer. The replacement tube must also be marked in accordance with 27 C.F.R. §§ 478.92 and 479.102. The required markings include an individual serial number and the name, city, and State of the manufacturer who replaced the tube. The replacement tube may not be marked with the name, city, and State of the original manufacturer of the silencer, as this would be a false marking. Although the new tube is a new silencer for purposes of the NFA, it would be a replacement firearm of the same type as the original silencer, and it may be returned directly to the registrant in interstate commerce in accordance with 18 U.S.C. § 922(a)(2). The original damaged silencer should be reported to the NFA Branch as destroyed.

Q5: May a repair change the dimensions or caliber of a silencer?

A: If alterations to a silencer would increase the overall length or change the diameter or caliber of a silencer, this is the making of a new silencer, as opposed to a repair. The new silencer must be registered and transferred in accordance with the NFA and the GCA. Alterations to a registered silencer that result in a minimal reduction in the overall length for purposes of rethreading are permissible as repairs. However, the reduction in length may not result in the removal, obliteration, or alteration of the existing serial number, as this would violate 18 U.S.C. § 922(k). If such a repair is necessary, the damaged silencer should be destroyed or returned to the registrant. If it is destroyed, destruction should be reported to the NFA Branch. Any replacement silencer must be registered and transferred in accordance with the NFA and the GCA. See Q2 and Q3 for further information on repairs.

Q6: If a silencer is found to be defective due to the manufacturing process, may it be replaced?

A: A silencer may be replaced only under the following circumstances:

(1) A manufacturer of silencers licensed as a manufacturer under the GCA who has paid special (occupational) tax under the NFA;

(2) prior to the time the silencer has left the manufacturer's premises;

(3) determines that a silencer of its own manufacture is defective.

If all the above criteria are satisfied, the manufacturer may destroy the defective silencer and replace it with another silencer. If the silencer has already been registered, the replacement silencer may be marked with the same serial number and markings as the original silencer. If the destruction is prior to registration on Form 2, the replacement silencer may be marked with the same serial number or another serial number. See also **Q2, Q3**, and **Q4**.

U.S. Department of Justice

Bureau of Alcohol, Tobacco,
Firearms and Explosives

Assistant Director

Washington, DC 20226
www.atf.gov

MAR 2 1 2017

90000:GM
5000

Mark Barnes, Esq.
Outside Counsel to SB Tactical, LLC
1350 Eye St. NW, Suite 260
Washington, D.C. 20005

Re: Reversal of ATF Open Letter on the Redesign of "Stabilizing Braces"

Dear Mr. Barnes:

I am writing in response to your letter dated January 5, 2017, to Thomas Brandon, the Acting Director of the Bureau of Alcohol, Tobacco, Firearms and Explosives (ATF) on behalf of your client SB Tactical, LLC. Your letter requests that ATF reconsider its position articulated in ATF's *"Open Letter on the Redesign of 'Stabilizing Braces'"* issued on January 16, 2015 (hereafter, the *"Open Letter"*). The *Open Letter* made it clear that stabilizing braces are perfectly legal accessories for large handguns or pistols. However, when employed as a shoulder stock with a firearm with a barrel less than 16 inches in length, the result would be making an unregistered NFA firearm. Your letter challenges the legal correctness of this latter conclusion and asks that ATF disavow it. Since receiving your letter we have re-examined the conclusions contained in the *Open Letter*. Although we stand by those conclusions, we agree that the *Open Letter* may have generated some confusion concerning the analytical framework by which those conclusions were reached. Thank you for the opportunity to clarify our analysis.

Background

As you are aware, the NFA, 26 USC § 5845, defines "firearm," in relevant part, as "a shotgun having a barrel or barrels of less than 18 inches in length" and "a rifle having a barrel or barrels of less than 16 inches in length." That section defines both "rifle" and "shotgun" as "a weapon designed or redesigned, made or remade, and intended to be fired from the shoulder...."
Pursuant to the plain language of the statute, ATF and its predecessor agency have long held that a pistol with a barrel less than 16 inches in length and an attached shoulder stock is an NFA "firearm."

Mark Barnes, Esq.

In 2012, ATF determined that a specific arm-stabilizing brace—marketed as "a shooter's aid" to assist in shooting large buffer tube equipped pistols—was not a shoulder stock and therefore could be attached to a firearm without that act constituting the making of an NFA firearm. Following this determination, the firearms industry and members of the public sought clarification on whether the stabilizing brace may lawfully be used as a shoulder stock. To respond to these inquiries, ATF published the January 2015 *Open Letter*. In that letter ATF confirmed its previous determination that the use of stabilizing braces, as designed, would not create a short-barreled rifle when attached to a firearm. ATF also advised, however, that because the stabilizing brace was not designed as a shoulder stock, "use" of the device as a shoulder stock would constitute a "redesign" of the firearm to which it was attached, resulting in the classification of that firearm as a short-barreled rifle.

Your letter asserts that ATF's analysis of "use" is untenable because the mere use of an otherwise lawfully possessed item for a purpose for which it was not designed does not constitute "redesign" as defined in the NFA. You support this argument with analogies involving items that are not firearms (*i.e.*, misuse of a screwdriver or hammer), and by distinguishing a prior ATF ruling, ATF Ruling 95-2, on which the *Open Letter* relies in its analysis of use. The unstated, but logical, result of your argument is that stabilizing braces, although designed, intended and marketed for use only to shoot from the arm, could be attached to a firearm and used as a shoulder stock without falling within the purview of the NFA. Under certain circumstances, such an absolute result is simply not consistent with the letter and intent of the NFA, as we illustrate in the next paragraph.

An accessory that can be attached to a firearm in any one of several configurations must be evaluated to determine whether attaching it in each of those configurations constitutes "making" an NFA firearm under both objective and subjective analyses. With respect to stabilizing braces, ATF has concluded that attaching the brace to a handgun as a forearm brace does not "make" a short-barreled rifle because in the configuration as submitted to and approved by FATD, it is not intended to be and cannot comfortably be fired from the shoulder. If, however, the shooter/possessor takes affirmative steps to configure the device for use as a shoulder-stock—for example, configuring the brace so as to permanently affix it to the end of a buffer tube, (thereby creating a length that has no other purpose than to facilitate its use as a stock), removing the arm-strap, or otherwise undermining its ability to be used as a brace – and then in fact shoots the firearm from the shoulder using the accessory as a shoulder stock, that person has objectively "redesigned" the firearm for purposes of the NFA. This conclusion is not based upon the mere fact that the firearm was fired from the shoulder at some point. Therefore, an NFA firearm has not necessarily been made when the device is not re-configured for use as a shoulder stock – even if the attached firearm happens to be fired from the shoulder.

Mark Barnes, Esq.

To the extent the January 2015 *Open Letter* implied or has been construed to hold that incidental, sporadic, or situational "use" of an arm-brace (in its original approved configuration) equipped firearm from a firing position at or near the shoulder was sufficient to constitute "redesign," such interpretations are incorrect and not consistent with ATF's interpretation of the statute or the manner in which it has historically been enforced.

In that regard, we also note that the "making" of an NFA firearm pursuant to 26 U.S.C. § 5821 includes the altering of an existing firearm such that, after the alteration, the firearm meets one of the enumerated descriptions in 26 U.S.C. § 5845(a), whether or not that alteration is permanent. So, for example, one "makes" a short-barreled shotgun subject to the NFA by replacing a 20 inch barrel with a 16 inch barrel, even though that configuration may not be permanent. Nothing in the NFA requires that the "making" be irreversible. Similarly, an item that functions as a stock if attached to a handgun in a manner that serves the objective purpose of allowing the firearm to be fired from the shoulder may result in "making" a short-barreled rifle, even if the attachment is not permanent. *See*, Revenue Ruling 61-45. The fact that the item may allow, or even be intended by its manufacturer for other lawful purposes, does not affect the NFA analysis.

Again, to the extent the *Open Letter* was confusing, we appreciate the opportunity to clarify our position. Thank you for your inquiry regarding this matter.

Sincerely,

Marvin G. Richardson
Assistant Director
Enforcement Programs and Services

APPENDIX C

ATF FORMS

ATF Form 1 (5320.1)
Application to Make and Register a Firearm

DEPARTMENT OF THE TREASURY
BUREAU OF ALCOHOL, TOBACCO AND FIREARMS
APPLICATION TO MAKE AND REGISTER A FIREARM
(Detach this sheet before completing form)

INSTRUCTIONS

1. **DEFINITIONS.**

   a. NATIONAL FIREARMS ACT (NFA). Title 26, United States Code, Chapter 53. The implementing regulations are found in Title 27, Code of Federal Regulations, Part 179.

   b. GUN CONTROL ACT (GCA). Title 18, United States Code, Chapter 44. The implementing regulations are found in Title 27, Code of Federal Regulations, Part 178.

   c. FIREARM. The term "firearm" means: (1) a shotgun having a barrel or barrels of less than 18 inches in length; (2) a weapon made from a shotgun if such weapon as modified has an overall length of less than 26 inches or a barrel or barrels of less than 18 inches in length; (3) a rifle having a barrel or barrels of less than 16 inches in length; (4) a weapon made from a rifle if such weapon as modified has an overall length of less than 26 inches or a barrel or barrels of less than 16 inches in length; (5) any other weapon, as defined in 18 U.S.C. 5845(e); (6) a machinegun; (7) a muffler or a silencer for any firearm whether or not such firearm is included within this definition; and (8) a destructive device.

   d. PERSON. The term "person" means a partnership, company, association, trust, estate, or corporation as well as a natural person.

   e. EMPLOYER IDENTIFICATION NUMBER (EIN). Required of taxpayer filing special (occupational) tax returns under 27 CFR § 179.35.

   f. SPECIAL (OCCUPATIONAL) TAX. Required by the NFA to be paid by a Federal firearms licensee engaged in the business of manufacturing (Class 2), importing (Class 1), or dealing (Class 3) in NFA firearms.

   g. FEDERAL FIREARMS LICENSE. A license issued under the provisions of the GCA to manufacture, import or deal in firearms.

   h. ATF OFFICER. An officer or employee of the Bureau of Alcohol, Tobacco and Firearms (ATF) authorized to perform any function relating to the administration of the NFA.

   i. MAKE. The term "make", and the various derivatives of such word, shall include manufacturing *(other than by one qualified to engage in such business under the NFA)*, putting together, altering, any combination of these, or otherwise producing a firearm.

   j. MISDEMEANOR CRIME OF DOMESTIC VIOLENCE. A crime that is a misdemeanor under Federal or State law and has, as an element, the use or attempted use of physical force, or the threatened use of a deadly weapon, committed by a current or former spouse, parent, or guardian of the victim, by a person with whom the victim shares a child in common, by a person who is cohabitating with or has cohabited with the victim as a spouse, parent, or guardian. The term includes all misdemeanors that involve the use or attempted use of physical force (e.g., simple assault, assault and battery), if the offense is committed by one of the defined parties. The person is NOT considered to have been convicted of such crime unless the person was represented by a lawyer or gave up the right to a lawyer, and, if the person was entitled to a jury trial, was tried by a jury or gave up the right to a jury trial.

   k. REACTIVATION. The restoration of a registered unserviceable NFA firearm to a functional condition. This action incurs the making tax liability.

   l. UNSERVICEABLE FIREARM. One which is incapable of discharging a shot by means of an explosive and incapable of being readily restored to firing condition. An acceptable method of rendering most firearms unserviceable is to fusion weld the chamber closed and fusion weld the barrel solidly to the frame.

2. **PREPARATION OF APPLICATION AND PAYMENT OF TAX.**

   a. AUTHORITY. As provided by 26 U.S.C. § 5822, any person *(other than a qualified manufacturer of firearms (see paragraph b))* seeking to make a firearm must complete, in duplicate, a separate application on this form for each firearm. The applicant maker must furnish all the information called for on this application form.

   b. REGISTRATION BY QUALIFIED MANUFACTURER. A person who has a Federal firearms license to manufacture firearms *(Type 07 or 10)* and who has paid special (occupational) tax to manufacture NFA firearms is exempt from the making tax and filing of the ATF F 1 application. Such qualified manufacturer must report and register each NFA firearm manufactured by filing ATF F 2, Notice of Firearms Manufactured or Imported, as required by 27 CFR § 179.102.

   c. PAYMENT OF/EXEMPTION FROM PAYMENT OF TAX. As provided in 26 U.S.C. § 5821, there is a $200.00 tax on each firearm made, except as provided in 26 U.S.C. §§ 5852 and 5853, when an NFA firearm may be made without payment of the tax when made by, or on behalf of the United States or any State or political subdivision thereof. Documentation that the firearm is being made for a government entity, such as a United States government contract or a State or local government agency purchase order, must accompany the application. The reactivation of a registered unserviceable firearm is subject to the making tax.

   d. PHOTOGRAPHS AND FINGERPRINTS. An individual maker must (1) attach to each copy in item 12 of the ATF F 1, a 2 inch x 2 inch photograph of his/her frontal view taken within 6 months prior to the date of the application and (2) submit two properly completed FBI Forms FD-258 *(Fingerprint Card with blue lines)* with the application. The fingerprints must be clear for accurate classification and taken by someone properly equipped to take them.

   e. SIGNATURES. All signatures required on ATF F 1 must be original in ink on both copies.

   f. REMITTANCE. If the application is subject to the making tax, a check or money order, made payable to the Bureau of Alcohol, Tobacco and Firearms, in the amount of $200.00 must be submitted with the ATF F 1. <u>Do not send cash</u>.

   g. PHOTOCOPIES OR COMPUTER GENERATED VERSIONS. The ATF F 1 may be photocopied or a computer-generated version *(as long as it is in the same format and contains all required information)* may be used. This form may also be downloaded from the ATF Internet website at www.atf.treas.gov.

   h. SERIAL NUMBERS AND OTHER MARKINGS. If an existing firearm is being modified into an NFA firearm, enter the existing serial number of the firearm into item 4g and the name and address of the original manufacturer into item 4a. DO NOT ALTER OR MODIFY THE EXISTING SERIAL NUMBER. If the NFA firearm is being made from parts, your name and address are to be entered into 4a and a serial number you create is to be entered into item 4g.

   i. SUBMISSION. All requested information must be entered in blue or black ink and must be legible. Illegible entries will be returned for correction. Send both copies of the ATF F 1 and attachments to the address located in the upper right hand corner on the face side of the ATF F 1. The return of the application or your sending it to any other address will only delay the processing.

3. APPROVAL OF APPLICATION. Upon approval of an application, the NFA Branch will affix the NFA tax stamp *(if any)* to the application, cancel it, and return the approved copy to the maker. The approval of the application effectuates registration of the firearm to the maker; however, the firearm must not be made until the application has been approved.

4. WITHDRAWAL OF APPLICATION. The application may be withdrawn prior to approval by submission of a written request from the maker. The NFA Branch will arrange for a refund of any tax paid.

5. CANCELLATION OF APPROVED APPLICATION. An approved application may be cancelled <u>only</u> if the firearms had not been made or modified. The maker must return the approved application with a written request for cancellation, citing the need and that the making of the firearm did not take place. The NFA Branch will arrange for a refund of any tax paid.

6. DISAPPROVAL OF APPLICATION. If the application is disapproved, the NFA Branch will note the reason for disapproval on the application and return one copy to the maker. The NFA Branch will arrange for a refund of any tax paid.

7. REASONS FOR DISAPPROVAL. 26 U.S.C. § 5822 provides that applications shall be denied if the making or possession of the firearm would place the maker in violation of law.

   a. STATE OR LOCAL LAW. If State or local law prohibits the making or possession of the firearm being made, the application will be disapproved.

   b. MACHINEGUNS AND SEMIAUTOMATIC ASSAULT WEAPONS.

      (1) 18 U.S.C. § 922(o) provides that machineguns may be made only for government use or export. An application will be denied unless the making meets these criteria.

      (2) 18 U.S.C. § 922(v) generally prohibits the manufacture of a semiautomatic assault weapon. The making of an NFA firearm does not provide relief from this prohibition.

   c. PERSONS PROHIBITED FROM MAKING A FIREARM. The application will be disapproved if the maker is a person prohibited from possessing a firearm by 18 U.S.C. § 922(g), which provides that is shall be unlawful for any person-

      (1) who has been convicted in any court of a crime punishable by imprisonment for a term exceeding one year;
      (2) who is a fugitive from justice;
      (3) who is an unlawful user of or addicted to any controlled substance;
      (4) who has been adjudicated as a mental defective or who has been committed to a mental institution;
      (5) who, being an alien, is illegally or unlawfully in the United States or, except as provided in 18 U.S.C. § 922(y)(2), has been admitted to the United States under a nonimmigrant visa *(as that term is defined in 8 U.S.C. §1101(a)(26)*;
      (6) who has been discharged from the Armed Forces under dishonorable conditions;
      (7) who, having been a citizen of the United States, has renounced his citizenship;
      (8) who is subject to a court order that-

         (A) was issued after a hearing of which such person received actual notice, and at which such person had an opportunity to participate;

ATF F 1 (5320.1) (3-2001)

INSTRUCTIONS (Continued)

(B) restrains such person from harassing, stalking, or threatening an intimate partner of such person or child of such intimate partner or person, or engaging in other conduct that would place an intimate partner in reasonable fear of bodily injury to the partner or child; and

(C) (i) includes a finding that such person represents a credible threat to the physical safety of such intimate partner or child; or (ii) by its terms explicitly prohibits the use, attempted use, or threatened use of physical force against such intimate partner or child that would reasonably be expected to cause bodily injury, or

(9) who has been convicted in any court of a misdemeanor crime of domestic violence, to ship or transport in interstate or foreign commerce, or possess in or affecting commerce, or possess in or affecting commerce, any firearm or ammunition; or to receive any firearm or ammunition which has been shipped or transported in interstate or foreign commerce.

8. **STATUS INQUIRIES AND QUESTIONS.** The NFA Branch telephone number is (202) 927-8330. Any inquiry relating to the status of an applicable to make an NFA firearm or about procedures in general should be directed to the NFA. Please be aware that the information relating to the registration of firearms is defined as "return" or "return information" by 26 U.S.C. § 6103 and disclosure is generally prohibited to anyone other than the registrant. Information relating to the NFA and other firearms laws is also available at the ATF Internet website www.atf.treas.gov.

9. **PENALTIES.** Any person who violates or fails to comply with any of the requirements of the NFA shall, upon conviction, be fined not more than $10,000 or be imprisoned for not more than 10 years, or both. Any firearm involved in a violation of the NFA shall be subject to seizure and forfeiture. It is unlawful for any person to make or cause the making of a false entry on any application or record required by the NFA knowing such entry to be false.

10. **COMPLIANCE WITH THE GUN CONTROL ACT.** All provisions of the GCA must also be complied with.

PRIVACY ACT INFORMATION

1. **AUTHORITY.** Solicitation of this information is made pursuant to the National Firearms Act *(26 U.S.C. §§ 5821 and 5822)*. Disclosure of this information by the applicant is mandatory for any person *(other than a manufacturer qualified under the National Firearms Act)* making a firearm as defined in the National Firearms Act.

2. **PURPOSE.** To verify payment of the tax imposed by 26 U.S.C. § 5821; to determine that the making would not be in violation of law; and to effect registration of the firearm.

3. **ROUTINE USES.** The information will be used by ATF to make the determinations set forth in paragraph 2. In addition, to effect registration of the firearm, information as to the identification of the firearm, date of registration, and the identification and address of person entitled to possess the firearm will be entered into the National Firearms Registration and Transfer Record. No information obtained from a application, registration, or records required to be submitted by a natural person in order to comply with any provision of the National Firearms Act or regulations issued thereunder, shall, except in connection with prosecution or other action for furnishing false information, be used, directly or indirectly, as evidence against that person in any criminal proceeding with respect to a violation of law occurring prior to or concurrently with the filing of the application. The information from this application may only be disclosed to Federal authorities for purpose of prosecution for violation of the National Firearms Act.

4. **EFFECTS OF NOT SUPPLYING INFORMATION REQUESTED.** Failure to supply complete information will delay processing and may cause denial of the application.

PAPERWORK REDUCTION ACT NOTICE

This form is in accordance with the Paperwork Reduction Act of 1995. The information you provide is used to establish that a transferee's receipt and possession of the firearm would be in conformance with Federal, State, and local law. The data is used as proof of lawful registration of a firearm to the manufacturer. The furnishing of this information is mandatory *(26 U.S.C. § 5822)*.

The estimated average burden associated with this collection of information 4 hours per respondent or recordkeeper, depending on individual circumstances. Comments concerning the accuracy of this burden estimate and suggestions for reducing this burden should be addressed to Reports Management Officer, Document Services Branch, Bureau of Alcohol, Tobacco and Firearms, Washington, DC 20226.

An agency may not conduct or sponsor, and a person is not required to respond to, a collection of information unless it displays a currently valid OMB control number.

ATF F 1 (5320.1) (3-2001)

OMB No. 1512-0024 (02/29/2004)

DEPARTMENT OF THE TREASURY
BUREAU OF ALCOHOL, TOBACCO AND FIREARMS
APPLICATION TO MAKE AND REGISTER A FIREARM
(Submit in duplicate. See Instructions attached.)

ATF CONTROL NUMBER

TO: National Firearms Act Branch, Bureau of Alcohol, Tobacco and Firearms, Washington, DC 20226

The undersigned hereby makes application, as required by Sections 5821 and 5822 of the National Firearms Act, Title 26 U.S.C., Chapter 53, to make and register the firearm described below.

1. TYPE OF APPLICATION *(Check one)*

   a. TAX PAID. Submit with your application a check or money order for $200 made payable to the Department of the Treasury. Upon approval of the application, this office will acquire, affix, and cancel the required "National Firearms Act" stamp for you.

   b. TAX EXEMPT because firearm is being made on behalf of the United States, or any department, independent establishment, or agency thereof.

   c. TAX EXEMPT because firearm is being made by or on behalf of any State or possession of the United States, or any political subdivison thereof, or any official police organization of such a government entity engaged in criminal investigations.

2. APPLICATION IS MADE BY:
   - INDIVIDUAL
   - CORPORATION OR OTHER BUSINESS ENTITY
   - GOVERNMENT ENTITY

3a. TRADE NAME *(If any)*

3b. APPLICANT'S NAME AND MAILING ADDRESS *(Type or print below and between the dots)*

3c. IF P.O. BOX IS SHOWN ABOVE, STREET ADDRESS MUST BE GIVEN HERE

3d. COUNTY

3e. TELEPHONE AREA CODE AND NUMBER

IMPORTANT: COMPLETE THE REVERSE SIDE. INDIVIDUALS *(INCLUDING FEDERALLY LICENSED COLLECTORS)* MUST ALSO SUBMIT, IN DUPLICATE, FBI FORM FD-258, FINGERPRINT CARD.

4. DESCRIPTION OF FIREARM *(Complete items a through i)*

   a. NAME AND LOCATION OF ORIGINAL MANUFACTURER OF FIREARM (RECEIVER) *(If prototype, furnish plans and specifications)* *(See Instruction 2h)*

   b. TYPE OF FIREARM TO BE MADE *(See instruction 1c)*

   c. CALIBER, GAUGE OR SIZE *(Specify)*

   d. MODEL

   e. LENGTH OF BARREL *(inches)*

   f. OVERALL:

   g. SERIAL NUMBER *(See Instruction 2h.)*

   h. ADDITIONAL DESCRIPTION *(Include all numbers and other identifying data which will appear on the firearm)*

   i. STATE WHY YOU INTEND TO MAKE FIREARM *(Use additional sheet if necessary)*

5. APPLICANT'S FEDERAL FIREARMS LICENSE *(If any)* *(Give complete 15-digit number)*

6. SPECIAL (OCCUPATIONAL) TAX STATUS
   a. EMPLOYER IDENTIFICATION NUMBER *(If applicable)*
   b. CLASS

IMPORTANT: GIVE FULL DETAILS ON SEPARATE SHEET FOR ALL "YES" ANSWERS IN ITEMS 7 AND 8

7. ARE YOU:	YES	NO	8. HAVE YOU:	YES	NO
a. Charged by information or under indictment in any court for a crime for which the judge could imprison you for more than one year. An information is a formal accusation of a crime made by a prosecuting attorney.			a. Been convicted in any court of a crime for which the judge could have imprisoned him/her for more than one year, even if the judge actually gave him/her a shorter sentence?		
b. A **fugitive** from justice?			b. Been discharged from the armed forces under **dishonorable** conditions?		
c. An alien who is **illegally** in the United States?					
d. Under 21 years of age?			c. Been adjudicated mentally defective or been committed to a mental institution?		
e. An unlawful user of or addicted to, marijuana, or any depressant, stimulant, or narcotic drug, or any other controlled substance?			d. Renounced his or her United States citizenship?		
f. Subject to a court order restraining you from harassing, stalking or threatening an intimate partner or child of such partner? *(See Instruction 7c)*			e. Been convicted in any court of a misdemeanor crime of domestic violence? *(See instruction 1m)*		

UNDER PENALTIES OF PERJURY, I DECLARE that I have examined this application, including accompanying documents, and to the best of my knowledge and belief it is true, accurate and complete and the making and possession of the firearm described above would not constitute a violation of Chapter 44, Title 18, U.S.C., Chapter 53, Title 26, U.S.C., or any provisions of State or local law.

9. SIGNATURE OF APPLICANT

10. NAME AND TITLE OF AUTHORIZED OFFICIAL OF FIRM OR CORPORATION *(If applicable)*

11. DATE

THE SPACE BELOW IS FOR THE USE OF THE BUREAU OF ALCOHOL, TOBACCO AND FIREARMS

By authority of the Director, Bureau of Alcohol, Tobacco and Firearms, this application has been examined and the applicant's making and registration of the firearm described above is:

- APPROVED *(With the following conditions, if any)*
- DISAPPROVED *(For the following reasons)*

AUTHORIZED ATF OFFICIAL

DATE

ATF F 1 (5320.1) (3-2001) PREVIOUS EDITIONS ARE OBSOLETE

ADDITIONAL REQUIREMENTS

12. PHOTOGRAPH

AFFIX
RECENT PHOTOGRAPH HERE
(Approximately 2" x 2")
(See instruction 2d)

13. LAW ENFORCEMENT CERTIFICATION *(See IMPORTANT note below)*

I certify that I am the chief law enforcement officer of the organization named below having jurisdiction in the area of residence of

_____
(Name of Maker)

I have no information indicating that the maker will use the firearm or device described on this application for other than lawful purposes. I have no information that POSSESSION OF THE FIREARM DESCRIBED IN ITEM 4 ON THE FRONT OF THIS FORM WOULD PLACE THE MAKER IN VIOLATION OF STATE OR LOCAL LAW.

_____
(Signature and Title of Chief Law Enforcement Officer - see IMPORTANT note below)

BY *(See IMPORTANT NOTE BELOW)* _____
(Signature and Title of Delegated Person)

_____
(Organization)

_____
(Street Address)

_____   _____
(City, State, and ZIP Code)   *(Date)*

IMPORTANT: The chief law enforcement officer is considered to be the Chief of Police for the maker's city or town of residence, the Sheriff for the maker's county of residence; the Head of the State Police for the maker's State of residence; a State or local district attorney or prosecutor having jurisdiction in the maker's area of residence; or another person whose certification is acceptable to the Director, Bureau of Alcohol, Tobacco and Firearms. If someone has specific delegated authority to sign on behalf of the Chief of Police, Sheriff, etc., this fact must be noted by printing the Chief's, Sheriff's, or other authorized official's name and title, followed by the word "by" and the full signature and title of the delegated person. Item 13 must be completed for an individual maker. The certification must be dated no more than one year prior to the date of receipt of the application.

IMPORTANT INFORMATION FOR CURRENTLY REGISTERED FIREARMS

If this registration document evidences the current registration of the firearm described on it, please note the following information.

ESTATE PROCEDURES: For procedures regarding the transfer of firearms in an estate resulting from the death of the registrant identified in item 3, the executor should contact the NFA Branch, Bureau of ATF, Washington, DC 20226.

CHANGE OF ADDRESS: The registrant shall notify the NFA Branch, Bureau of Alcohol, Tobacco and Firearms, Washington, DC 20226, in writing, of any change to the address in item 3a.

INTERSTATE MOVEMENT: If the firearm identified in item 4 is a machinegun, short-barreled rifle, short-barreled shotgun, or destructive device, the registrant may be required by 18 U.S.C. § 922(a)(4) to obtain permission from ATF prior to any transportation in interstate or foreign commerce.

CHANGE OF DESCRIPTION: The registrant shall notify the NFA Branch, Bureau of Alcohol, Tobacco and Firearms, Washington, DC 20226, in writing, of any change to the description of the firearms in item 4.

RESTRICTIONS ON POSSESSION: Any restriction *(see approval block on face of form)* on the possession of the firearm identified in item 4 continues with the further transfer of the firearm.

PERSONS PROHIBITED FROM POSSESSING FIREARMS: If the registrant becomes prohibited by 18 U.S.C. § 922 from possessing a firearm, the registrant shall notify the NFA Branch, Bureau of Alcohol, Tobacco and Firearms, Washington, DC 20226, in writing, immediately upon becoming prohibited for guidance on the disposal of the firearm.

PROOF OF REGISTRATION: This approved application is the registrant's proof of registration and it shall be made available to any ATF officer upon request.

ATF F 1 (5320.1) (3-2001)

ATF Form 2 (5320.2)
Notice of Firearms Manufactured or Imported

INSTRUCTIONS

1. Preparation of Notice of Firearms Manufactured or Imported.

   a. This form is required to effect the registration of all firearms imported, manufactured, remanufactured or reactivated by qualified Federal firearms licensees who have paid the special (occupational) tax to import or manufacture firearms.

   b. Reactivation of an NFA firearm - Any NFA firearm (including the frame or receiver of such firearm) must be registered to the possessor in order to be lawfully possessed. A Form 2 to register a reactivated NFA firearm will not be accepted if the unserviceable firearm is not registered to the applicant. The firearm in that event, would be considered contraband and would be subject to seizure and forfeiture provisions of the law.

   c. Remanufacture of a firearm - Any NFA firearm has been properly destroyed, and thereby removed from the purview of the NFA, which are subsequently restored. (This could also include the converting of semi-automatic firearms to full automatic firearms). Public Law 99-308, §922(o) restrictions apply.

   d. Manufacture of NFA firearms - Other types of manufacturing operations which result in the manufacture or making of an NFA firearm. (This includes producing firearms from scratch).

   e. A separate Form 2 must be submitted for the four categories of manufacture, remanufacture, reactivation and importation of firearms.

   f. If the importation involves more than one import permit, a separate Form 2 must be filed to report those firearms imported under each permit.

   g. Serial numbers - Sections 178.92 and 179.102 of the regulations require that an individual serial number, *not duplicating any serial number placed by the manufacturer or importer on any other firearm*, must be placed on the firearm. However, please do not alter existing serial numbers.

   h. When large numbers of firearms of the same type and model are reported, lists of serial numbers (double-spaced) may be attached to this form. The number of firearms in item 3b should agree with total number of firearms reported. Lists must be referenced to this form by date and manufacturer or importer in such a way that if pages become separated they can be matched up to the Form 2.

   i. Photostatic or carbon signatures are not acceptable. Although typed forms are preferred, pen and ink may be used; forms completed in pencil will not be accepted. Facsimile copies will be accepted, if an original affidavit is on file with us.

   j. If any questions arise concerning the preparation of this form, please contact the nearest ATF Office or the National Firearms Act Branch at (202) 927-8330.

2. Where to File Form - Submit completed forms to the National Firearms Act Branch, Bureau of Alcohol, Tobacco and Firearms, Room 5440, 650 Massachusetts Ave., N.W., Washington, DC 20226.

3. When to File Forms -

   a. All firearms manufactured, remanufactured or reactivated during a single day must be filed no later than the close of the next business day. (27 CFR 179.112).

4. Disposition of Form - The manufacturer or importer must prepare the form, in duplicate, file the original with the National Firearms Act Branch and keep the copy with the firearms records required to be retained at the premises covered by the required special (occupational) tax stamp.

5. Receipt of Form by the Bureau of Alcohol, Tobacco and Firearms-

   a. The receipt of this form properly prepared and executed by a manufacturer will register the firearms listed on the form to the manufacturer or importer, with the exception noted in item 1f. of these instructions.

   b. Timely receipt by ATF of a properly prepared and executed form and timely receipt by the Imports Branch of a copy of ATF Form 6a (required by 27 CFR 178.112) covering the firearm(s) reported on the form by the importer, will register the listed firearms to the importer.

Paperwork Reduction Act Notice

This request is in accordance with the Paperwork Reduction Act of 1980. The information you provide as a qualified licensed firearms manufacturer or importer is to register, as required by law, firearms within the jurisdiction of the National Firearms Act, which have been lawfully manufactured or imported. The data is used to determine applicant's eligibility to register the firearms described. The furnishing of the information is mandatory (26 U.S.C. 5841c).

The estimated average burden associated with this collection of information is 30 minutes per respondent or recordkeeper depending on individual circumstances. Comments concerning the accuracy of this burden estimate and suggestions for reducing this burden should be addressed to Reports Management Officer, Information Programs Branch, Bureau of Alcohol, Tobacco and Firearms, Washington, D.C. 20226, and the Office of Management and Budget, Paperwork Reduction Project (1512-0025), Washington, D.C. 20503.

Form Approved: OMB No. 1512-0025 (02/28/95)

DEPARTMENT OF THE TREASURY
BUREAU OF ALCOHOL, TOBACCO AND FIREARMS
NOTICE OF FIREARMS MANUFACTURED OR IMPORTED
(Complete in duplicate - See Instructions on reverse)

TO: THE DIRECTOR, BUREAU OF ALCOHOL, TOBACCO AND FIREARMS, WASHINGTON, DC 20226

The undersigned hereby serves notice of the manufacture, reactivation, or importation of firearms as required by section 5841 of the National Firearms Act, Title 26, U.S.C. Chapter 53.

1. TYPE OF NOTICE

a. FIREARMS ON THIS NOTICE ARE: *(Check one)*
- ☐ MANUFACTURED
- ☐ REMANUFACTURED
- ☐ REACTIVATED
- ☐ IMPORTED *(If imported complete items c and d)*

2. PRINT NAME AND TITLE OF PERSON AUTHORIZED TO SIGN FOR A BUSINESS OR FIRM

3. NAME AND ADDRESS *(Include trade name)*

b. NUMBER OF FIREARMS COVERED BY THIS NOTICE *(See Instruction 1.c.)*

FOR IMPORTED FIREARMS ONLY

c. IMPORTATION PERMIT NUMBER *(See Instruction 1.d. on reverse)*

☐ SOLE PROPRIETOR   ☐ PARTNERSHIP   ☐ CORPORATION

4. WHERE ARE FIREARMS KEPT?   4a. TELEPHONE NUMBER *(Include area code)*   d. PERMIT EXPIRATION DATE

5. DESCRIPTION OF FIREARMS *(Complete all items)*

DATE OF MANUFACTURE OR REACTIVATION (If imported, give date released from Customs custody & manufacturer's name) (If remanufactured or reactivated, indicate name of original manufacturer)	TYPE OF FIREARM (Shortbarreled rifle, machine gun, destructive device, etc.)	CALIBER GAUGE OR SIZE	MODEL	LENGTH (In.)		SERIAL NUMBER (See Instructions 1.e. and 1.g.)
				OF BARREL	OVER-ALL	
a	b	c	d	e	f	g

ADDITIONAL DESCRIPTION ON THE FIREARM(S) DESCRIBED ABOVE; I.E. IF CONVERTED BY KIT. *(Attach additional sheets if necessary)*

6. FEDERAL FIREARMS LICENSE			7. SPECIAL (OCCUPATIONAL) TAX STAMP	
LICENSE NUMBER	TYPE OF BUSINESS	EXPIRATION DATE	EMPLOYER IDENTIFICATION NUMBER	CLASS

UNDER PENALTIES OF PERJURY, I DECLARE that I have examined this notice of firearms manufactured, remanufactured, reactivated or imported and, to the best of my knowledge and belief, it is true, correct and complete.

8. SIGNATURE OF MANUFACTURER OR IMPORTER *(Or authorized official shown in Item 2)*	9. DATE

ATF F2 (5320.2) (8-93)

ATF Form 3 (5320.3)
Application for Tax-Exempt Transfer of Firearm and Registration to Special (Occupational) Taxpayer

INSTRUCTIONS

This form must be completed, in duplicate, and used only between those who have paid the appropriate fees to maintain a current Federal firearms license which is issued every three years and valid special *(occupational)* tax stamp which must be renewed every July 1st. The FFL and SOT stamp qualifies a person to import, manufacture or deal in National Firearms Act (NFA) firearms. The applicant must furnish all the information called for on the form. The transferor's and transferee's names must be shown exactly as they appear on the federal firearms license.

1. PRINT or type firearm **buyer's** *full name* including middle name and *address*. P.O. Box number, rural route or highway and box number and *trade name*.

2a. PRINT or type firearm **owner's** *full name* including middle and complete *address*, former and current *trade name*.

2b. The **form** will not be mailed to this address. It will be **returned to the** address in item 2a.

2c. The firearm **seller's** *telephone number*.

3a - g. PRINT or type original **manufacturer's** or importer's *name* and/or tradename and address and ensure that all of the information referencing the firearm is complete and accurate. See General Information below for more details.

3h. PRINT or type additional information referencing the firearm, such as a complete description including serial number of the Title I firearm into which a registered auto sear may be placed.

4. PRINT or type firearm **buyer's** *VALID* 15 digit FFL #.

5a. PRINT or type firearm **buyer's** *VALID* 9 digit EIN #.

5b. Is the firearm **buyer** a **Class** 1, 2, or 3?

6. PRINT or type firearm **owner's** *VALID* 15 digit FFL #.

7a. PRINT or type firearm **owner's** *VALID* 9 digit EIN #.

7b. Is the firearm **owner** a **Class** 1, 2, or 3?

8. Firearm **owner's** original *signature*.

9. PRINT or type firearm **owner's** *name* and *title*.

10. DATE firearm **owner** *prepared*.

GENERAL INFORMATION

1. Ensure that the **state** in which the firearm buyer resides **deos** not prohibit **NFA firearms**. See "Firearms State Laws and Published Ordinances", ATF P 5300.5.

2. Prior to completing and **mailing** the Form 3 to the NFA Branch, BATF, Wash., DC 20226, please **make a physical examination of the firearm** to ensure that the information in **Items 3a - g** is **complete and accurate** and **matches the information permanently placed on the firearm.**

3. The firearm **owner can not deliver** the firearm to the firearm buyer until the approved form is received from the Bureau of ATF.

4. If the firearm transaction cannot be completed immediately, please void the transfer.

5. Always **initial** and **date** any *corrections* you make on the form.

6. **RECORDKEEPING REQUIREMENTS:** Pursuant to Title 18, U.S.C., Chapter 44, the transferor and the transferee, as firearm licensees, shall record their disposition and acquisition of the described firearm as required by subpart H of Title 27 CFR, Part 178.

PAPERWORK REDUCTION ACT NOTICE

This form is in accordance with the Paperwork Reduction Act of 1995. The information you provide will be used to apply to transfer firearms tax exempt from one Federal firearms licensee and special *(occupational)* taxpayer qualified to deal in NFA firearms to another qualified special taxpayer. The data is used to verify lawful transfer and registration of firearms. The information being furnished is mandatory (26 U.S.C. 5812).

The estimated average burden associated with this collection of information is 30 minutes per respondent or recordkeeper, depending on individual circumstances. Comments concerning the accuracy of this burden estimate and suggestions for reducing this burden should be addressed to the Reports Management Officer, Document Services Branch, Bureau of Alcohol, Tobacco and Firearms, Washington, DC 20226.

An agency may not conduct or sponsor, and a person is not required to respond to, a collection of information unless it displays a currently valid OMB control number.

PRIVACY ACT INFORMATION

1. **AUTHORITY.** Solicitation of this information is made pursuant to the National Firearms Act (26 U.S.C. §5812 and 5851 and 5852). Disclosure of this information by the applicant is mandatory for any person *(other than a manufacturer qualified under the National Firearms Act)* making a firearm as defined in the National Firearms Act.

2. **PURPOSE.** To verify the tax exemption imposed by 26 U.S.C. § 5851; to determine that the transfer would not be in violation of law; and to effect registration of the firearm.

3. **ROUTINE USES.** The information will be used by ATF to make the determinations set forth in paragraph 2. In addition, to effect registration of the firearm, information as to the identification of the firearm, date of registration, and the identification and address of person entitled to possess the firearm will be entered into the National Firearms Registration and Transfer Record. No information obtained from an application, registration, or records required to be submitted by a natural person in order to comply with any provision of the National Firearms Act or regulations issued thereunder, shall, except in connection with prosecution or other action for furnishing false information, be used, directly or indirectly, as evidence against that person in any criminal proceeding with respect to a violation of law occuring prior to or concurrently with the filing of the application. The information from this application may only be disclosed to Federal authorities for purpose of prosecution for violation of the National Firearms Act.

4. **EFFECTS OF NOT SUPPLYING INFORMATION REQUESTED.** Failure to supply complete information will delay processing and may cause denial of the application.

ATF F 3 (5320.3) (2-98)

OMB No. 1512-0026 (09/30/98)

DEPARTMENT OF THE TREASURY
BUREAU OF ALCOHOL, TOBACCO AND FIREARMS
**APPLICATION FOR TAX-EXEMPT TRANSFER OF FIREARM AND
REGISTRATION TO SPECIAL (OCCUPATIONAL) TAXPAYER** National Firearms Act (Title 26, U.S.C. Chapter 53)

1. TRANSFEREE'S NAME AND ADDRESS *(Show Trade Name, if any, and give number, street, city, State and ZIP Code, P.O. Box alone is not sufficient.)*

To be submitted in duplicate by transferor of firearm

TO: National Firearms Act Branch
Bureau of Alcohol, Tobacco and Firearms
Washington, D.C. 20226

☐ SOLE PROPRIETOR ☐ PARTNERSHIP ☐ CORPORATION

2a. TRANSFEROR'S NAME AND MAILING ADDRESS *(Show Trade Name, if any)*

2b. NUMBER, STREET, CITY, STATE AND ZIP CODE OF LICENSED PREMISES IF DIFFERENT FROM ITEM 2a.

2c. TELEPHONE NO. *(Include Area Code)*

☐ SOLE PROPRIETOR ☐ PARTNERSHIP ☐ CORPORATION

The above-named and undersigned transferor and special (occupational) taxpayer hereby makes application as required by Section 5812 of the National Firearms Act to transfer, without payment of tax, and register the firearm described below to the special *(occupational)* taxpayer identified as the transferee in this application.

3. DESCRIPTION OF FIREARM *(Complete items a through h, if applicable)*

a. NAME AND ADDRESS OF MANUFACTURER AND/OR IMPORTER OF FIREARM	b. TYPE OF FIREARM *(Shortbarreled rifle, machine gun, destructive device, any other weapon, etc.)*	c. CALIBER, GAUGE OR SIZE *(Specify)*	d. MODEL
			LENGTH *(Inches)* e. OF BARREL: f. OVERALL:
			g. SERIAL NUMBER

h. ADDITIONAL DESCRIPTION OR DATA APPEARING ON FIREARM *(Attach additional sheet if necessary)*

4. TRANSFEREE'S FEDERAL FIREARMS LICENSE *(If any)*				5. TRANSFEREE'S SPECIAL (OCCUPATIONAL) TAX STATUS	
(Give complete 15-digit number)				a. EMPLOYER IDENTIFICATION NUMBER	b. CLASS
First 6 digits	2 digits	2 digits	5 digits		
6. TRANSFEROR'S FEDERAL FIREARMS LICENSE *(If any)*				7. TRANSFEROR'S SPECIAL (OCCUPATIONAL) TAX STATUS	
(Give complete 15-digit number)				a. EMPLOYER IDENTIFICATION NUMBER	b. CLASS
First 6 digits	2 digits	2 digits	5 digits		

I believe I am entitled to exemption from payment of the transfer tax imposed by Section 5811, National Firearms Act (NFA), on the firearm described above because the transferee named herein is qualified under the NFA to manufacture, import or deal in that type of firearm.

UNDER PENALTIES OF PERJURY, I DECLARE that I have examined this application, and to the best of my knowledge and belief it is true, correct and complete.

8. ORIGINAL SIGNATURE OF TRANSFEROR *(Or authorized official)*	9. NAME AND TITLE OF AUTHORIZED OFFICIAL *(Print or type)*	10. DATE

THE SPACE BELOW IS FOR THE USE OF THE BUREAU OF ALCOHOL, TOBACCO AND FIREARMS

BY AUTHORITY OF THE DIRECTOR, THIS APPLICATION HAS BEEN EXAMINED, AND THE TRANSFER AND REGISTRATION OF THE FIREARM DESCRIBED HEREIN AND THE INTERSTATE MOVEMENT OF THAT FIREARM, WHEN APPLICABLE, TO THE TRANSFEREE ARE:

☐ APPROVED *(with the following conditions, if any)*   ☐ DISAPPROVED *(For the following reasons)*

AUTHORIZED ATF OFFICIAL	DATE

ATF F 3 (5320.3) (2-98) PREVIOUS EDITION IS USEABLE

ATF Form 4 (5320.4)
Application for Tax paid Transfer and Registration of Firearm

Form Approved: OMB 1512-0027(01/31/00)

DEPARTMENT OF THE TREASURY — BUREAU OF ALCOHOL, TOBACCO AND FIREARMS

APPLICATION FOR TAX PAID TRANSFER AND REGISTRATION OF FIREARM

DETACH THIS SHEET BEFORE COMPLETING FORM
INSTRUCTIONS

1. DEFINITIONS

a. FIREARM. The term "firearm" means: (1) a shotgun having a barrel or barrels of less than 18 inches in length; (2) a weapon made from a shotgun if such weapon as modified has an overall length of less than 26 inches or a barrel or barrels of less than 18 inches in length; (3) a rifle having a barrel or barrels of less than 16 inches in length; (4) a weapon made from a rifle if such weapon as modified has an overall length of less than 26 inches or a barrel or barrels of less than 16 inches in length; (5) any other weapon, as defined in b. below; (6) a machinegun; (7) a muffler or a silencer for any firearm whether or not such firearm is included within this definition; and (8) a destructive device. The term "firearm" shall not include an antique firearm or any device (other than a machinegun or destructive device) which, although designed as a weapon, the Director, Bureau of Alcohol, Tobacco and Firearms, or authorized delegate, finds by reason of the date of its manufacture, value, design and other characteristics is primarily a collector's item and is not likely to be used as a weapon.

b. ANY OTHER WEAPON. The term "any other weapon" means any weapon or device capable of being concealed on the person and from which a shot can be discharged through the energy of an explosive; a pistol or revolver having a barrel with a smooth bore designed or redesigned to fire a fixed shotgun shell; weapons with combination shotgun and rifle barrels 12 inches or more, less than 18 inches in length, from which only a single discharge can be made from either barrel without manual reloading; and shall include any such weapon which may be readily restored to fire. Such term shall not include a pistol or a revolver having a rifled bore, or rifled bores, or weapons designed, made, or intended to be fired from the shoulder and not capable of firing fixed ammunition.

c. TRANSFEROR. The term "transferor" means the registered owner of a firearm who is applying to transfer it.

d. TRANSFEREE. The term "transferee" means the person desiring to acquire the firearm.

e. PERSON. The term "person" means any individual, company, corporation, association, firm, partnership, joint stock company, trust or society other than a special (occupational) taxpayer qualified to deal in NFA firearms.

2. PREPARATION OF APPLICATION FOR TAX PAID TRANSFER AND REGISTRATION OF A FIREARM.

a. Reference §§5811 and 5812, National Firearms Act, United States Code, Chapter 53), persons seeking to transfer a firearm tax paid must complete, in duplicate, a separate application on this form for each firearm. The applicant transferor must furnish all the information called for on this application form.

b. If the transferor of a destructive device, machinegun, shortbarreled shotgun or short-barreled rifle is a licensee under 18 U.S.C., Chapter 44, and the transferee is anyone other than a qualified licensee under the National Firearms Act (special (occupational) taxpayer], the transferee must complete item 2 (Applicant Certification) on the reverse side of ATF Form 4 (5320.4). Item 3 (Law Enforcement Certification) must be completed for the transfer of any NFA firearm to an individual other than a special (occupational) taxpayer.

c. If the transferee is an individual, including a collector licensed under 18 U.S.C., Chapter 44, in addition to satisfying the requirements of 2b, above, a recent 2" x 2" photograph must be affixed in item 1 on the reverse of ATF Form 4 (5320.4) and completed FBI Form FD-258, Fingerprint Card, must be submitted in duplicate. The fingerprints should be taken by a person qualified to do so, and must be clear, unsmudged and classifiable.

d. All signatures required on this form must be entered in ink on both copies. Photocopies or other facsimile signatures are not acceptable. It is preferred that the form be prepared by the use of a typewriter, using carbon paper to make an exact duplicate. Pen and ink may be used, but under no circumstances will a form filled in by use of a lead pencil be accepted. All changes made on this form must be initialed and dated.

e. If the transferee is acquiring the firearm as other than an individual, the trade name and business address should be shown in item 2 on the face of ATF Form 4 (5320.4). Firearms may not be acquired as a part of the business inventory of a firearms licensee who is not a special (occupational) taxpayer. In such case, the home address of the transferee should be shown.

f. If the firearm is being transferred from an estate, item 3a. should show the transferor as: Executor's name, title (Executor (or executrix, administrator, administratrix) of the Estate of (name)), and the executor's address. Item 3c. should reflect the last address of the decedent and date of death.

g. If any questions arise concerning the preparation of this form, please contact the NFA Branch, Bureau of Alcohol, Tobacco and Firearms, Washington, DC 20226 or the nearest Alcohol, Tobacco and Firearms office.

3. DISPOSITION OF APPLICATION FOR TRANSFER AND REGISTRATION OF FIREARM.
The transferor will forward both copies of the form to the National Firearms Act Branch, Bureau of Alcohol, Tobacco and Firearms, P.O. Box 73201 Chicago, IL 60673-7201. This office will deposit the tax and forward the application to the Bureau of Alcohol, Tobacco and Firearms, National Firearms Act Branch, Washington, DC 20226 for processing. If approved, the original of the approved form will be returned to the transferor for delivery to the transferee with the firearm, and this office will retain the duplicate. Approval of this form will effect registration of the firearm to the transferee. The transferor shall not under any circumstances deliver the firearm to the transferee until the approved form is received. This form must be retained by the transferee and be available for inspection by Government officers until such time as the firearm may later be transferred after approval by this office. (If the application is disapproved, the original with any accompanying check or money order, will be returned to the transferor with the reason for disapproval.)

4. APPROVED TRANSFER NOT PHYSICALLY ACCOMPLISHED.
The transferor should mark the front of the form "VOID," sign and date the form and return the voided form to the Director. This will assure that the firearm will remain registered in the name of the transferor who submitted the application. Upon receipt of the voided form, instructions for obtaining a tax refund will be provided.

5. LATER TRANSFERS OF THE FIREARM.
If the firearm is to be transferred later by the new owner, a new application form covering the proposed transfer must be filed with the Director.

ATF Form 4 (5320.4) (7-88)

INSTRUCTIONS (Continued)

6. RATE OF TAX ON THE TRANSFER OF A FIREARM. The tax on the transfer of a firearm is $200, except that the transfer tax is $5 on any firearm classified as "any other weapon" as defined in instruction 1b.

7. PERSONS PROHIBITED FROM RECEIVING FIREARMS. Under 18 U.S.C., Chapter 44 and Title VII of Public Law 90-351, as amended, (18 U.S.C., Appendix), the following persons are prohibited from receiving a firearm, including an unserviceable firearm which has a frame or receiver: (1) fugitives from justice (any crime); (2) persons under indictment for, or who have been convicted of, a crime punishable by imprisonment, for a term exceeding 1 year; (3) narcotic addicts or unlawful drug users; (4) persons adjudicated mental defectives or mentally incompetent, or who have been committed to any mental institution; (5) veterans discharged under dishonorable conditions; (6) persons who have renounced their United States citizenship; (7) aliens illegally or unlawfully in the United States; and (8) where the transferor is a firearms licensee, persons under 21 years of age in the case of any firearm other than a shotgun or a rifle and under 18 years of age in the case of a shotgun or a rifle. In addition, section 5812 of the National Firearms Act requires that an application to transfer a firearm be denied if the transfer, receipt or possession of the firearm would place the transferee in violation of law. The term "law" in this statute includes Federal laws as well as State statutes and local ordinances applicable to the locality where the transferee resides.

8. INQUIRIES ABOUT STATUS OF A TRANSFER APPLICATION. The transfer application form will be reviewed and returned to the transferor promptly if additional information or corrections are required. However, because of the necessity for an FBI record check on an individual transferee's fingerprints, approximately 60 days must be allowed for processing such applications. Under the provisions of Section 6103(a), Title 26, United States Code, disclosure of any "return" or "return information" is generally prohibited to anyone except the person filing the return. Therefore, information about the status of a transfer application may be given only to the transferor. Such information cannot be divulged to the transferee.

9. PENALTIES. Any person who violates or fails to comply with any of the requirements of the National Firearms Act shall, upon conviction, be fined not more than $10,000 or be imprisoned for not more than 10 years, or both, in the discretion of the court. Moreover, any firearm involved in any violation of the provisions of the National Firearms Act or any regulations issued thereunder shall be subject to seizure and forfeiture. It is unlawful for any person to make or cause the making of a false entry on any application or record required by the National Firearms Act knowing such entry to be false.

NOTE: All provisions of Title I of the Gun Control Act must also be complied with, including the recordkeeping requirements for licenses and retention of ATF Form 4473 (5300.9) by licensees for dispositions to nonlicensees.

SPECIAL NOTE: A direct interstate transfer will be approved only to a licensee who is also a special (occupational) taxpayer qualified to deal in the particular type NFA firearm; or a government entity; or a lawful heir; or, in the case of a firearm which has been designated as a "curio or relic," to a licensed collector.

PAPERWORK REDUCTION ACT NOTICE

This information request is in accordance with the Paperwork Reduction Act of 1980. The information you provide is used in applying to transfer serviceable firearms taxpaid to persons other than special taxpayers qualified to deal in NFA firearms or government entities. Data is used to identify transferor, transferee, and firearm, and to ensure legality for transfer under Federal, State and local laws. The furnishing of this information is mandatory. (26 U.S.C. 5812)

The following information is provided pursuant to Section 3 of the Privacy Act of 1974 (5 U.S.C. §552(e)(3)):

1. *AUTHORITY.* Solicitation of this information is made pursuant to the National Firearms Act (26 U.S.C. §5812). Disclosure of this information by the applicant is mandatory for transfer of an NFA firearm, unless the transfer is otherwise exempt from tax.

2. *PURPOSE.* To insure payment of the tax imposed by 26 U.S.C. §5811; to insure that the transfer would not be in violation of law; and to effect registration of the firearm.

3. *ROUTINE USES.* The information will be used by ATF to make the determinations set forth in paragraph 2. In addition, to effect registration of the firearm, information as to the identification of the firearm, date of registration, and the identification and address of person entitled to possess the firearm will be entered into the National Firearms Registration and Transfer Record. No information obtained from an application, registration, or records required to be submitted by a natural person in order to comply with any provision of the National Firearms Act or regulations issued thereunder, shall, except in connection with prosecution or other action for furnishing false information, be used, directly or indirectly, as evidence against that person in any criminal proceeding with respect to a violation of law occurring prior to or concurrently with the filing of the application. The information from this application may only be disclosed to Federal authorities for purposes of prosecution for violation of the National Firearms Act.

4. *EFFECTS OF NOT SUPPLYING INFORMATION REQUESTED.* Failure to supply complete information will delay processing and may cause denial of the application.

ATF Form 4 (5320.4) (7-88)

DEPARTMENT OF THE TREASURY — BUREAU OF ALCOHOL, TOBACCO AND FIREARMS
APPLICATION FOR TAX PAID TRANSFER AND REGISTRATION OF FIREARM

SEE INSTRUCTIONS ATTACHED.
TO BE SUBMITTED IN DUPLICATE
TO: National Firearms Act Branch
Bureau of Alcohol, Tobacco and Firearms
P.O. Box 73201
Chicago, IL 60673-7201

2a. TRANSFEREE'S NAME AND ADDRESS (If transferee is a Special (Occupational) Taxpayer who is acquiring firearm for personal use, rather than as part of his business inventory, show personal name below and check here: ☐)

1. TYPE OF TRANSFER (Check one) (See instructions 1 and 6)
☐ $5   ☐ $200

2b. TRADE NAME (See instruction 2e)

2c. COUNTY

3a. TRANSFEROR'S NAME AND MAILING ADDRESS (If the firearm is registered under your trade name, enter your trade name. EXECUTORS: See instruction 2f.)

Submit with your application a check or money order for the appropriate amount made payable to the Department of the Treasury. Upon approval of this application, this office will acquire, affix and cancel the required "National Firearms Act" stamp for you. (See Instruction 6)

3b. NUMBER, STREET, CITY, STATE AND ZIP CODE IF DIFFERENT FROM ITEM 3a.

3c. IF APPLICABLE: DECEDENT'S NAME, ADDRESS, AND DATE OF DEATH

The above-named and undersigned transferor hereby makes application as required by Section 5812 of the National Firearms Act to transfer and register the firearm described below to the transferee.

4. DESCRIPTION OF FIREARM (Complete items a through h)

a. NAME AND ADDRESS OF MANUFACTURER AND/OR IMPORTER OF FIREARM

b. TYPE OF FIREARM (Short-barreled rifle, machine gun, destructive device, any other weapon, etc.)

c. CALIBER, GAUGE OR SIZE (Specify)

d. MODEL

LENGTH (Inches)   e. OF BARREL: f. OVERALL:

g. SERIAL NUMBER

h. ADDITIONAL DESCRIPTION OR DATA APPEARING ON FIREARM (Attach additional sheet if necessary)

5. TRANSFEREE'S FEDERAL FIREARMS LICENSE (If any)
(Give complete 15-digit number)
First 6 digits	2 digits	2 digits	5 digits

6. TRANSFEREE'S SPECIAL (OCCUPATIONAL) TAX STATUS
a. ATF IDENTIFICATION NUMBER   b. CLASS

7. TRANSFEROR'S FEDERAL FIREARMS LICENSE (If any)
(Give complete 15-digit number)
First 6 digits	2 digits	2 digits	5 digits

8. TRANSFEROR'S SPECIAL (OCCUPATIONAL) TAX STATUS
a. ATF IDENTIFICATION NUMBER   b. CLASS

UNDER PENALTIES OF PERJURY, I DECLARE that I have examined this application, and to the best of my knowledge and belief it is true, correct and complete, and that the transfer of the described firearm to the transferee and receipt and possession of it by the transferee are not prohibited by the provisions of Chapter 44, Title 18, United States Code; Chapter 53, Title 26, United States Code; or Title VII of the Omnibus Crime Control and Safe Streets Act, as amended; or any provisions of State or local law.

9. SIGNATURE OF TRANSFEROR (Or authorized official)

10. NAME AND TITLE OF AUTHORIZED OFFICIAL (Print or type)

11. DATE

THE SPACE BELOW IS FOR THE USE OF THE BUREAU OF ALCOHOL, TOBACCO AND FIREARMS

BY AUTHORITY OF THE DIRECTOR, THIS APPLICATION HAS BEEN EXAMINED, AND THE TRANSFER AND REGISTRATION OF THE FIREARM DESCRIBED HEREIN AND THE INTERSTATE MOVEMENT OF THAT FIREARM, WHEN APPLICABLE, TO THE TRANSFEREE ARE:

STAMP NUMBER

☐ APPROVED (With the following conditions, if any)

☐ DISAPPROVED (For the following reasons)

SIGNATURE OF DIRECTOR, BUREAU OF ALCOHOL, TOBACCO AND FIREARMS

DATE

ATF Form 4 (5320.4) (7-88)

CERTIFICATIONS

1. PHOTOGRAPH

If the transferor of a destructive device, machinegun, short-barreled shotgun or short-barreled rifle is a Federal firearms licensee, and the transferee is anyone other than a licensee qualified to deal in the firearm to be transferred, the transferee must sign the Applicant Certification (item 2 below) in the presence of the law enforcement officer signing item 3 below. The Law Enforcement Certification (item 3 below) must be completed for the transfer of any registered firearm to an individual other than a licensee qualified to deal in the firearm to be transferred. In addition, the individual transferee must affix a recent photograph (taken within the past year) in item 1 and submit, in duplicate (to the transferor) two completed copies of FBI Form FD-258, Fingerprint Card. (See Important note below.)

AFFIX RECENT PHOTOGRAPH HERE (Approximately 2" x 2")

2. APPLICANT CERTIFICATION

I, _____ (Name of Transferee), have a reasonable necessity to possess the device or weapon described on this application for the following reason(s) _____

and my possession of the device or weapon would be consistent with public safety (18 U.S.C. 922(b) (4) and 27 CFR 178.98).

UNDER PENALTIES OF PERJURY, I declare that I have examined this application, and to the best of my knowledge and belief it is true, correct and complete, and that receipt and possession of the firearm described on this form will not place me in violation of the provisions of Chapter 44, Title 18, U.S.C.; Chapter 53, Title 26, U.S.C.; or Title VII of the Omnibus Crime Control and Safe Streets Act, as amended, or any provisions of State or local law.

_____ (Signature of Transferee or official authorized to sign for firm)   Date

3. LAW ENFORCEMENT CERTIFICATION (See IMPORTANT note below)

I certify that I am the chief law enforcement officer of the organization named below having jurisdiction in the area of residence of _____ (Name of Transferee). I have no information indicating that the transferee will use the firearm or device described on this application for other than lawful purposes. I have no information that the receipt and/or possession of the firearm described in item 4 of this form would place the transferee in violation of State or local law.

_____ (Signature and Title of Chief Law Enforcement Officer — See IMPORTANT note below)

_____ (Date)

_____ (Organization and Street Address)

_____ (County)   _____ (Phone — include area code)

IMPORTANT: The chief law enforcement officer is considered to be the Chief of Police for the transferee's city or town of residence, the Sheriff for the transferee's county of residence; the Head of the State Police for the transferee's State of residence; a State or local district attorney or prosecutor having jurisdiction in the transferee's area of residence; or another person whose certification is acceptable to the Director, Bureau of Alcohol, Tobacco and Firearms. If someone has specific delegated authority to sign on behalf of the Chief of Police, Sheriff, etc., this fact must be noted by printing the Chief's, Sheriff's, or other authorized official's name and title, followed by the word "by" and the full signature and title of the delegated person.

ATF Form 4 (5320.4) (7-88)

ATF Form 5 (5320.5)
Application for Tax Exempt Transfer and Registration of a Firearm

OMB No. 1512-0028 (01/31/00)

DEPARTMENT OF THE TREASURY — BUREAU OF ALCOHOL, TOBACCO AND FIREARMS
APPLICATION FOR TAX EXEMPT TRANSFER AND REGISTRATION OF A FIREARM

DETACH THIS SHEET BEFORE COMPLETING
INSTRUCTIONS

1. DEFINITIONS.

a. FIREARM. The term "firearm" means: (1) a shotgun having a barrel or barrels of less than 18 inches in length; (2) a weapon made from a shotgun if such weapon as modified has an overall length of less than 26 inches or a barrel or barrels of less than 18 inches in length; (3) a rifle having a barrel or barrels of less than 16 inches in length; (4) a weapon made from a rifle if such weapon as modified has an overall length of less than 26 inches or a barrel or barrels of less than 16 inches in length; (5) any other weapon, as defined in b. below; (6) a machinegun; (7) a muffler or a silencer or any firearm whether or not such firearm is included within this definition; and (8) a destructive device. The term "firearm" shall not include an antique firearm or any device (other than a machinegun or destructive device) which, although designed as a weapon, the Director, Bureau of Alcohol, Tobacco and Firearms, or authorized delegate, finds by reason of the date of its manufacture, value, design and other characteristics is primarily a collector's item and is not likely to be used as a weapon.

b. ANY OTHER WEAPON. The term "any other weapon" means any weapon or device capable of being concealed on the person and from which a shot can be discharged through the energy of an explosive; a pistol or revolver having a barrel with a smooth bore designed or redesigned to fire a fixed shotgun shell; weapons with combination shotgun and rifle barrels 12 inches or more, less than 18 inches in length, from which only a single discharge can be made from either barrel without manual reloading; and shall include any such weapon which may be readily restored to fire. Such term shall not include a pistol or a revolver having a rifled bore, or rifled bores, or weapons designed, made, or intended to be fired from the shoulder and not capable of firing fixed ammunition.

c. TRANSFEROR. The term "transferor" means the registered owner of a firearm who is applying to transfer it.

d. TRANSFEREE. The term "transferee" means the person desiring to acquire the firearm.

e. PERSON. The term "person" means any individual, company, corporation, association, firm, partnership, joint stock company, trust or society which is not a special (occupational) taxpayer.

2. PREPARATION OF APPLICATION FOR TAX-EXEMPT TRANSFER AND REGISTRATION OF A FIREARM.

a. As set forth in section 5812, National Firearms Act (26 U.S.C., Chapter 53), and except as otherwise provided, persons seeking to transfer a firearm without payment of tax must complete, in duplicate, a separate application on this form for each firearm. The applicant transferor must furnish all the information called for on this application form.

b. If the transferor of a destructive device, machinegun, shortbarreled shotgun or short-barreled rifle is a licensee under 18 U.S.C., Chapter 44, and the transferee is anyone other than a qualified licensee under the National Firearms Act [special (occupational) taxpayer], the transferee must complete item 2 (Applicant Certification) on the reverse side of ATF Form 5 (7560.5).

Item 3 (Law Enforcement Certification) must be completed for the transfer of any NFA firearm to an individual other than a special (occupational) taxpayer.

c. If the transferee is an individual (including a licensed collector), in addition to satisfying the requirements of 2b. above, a recent 2" x 2" photograph must be affixed in item 1 on the reverse of ATF Form 5 and completed FBI Form FD-258, Fingerprint Card, in duplicate, must be submitted. The fingerprints should be taken by a person qualified to do so, and must be clear, unsmudged and classifiable.

d. It is preferred that the form be prepared by the use of a typewriter, using carbon paper to make an exact duplicate. Pen and ink may be used, but under no circumstances will a form filled in by use of a lead pencil be accepted. All signatures on both copies MUST be original. Photocopies or other facsimiles are not acceptable. All changes made on the face of the form by the transferor must be initialed and dated.

e. If the transferee is acquiring the firearm as other than an individual, the trade name should be shown in item 2b. on the face of ATF Form 5 and the business address should appear in items 2a. and 2c. A firearms licensee who is not a special (occupational) taxpayer may not acquire firearms as part of the business inventory and item 2b. should be left blank. Items 2a. and 2c. should, in such case, reflect the home address.

f. If the firearm is being transferred from an estate, item 3a. should show the transferor as: Executor's name, title (Executor (or executrix, administrator, administratrix) of the Estate of (name)), and the executor's address. Item 3b. should reflect the last address of the decedent and date of death.

g. If any questions arise concerning the preparation of this form, please contact the NFA Branch, Bureau of Alcohol, Tobacco and Firearms, Washington, DC 20226 or the nearest Alcohol, Tobacco and Firearms office.

3. DISPOSITION OF APPLICATION FOR TRANSFER AND REGISTRATION OF FIREARM.

The transferor will forward both copies of the form to the NFA Branch, Bureau of Alcohol, Tobacco and Firearms, Washington, DC 20226. If approved, the original of the approved form will be returned to the transferor for delivery to the transferee with the firearm, and this office will retain the duplicate. Approval of this form will effect registration of the firearm to the transferee. The transferor shall not under any circumstances deliver the firearm to the transferee until the approved form is received. This form must be retained by the transferee and be available for inspection by Government officers until such time as the firearm may later be transferred after approval by this office. If the application is disapproved, the original will be returned to the transferor with the reason for disapproval.

4. APPROVED TRANSFER NOT PHYSICALLY ACCOMPLISHED.

The transferor should mark the front of the form "VOID," sign and date the form and return the voided form to the Director. This will assure that the firearm will remain registered in the name of the transferor who submitted the application.

ATF FORM 5 (5320.5) (4-89)   PREVIOUS EDITIONS ARE OBSOLETE

INSTRUCTIONS (Continued)

5. LATER TRANSFERS OF THE FIREARM. If the firearm is to be transferred later by the new owner, a new application form covering the proposed transfer must be filed with the Director.

6. TRANSFERS EXEMPT FROM TAX. A registered firearm may be transferred without payment of tax under any of the following conditions:

a. If it is an unserviceable firearm being transferred as a curio or ornament. (NOTE: an unserviceable firearm is defined as one which is incapable of discharging a shot by means of an explosive and incapable of being readily restored to a firing condition. An acceptable method of rendering most firearms unserviceable is to fusion weld the chamber closed and fusion weld the barrel solidly to the frame. Certain unusual firearms require other methods to render the firearm unserviceable. Contact ATF for instructions when in doubt.)

b. To or from the United States, or any department, independent establishment or agency thereof.

c. To or from any State or possession of the United States or any political subdivision thereof, or any official police organization of such a government entity engaged in criminal investigations.

d. To a lawful heir as defined in the laws of the State of residence of the decedent.

e. The National Firearms Act also provides that registered firearms may be transferred tax exempt between firearms dealers who have also paid special (occupational) tax. In such instances, however, the application must be submitted on ATF Form 3.

7. PERSONS PROHIBITED FROM RECEIVING FIREARMS. Under 18 U.S.C., Chapter 44 and Title VII of Public Law 90-351, as amended, (18 U.S.C., Appendix), the following persons are prohibited from receiving a firearm, including an unserviceable firearm which has a frame or receiver: (1) fugitives from justice (any crime); (2) persons under indictment for, or who have been convicted of, a crime punishable for a term exceeding 1 year; (3) narcotic addicts or unlawful drug users; (4) persons adjudicated mental defectives or mentally incompetent, or who have been committed to any mental institution; (5) veterans discharged under dishonorable conditions; (6) persons who have renounced their United States citizenship; (7) aliens illegally or unlawfully in the United States; and (8) where the transferor is a firearms licensee, persons under 21 years of age in the case of any firearm other than a shotgun or a rifle and under 18 years of age in the case of a shotgun or a rifle. In addition, section 5812 of the National Firearms Act requires that an application to transfer a firearm be denied if the transfer, receipt or possession of the firearm would place the transferee in violation of law. The term "law" in this statute includes Federal laws as well as State statutes and local ordinances applicable to the locality where the transferee resides.

8. PENALTIES. Any person who violates or fails to comply with any of the requirements of the National Firearms Act shall, upon conviction, be fined not more than $10,000 or be imprisoned for not more than 10 years, or both, in the discretion of the court. Moreover, any firearm involved in any violation of the provisions of the National Firearms Act or any regulations issued thereunder shall be subject to seizure and forfeiture. It is unlawful for any person to make or cause the making of a false entry on any application or record required by the National Firearms Act knowing such entry to be false.

NOTE: All provisions of Title I of the Gun Control Act must also be complied with, including the recordkeeping requirements for licenses.

SPECIAL NOTE: A direct interstate transfer will be approved only to a licensee who is also a special (occupational) taxpayer qualified to deal in the particular type NFA firearm; or a government entity; or a lawful heir; or, in the case of a firearm which has been designated as a "curio or relic," to a licensed collector.

PAPERWORK REDUCTION ACT NOTICE

This form meets the clearance requirements of Section 3507, PL 96-511, 12/11/80. The information you provide is used to apply the tax-exempt transfer of an unserviceable firearm to anyone other than a Federal firearms licensee who has paid the required special (occupational) tax to deal in NFA firearms. The data is used to ensure legality of transfer under Federal, State and local law. The furnishing of this information is mandatory (26 USC 5812).

The estimated average burden associated with this collection of information is 4 hours per respondent or recordkeeper, depending on individual circumstances. Comments concerning the accuracy of this burden estimate and suggestions for reducing this burden should be addressed to Reports Management Officer, Document Services Branch, Bureau of Alcohol, Tobacco and Firearms, Washington, DC 20226.

An agency may not conduct or sponsor, and a person is not required to respond to, a collection of information unless it displays a currently valid OMB control number.

PRIVACY ACT INFORMATION

The following information is provided pursuant to Section 3 of the Privacy Act of 1974 (5 U.S.C. §552(e)(3)):

1. *AUTHORITY.* Solicitation of this information is made pursuant to the National Firearms Act (26 U.S.C. §5812). Disclosure of this information by the applicant is mandatory for any transfer without payment of transfer tax as provided in 26 U.S.C. §5852.

2. *PURPOSE.* To verify that the proposed transfer is exempt from transfer tax; to verify that the transfer would not be in violation of law; and to effect registration of the firearm.

3. *ROUTINE USES.* The information will be used by ATF to make the determinations set forth in paragraph 2. In addition, to effect registration of the firearm, information as to the identification of the firearm, date of registration, and the identification and address of person entitled to possess the firearm will be entered into the National Firearms Registration and Transfer Record. No information obtained from an application, registration, or records required to be submitted by a natural person in order to comply with any provision of the National Firearms Act or regulations issued thereunder, shall, except in connection with prosecution or other action for furnishing information, be used, directly or indirectly, as evidence against that person in any criminal proceeding with respect to a violation of law occurring prior to or concurrently with the filing of the application. The information from this application may only be disclosed to Federal authorities for purposes of prosecution for violation of the National Firearms Act.

4. *EFFECTS OF NOT SUPPLYING INFORMATION REQUESTED.* Failure to supply complete information will delay processing and may cause denial of the application.

PREVIOUS EDITIONS ARE OBSOLETE   ATF FORM 5 (5320.5) (4-89)

Form Approved: OMB No. 1512-0028 (09/30/95)

DEPARTMENT OF THE TREASURY — BUREAU OF ALCOHOL, TOBACCO AND FIREARMS

APPLICATION FOR TAX EXEMPT TRANSFER AND REGISTRATION OF A FIREARM

SEE INSTRUCTIONS ATTACHED. TO BE SUBMITTED IN DUPLICATE
TO: National Firearms Act Branch
Bureau of Alcohol, Tobacco and Firearms
Washington, DC 20226

2a. TRANSFERRE'S NAME AND ADDRESS (If transferee is a Special (Occupational) Taxpayer who is acquiring firearm for personal use, rather than as part of his business inventory, show personal name below and check here: ☐)

1. TYPE OF TRANSFER: TAX EXEMPT

I believe that I am entitled to exemption from the payment of the transfer tax imposed by Section 5811 (26 U.S.C. Chapter 53) on the firearm described herein for the following reason See Instruction 6):

☐ FIREARM IS UNSERVICEABLE AND IS BEING TRANSFERRED AS A CURIO OR ORNAMENT (6a)

2b. TRADE NAME (See instruction 2e)

2c. COUNTY

☐ FIREARM IS BEING TRANSFERRED TO OR FROM A GOVERNMENT ENTITY (6b & 6c)

3a. TRANSFEROR'S NAME AND MAILING ADDRESS (If firearm is registered under your trade name, enter your trade name. EXECUTORS: See instruction 2f.)

☐ FIREARM IS BEING TRANSFERRED TO A LAWFUL HEIR (6d)

☐ OTHER (Specify)

3c. NUMBER, STREET, CITY, STATE AND ZIP CODE OF RESIDENCE (OR FIREARMS BUSINESS PREMISES) IF DIFFERENT FROM ITEM 3a.

3b. IF APPLICABLE: DECEDENT'S NAME, ADDRESS, AND DATE OF DEATH

The above-named and undersigned tranferor hereby makes application as required by Section 5812 of the National Firearms Act to transfer and register the firearm described below to the transferee.

4. DESCRIPTION OF FIREARM (Complete items a through i)

a. NAME AND ADDRESS OF MANUFACTURER AND/OR IMPORTER OF FIREARM	b. TYPE OF FIREARM (Short-barreled rifle, machine gun, destructive device, any other weapon, etc.)	c. CALIBER, GAUGE OR SIZE (Specify)	d. MODEL
			LENGTH (Inches) e. OF BARREL: f. OVERALL:
		g. SERIAL NUMBER	

h. ADDITIONAL DESCRIPTION OR DATA APPEARING ON FIREARM (Attach additional sheet if necessary)

i. IS THE FIREARM UNSERVICEABLE AS DEFINED IN INSTRUCTION 6a? ☐ YES ☐ NO (If "No," describe any other method by which firearm has been rendered unserviceable. Use additional sheets.)

5. TRANSFEREE'S FEDERAL FIREARMS LICENSE (If any)
(Give complete 15-digit number)
First 6 digits | 2 digits | 2 digits | 5 digits

6. TRANSFEREE'S SPECIAL (OCCUPATIONAL) TAX STATUS
a. ATF IDENTIFICATION NO. | b. CLASS

7. TRANSFEROR'S FEDERAL FIREARMS LICENSE (If any)
(Give complete 15-digit number)
First 6 digits | 2 digits | 2 digits | 5 digits

8. TRANSFEROR'S SPECIAL (OCCUPATIONAL) TAX STATUS
a. ATF IDENTIFICATION NO. | b. CLASS

UNDER PENALTIES OF PERJURY, I DECLARE that I have examined this application, and to the best of my knowledge and belief it is true, correct and complete, and that the transfer of the described firearm to the transferee and receipt and possession of it by the transferee are not prohibited by the provisions of Chapter 44, Title 18, United States Code; Chapter 53, Title 26, United States Code; or Title VII of the Omnibus Crime Control and Safe Streets Act, as amended; or any provisions of State or local law.

9. SIGNATURE OF TRANSFEROR (Or authorized official)

10. NAME AND TITLE OF AUTHORIZED OFFICIAL (Print or type)

11. DATE

THE SPACE BELOW IS FOR THE USE OF THE BUREAU OF ALCOHOL, TOBACCO AND FIREARMS

BY AUTHORITY OF THE DIRECTOR, THIS APPLICATION HAS BEEN EXAMINED, AND THE TRANSFER AND REGISTRATION OF THE FIREARM DESCRIBED HEREIN AND THE INTERSTATE MOVEMENT OF THAT FIREARM, WHEN APPLICABLE, TO THE TRANSFEREE ARE:

☐ APPROVED (With the following conditions, if any)

☐ DISAPPROVED (For the following reasons)

EXAMINER | DATE | AUTHORIZED ATF OFFICIAL | DATE

ATF FORM 5 (5320.5) (4-89)   PREVIOUS EDITIONS ARE OBSOLETE

CERTIFICATIONS

1. PHOTOGRAPH

If the transferor of a destructive device, machinegun, short-barreled shotgun or short-barreled rifle is a Federal firearms licensee, and the transferee is anyone other than a licensee qualified to deal in the firearm to be transferred, the transferee must sign the Applicant Certification (item 2 below) in the presence of the law enforcement officer signing item 3 below. The Law Enforcement Certification (item 3 below) must be completed for the transfer of any registered firearm to an individual other than a licensee qualified to deal in the firearm to be transferred. In addition, the individual transferee must affix a recent photograph (taken within the past year) in item 1 and submit, in duplicate (to the transferor) two completed copies of FBI Form FD-258, Fingerprint Card. (See Important note below.)

AFFIX
RECENT PHOTOGRAPH HERE
(Approximately 2'' x 2'')

2. APPLICANT CERTIFICATION

I, _____ (Name of Transferee), have a reasonable necessity to possess the device or weapon described on this application for the following reason(s) _____

and my possession of the device or weapon would be consistent with public safety (18 U.S.C. 922(b) (4) and 27 CFR 178.98).

UNDER PENALTIES OF PERJURY, I declare that I have examined this application, and to the best of my knowledge and belief it is true, correct and complete, and that receipt and possession of the firearm described on this form will not place me in violation of the provisions of Chapter 44, Title 18, U.S.C.; Chapter 53, Title 26, U.S.C.; or Title VII of the Omnibus Crime Control and Safe Streets Act, as amended, or any provisions of State or local law.

_____ (Signature of Transferee or official authorized to sign for firm)   Date

3. LAW ENFORCEMENT CERTIFICATION (See IMPORTANT note below)

I certify that I am the chief law enforcement officer of the organization named below having jurisdiction in the area of residence of _____ (Name of Transferee). I have no information indicating that the transferee will use the firearm or device described on this application for other than lawful purposes. I have no information that the receipt and/or possession of the firearm described in item 4 of this form would place the transferee in violation of State or local law.

_____ (Signature and Title of Chief Law Enforcement Officer — See IMPORTANT note below)

_____ (Date)

_____ (Organization and Street Address)

_____ (County)   _____ (Phone — include area code)

IMPORTANT: The chief law enforcement officer is considered to be the Chief of Police for the transferee's city or town of residence, the Sheriff for the transferee's county of residence; the Head of the State Police for the transferee's State of residence; a State or local district attorney or prosecutor having jurisdiction in the transferee's area of residence; or another person whose certification is acceptable to the Director, Bureau of Alcohol, Tobacco and Firearms. If someone has specific delegated authority to sign on behalf of the Chief of Police, Sheriff, etc., this fact must be noted by printing the Chief's, Sheriff's, or other authorized official's name and title, followed by the word ''by'' and the full signature and title of the delegated person.

PREVIOUS EDITIONS ARE OBSOLETE   ATF FORM 5 (5320.5) (4-89)

ATF Form 9 (5320.9)
Application and Permit for Permanent Exportation of Firearms

INSTRUCTIONS (*See 27 CFR Part 479*)

Any person desiring to permanently export a firearm without payment of the transfer tax must submit ATF Form 9, in to the Director, Bureau of Alcohol, Tobacco and Firearms, Washington, D.C. 20226, for a permit providing for deferment of the transfer tax. No shipment may be made until that permit is received from the Director.

a. ATF Form 9 must be submitted until a State Department License for the exportation has been received by the applicant.

b. Part 1 of ATF Form 9 must be completed by the applicant and submitted to ATF with a certified copy of a written order, contract of sale, or other evidence showing firearm is to be shipped to a foreign destination. The transferor's written certification attesting to that fact must appear on the documentation. If the applicant wishes to transfer the firearm(s) tax free to another person who will export the firearm, the applicant must submit Form 9 with documentation that the transfer is a part of the exportation process.

c. The form must be completed by typewriter or pen and ink; penciled entries are unacceptable. The signature in item 10 must be entered in ink on all four copies. Photostatic, facsimile or carbon copy signatures are not acceptable. Where the exporter is a Federal Firearms Licensee, only those individuals Form 7, Application for License, or an individual whom the licensee has certified to ATF as a responsible official, may sign as the authorized official in item 10, Part 1.

d. Applications approved by ATF will serve as the permit to export the firearm(s) described on the application.

e. In the event exportation is not effected, all copies of the form must be *immediately* returned to ATF for cancellation. (27 CFR 179.116).

When the firearms are to be exported by other than parcel post, two copies each of the permit and the Shipper's Export Declaration (Commerce Form 7525-V), and a copy of the State Department License, must be submitted to the District Director of U.S. Customs Service at the port of exportation, an must precede or accompany the shipment in order to permit appropriate inspection prior to lading. The Customs official, after execution Part 3, will retain one copy of the permit and return one copy to the Director, Bureau of Alcohol, Tobacco and Firearms, NFA Branch, Washington, DC 20226, as provided in Customs Manual Supplement No. 3284.02 dated March 12, 1979.

When the firearms are to be exported by parcel post, one copy of the permit must be presented to the postmaster at the office receiving the parcel. The postmaster will execute Part 4 of ATF Form 9 and return the permit to the exporter.

Proof of exportation must be furnished by the exporter to ATF within a 6-month period from date of issuance of the permit by ATF. Satisfactory evidence of exportation would be:

a. The certificate of exportation executed by a Customs Official.

b. The certificate of mailing by parcel post executed by a postmaster.

c. A certificate of landing executed by a Customs official of the foreign country to which the firearm is exported.

d. A sworn statement of the foreign consignee covering the receipt of the firearm.

e. A return receipt, or photostatic copy, signed by the addressee or an authorized agent of the addressee, if the shipment of a firearm was made by insured or registered parcel post.

)TE: ATF receipt of the required documentation that the firearm(s) has/have been exported will relieve the transferor from the transfer tax liability. IF SATISFACTORY EVIDENCE IS NOT FURNISHED WITHIN THE STATED PERIOD, THE TRANSFER TAX WILL BE ASSESSED.

ACTION BY U.S. CUSTOMS SERVICE

on receipt of an approved ATF Form 9, in duplicate, the Customs official may order such inspection as deemed necessary prior to lading of the merchandise. If satisfied that the shipment is oper and the information contained in the permit to export is in agreement with the information shown in the shipper's export declaration, the Customs official will, after the merchandise has en exported, execute Part 3 of ATF Form 9. One copy will be retained with the shipper's export declaration. Customs will forward the remaining copy to the Bureau of Alcohol, Tobacco and earms, NFA Branch, Washington, DC 20226.

PRIVACY ACT INFORMATION

e following information is provided pursuant to Section 3 of the Privacy Act of 1974 (5 U.S.C. §552a(e)(3)):

AUTHORITY. Solicitation of this information is made pursuant to the National Firearms Act (26 U.S.C. §5854). Disclosure of this information is mandatory for the exportation of a firearm exempt from transfer tax.

PURPOSE. To determine whether the proposed transfer qualifies as an exportation exempt from tax.

ROUTINE USES. The information will be used by ATF to make the determination set forth in para. 2. In addition, ATF will use the information to annotate the National Firearms Registration and Transfer Record. No information obtained from an application, registration, or records required to be submitted by a natural person in order to comply with any provision of the National Firearms Act, or regulations issued thereunder, shall, except in connection with prosecution, or other action, for furnishing false information, be used, directly or indirectly, as evidence against that person in any criminal proceeding with respect to a violation of law occurring prior to or concurrently with the filing of the application. The information from this application may only be disclosed to Federal authorities as provided in Section 6103, 26 USC (as amended by the Tax Reform Act of 1979).

EFFECTS OF NOT SUPPLYING INFORMATION REQUESTED. Failure to supply complete information will delay processing and may cause denial of the application.

PAPERWORK REDUCTION ACT NOTICE

s form meets the clearance requirements of Section 3507, PL 96-511, 12/11/80. The information you provide is used to verify exportation of a firearm and justify removal of the firearm from National Firearms Registration and Transfer Record (NFRTR). The information is required to show satisfactory proof that a firearm may be exported without payment of the transfer tax in manner as prescribed by the Secretary of the Treasury. The furnishing of this information is mandatory (26 USC 5854).

e estimated average burden associated with this collection of information is 3.4 hour(s) per respondent or recordkeeper, depending on individual circumstances. Comments concerning the curacy of this burden estimate and suggestion for reducing this burden should be addressed to Reports Management Officer, Information Programs Branch, Bureau of Alcohol, Tobacco and earms, Washington, D.C. 20226, and the Office of Management and Budget, Paperwork Reduction Project (1512-0020), Washington, D.C. 20503.

TF F 9 (5320.9) (7/84)

Form Approved OMB No. 1512-0020 (05/31/93)

DEPARTMENT OF THE TREASURY - BUREAU OF ALCOHOL, TOBACCO AND FIREARMS
APPLICATION AND PERMIT FOR PERMANENT EXPORTATION OF FIREARMS
(CHAPTER 53, TITLE 26, UNITED STATES CODE)
(SUBMIT IN QUADRUPLICATE. SEE INSTRUCTIONS ON REVERSE.)

TO: DIRECTOR, BUREAU OF ALCOHOL, TOBACCO AND FIREARMS, WASHINGTON, DC 20226

PART 1 - APPLICATION. The undersigned transferor hereby makes application to export the firearm(s) described herein. The application is supported by the attached certified copy of written order or contract of sale of such firearm(s) to consignee.

1. NAME AND ADDRESS OF FOREIGN CONSIGNEE	2. INTENDED PORT OF EXPORTATION (Including air freight)	3. NUMBER OF FIREARMS INCLUDED IN THIS APPLICATION

4. DESCRIPTION OF FIREARM(S) (If additional space is needed, continue on a separate sheet using the format below.)

LINE NO.	TYPE (Machine gun, destructive device, short barreled shotgun or rifle, etc.) (a)	CALIBER, GAUGE OR SIZE (b)	MODEL (c)	LENGTH OF BARREL(S) (d)	OVERALL LENGTH (e)	SERIAL NUMBER (f)
1						
2						
3						
4						
5						

5. NAME OF EXPORTER (And trade name if any)	6. ADDRESS (Number, street, city, county, state, ZIP Code)

7. FEDERAL FIREARMS LICENSE (if any) (Give complete 15-digit number)	8. ATF IDENTIFICATION NUMBER (If any)	9. STATE DEPARTMENT LICENSE NUMBER FOR THIS SPECIFIC SHIPMENT

Under penalties of perjury, I certify that I am the lawful possessor of the firearm(s) described on this form and any accompanying sheets, and that I have examined this application and, to the best of may knowledge and belief, it is true, correct and complete.

10. SIGNATURE AND TITLE (Owner or authorized official) (See instruction 1c.)	11. DATE OF APPLICATION

PART 2 - PERMIT (This portion to be completed by Bureau of Alcohol, Tobacco and Firearms)

12. THIS APPLICATION IS: ☐ APPROVED ☐ DISAPPROVED: (Reason)	13. ASSESSMENT OF TAX INCURRED BY THIS TRANSFER WILL BE MADE UNLESS PROPER EVIDENCE OF EXPORTATION IS RECEIVED ON OR BEFORE:

14. EXAMINER	15. DATE	16. AUTHORIZED ATF OFFICIAL	17. DATE

PART 3 - CERTIFICATION BY CUSTOMS

I hereby certify that the described merchandise, covered by a shipper's export declaration on file in this office, was laden and cleared as described below:

LADEN IN (Name and/or type of carrier)	DATE CLEARED	FOREIGN DESTINATION	
SIGNATURE OF CUSTOMS OFFICIAL	PORT OF		DATE

PART 4 - CERTIFICATION OF MAILING BY PARCEL POST/EXPORTATION

I certify that there has (have) been posted at this office today, parcel(s) addressed as indicated in Item 1, Part 1 of this application, declared to be firearms by the transferor named in Item 5, Part 1, or the transferor's authorized agent, who has waived the right to withdraw same from the mails.

POST OFFICE NAME OR STAMP	SIGNATURE OF POSTMASTER, BY	DATE POSTED

ATF F 9 (5320.9) (7-84)

ATF Form 10 (5320.10)
Application for Registration of Firearms Acquired by Certain Government Entities

SPECIAL NOTICE

1. If a firearm is registered to the person from whom you obtained it, that person may submit ATF Form 5 for the tax exempt transfer of the firearm to you, in lieu of your submission of ATF Form 10. If the transfer is approved, the restriction on further transfer of the firearm which applies to firearms registered on ATF Form 10 would not apply.

2. Title 27 CFR 179.104 provides that any state, any political subdivision thereof, or any official police organization of such a governmental entity engaged in criminal investigations which acquires for official use a National Firearms Act weapon not registered to it, such as by abandonment or by forfeiture, will register such firearm with the Director by filing ATF Form 10, Application for Registration of Firearms Acquired by Certain Governmental Entities, and that such registration shall become a part of the National Firearms Registration and Transfer Record. Registration of such firearms has been required since passage of the original National Firearms Act in 1934. On April 15, 1971, the Supreme Court decided in the matter of *U.S. vs. Freed, et al.*, and noted that, "only possessors who lawfully make, manufacture, or import firearms can and must register them." However, in order to assist law enforcement agencies, while curtailing the flow of "gangster type" weapons into interstate commerce, the cited regulation was promulgated to permit the limited registration of firearms by governmental entities for official use only. When registration of a firearm on this form by a governmental entity is approved, the Bureau will approve subsequent transfer of such firearm to another qualified governmental entity only, for official use. Otherwise, such firearm must be destroyed or abandoned to ATF.

INSTRUCTIONS

1. Preparation of this form.

    a. This form must be submitted in duplicate. Photostatic copies of this form are not acceptable.

    b. Only one firearm may be listed on each form.

    c. It is preferred that the original and carbon copy be typed, although pen and ink entries are acceptable.

    d. The signature on each copy must be in ink. Pencilled, photostatic, or facsimile signatures are not acceptable.

    e. Serial Number - If the firearm being registered does not bear a serial number, please contact the nearest Alcohol, Tobacco and Firearms office to have an ATF serial number assigned and placed on the frame or receiver of the firearm prior to the submission of the form.

2. Disposition of this form - The applicant will forward the original and one copy of the form to the Director, Bureau of Alcohol, Tobacco and Firearms, Washington, DC 20226, Attention: Technical Services Division. The Director will return the original form, showing approval or disapproval, to the applicant. Approval authorized by the Director will effect the registration of the firearm to the governmental entity. The approved form must be retained with the permanent records of the entity. Subsequent transfer of the firearm will be approved to another qualified governmental entity only.

3. Firearms Held for Use as Evidence - Firearms being held for use as evidence in a criminal proceeding need not be registered if they are to be destroyed or abandoned to ATF when no longer needed as evidence.

DEFINITIONS

The following types of firearms, whether serviceable or unserviceable, fall within the purview of the National Firearms Act and must be registered to the possessor to be lawfully possessed:

1. Short-barreled shotgun - Shotguns with barrels less than 18 inches long or any weapon made from a shotgun having an overall length of less than 26 inches or a barrel less than 18 inches in length.

2. Short-barreled rifle - Rifles with barrels less than 16 inches long. This includes a pistol with a shoulder stock unless it has been specifically exempted; or any weapon made from a rifle having an overall length of less than 26 inches or a barrel less than 16 inches in length.

3. Any other weapon - Any other weapon, except a conventional pistol or revolver having a rifled bore, capable of firing a shot and being concealed on the person. Examples include: "pen" guns ostensibly designed to expel tear gas but which fire fixed ammunition, H & R Handy Guns; Ithaca Auto-Burglar guns; cane guns; and gadget-type firearms.

4. Machinegun - Any weapon which shoots, is designed to shoot, or can be readily restored to shoot, automatically more than one shot, without manual reloading, by a single function of the trigger. The term also includes the frame or receiver of any such weapon, any combination of parts designed and intended for use in converting a weapon into a machinegun, and any combination of parts from which a machinegun can be assembled if such parts are in the possession or under the control of a person.

5. Destructive device - Destructive devices include explosive, incendiary (including so called "molotov cocktails") or poison gas bombs, grenades, rockets, missiles, mines, and similar devices. Included in this category are anti-tank guns, bazookas and mortars and other military type weapons with a bore of more than one-half inch diameter, other than a sporting shotgun or shotgun ammunition.

6. Muffler or silencer - A muffler or silencer for any firearm whether or not such a firearm is included within this listing.

PAPERWORK REDUCTION ACT NOTICE

This form meets the clearance requirements of the Paperwork Reduction Act of 1995. The information you provide is used to properly identify the registrant and the firearms to be registered. The form when approved, registers the firearm to the law enforcement agency. The furnishing of this information is mandatory (26 U.S.C. 5853a).

The estimated average burden associated with this collection of information is 30 minutes per respondent or recordkeeper, depending on individual circumstances. Comments concerning the accuracy of this burden estimate and suggestions for reducing this burden should be addressed to Reports Management Officer, Document Services Branch, Bureau of Alcohol, Tobacco and Firearms, Washington, DC 20226.

An agency may not conduct or sponsor, and a person is not required to respond to, a collection of information unless it displays a currently valid OMB control number.

ATF F 10 (5320.10) (10-83)

OMB No. 1512-0029 (01/31/05)

DEPARTMENT OF THE TREASURY
BUREAU OF ALCOHOL, TOBACCO AND FIREARMS
APPLICATION FOR REGISTRATION OF FIREARMS ACQUIRED BY CERTAIN GOVERNMENTAL ENTITIES
(Submit in duplicate)
PLEASE READ INSTRUCTIONS ON REVERSE CAREFULLY BEFORE COMPLETING THIS FORM

TO: The Director, Bureau of Alcohol, Tobacco and Firearms, Washington, DC 20226

The undersigned hereby makes application to register to the governmental entity identified in this application the firearm described below.

1. NAME AND COMPLETE ADDRESS *(Including ZIP code)* OF DEPARTMENT OR AGENCY MAKING APPLICATION TO REGISTER FIREARM

27 CFR 179.104 Provides for limited registration of otherwise unregistrable firearms by certain governmental entities, for official use only. If this application is approved, it is with the condition that the firearm is for "OFFICIAL USE ONLY."

2. TELEPHONE NUMBER *(Include Area Code)*

3. DESCRIPTION OF FIREARM *(Complete Items (a) through (h).)*

NAME AND ADDRESS OF MANUFACTURER AND/OR IMPORTER OF FIREARM	TYPE OF FIREARM *(See Definitions)*	*(Check One)* ☐ CALIBER ☐ GAUGE ☐ SIZE	MODEL	LENGTH *(inches)* OF BARREL	OVERALL	SERIAL NUMBER *(See Instruction 1)*
a	b	c	d	e	f	g

h. ADDITIONAL DESCRIPTION *(Include all numbers on firearm, and location of each number. If firearm is unserviceable, describe how it was made unserviceable.)*

4. LOCATION WHERE FIREARM IS USUALLY KEPT

5. FROM WHOM WAS FIREARM RECEIVED? *(Optional response - This information may assist ATF in removing records relating to previous registrations of this firearm.)*

I CERTIFY THAT the above described firearm is for OFFICIAL USE ONLY and that I have examined this application and, to the best of my knowledge and belief, it is true, correct and complete.

6. SIGNATURE OF AUTHORIZED OFFICIAL *(See Instruction 1)*	7. PRINT NAME AND TITLE OF AUTHORIZED OFFICIAL	8. DATE

SPACE BELOW IS FOR USE BY THE BUREAU OF ATF - PLEASE DO NOT WRITE BELOW

By authority of the Director, Bureau of Alcohol, Tobacco and Firearms, this application has been examined and the registration of the described firearm to the government entity described above is:

☐ APPROVED FOR OFFICIAL USE

☐ DISAPPROVED

REMARKS

AUTHORIZED ATF OFFICIAL

DATE

ATF F 10 (5320.10) (10-83)

ATF Form 5320.20
Application To Transport Interstate or to Temporarily Export Certain NFA Firearms

INSTRUCTIONS

a. A written request and prior authorization from ATF to transport interstate or in foreign commerce any destructive device, machinegun, short-barreled rifle, or short-barreled shotgun is required under the provisions of Section 922(a)(4), Title 18, U.S.C., and Section 178.28, Title 27, CFR. A letter of request, in duplicate, containing all information required on this form, may be submitted in lieu of the form.

b. The registered owner of NFA firearm(s) shall complete two copies of ATF F 5320.20 and forward the forms to the Director, Bureau of Alcohol, Tobacco and Firearms, Washington, D.C. 20226 (Attention: NFA Branch).

c. All signatures on both copies of the form shall be in ink. A facsimile signature is not acceptable. All other entries on the form shall be printed in ink or typewritten.

d. The original of ATF F 5320.20 will be returned to the registered owner. Approval authorizes the registered owner to transport the designated firearm(s) only during the time period specified in item 3. THE AUTHORIZATION DOES NOT CARRY OR IMPORT RELIEF FROM ANY STATUTORY OR REGULATORY PROVISIONS RELATING TO FIREARMS OTHER THAN 27 CFR 178.28.

e. In the event item 2 is checked "yes" and the firearm(s) is not returned to the original location by the date specified, the registered owner shall submit a new application on ATF F 5320.20 to receive approval to return the firearm(s).

f. If a contract or common carrier is used to transport the firearm(s) a copy of ATF F 5320.20 shall be furnished to the carrier and shall be in the possession of the carrier for the duration of the transportation. This will meet the requirements of sections 922(e) and (f) of the Gun Control Act of 1968.

PRIVACY ACT INFORMATION

The following information is provided pursuant to Section 3 of the Privacy Act of 1974 (5 U.S.C. 552a(e)(3)):

1. AUTHORITY. Solicitation of this information is made pursuant to the Gun Control Act of 1968 (18 U.S.C. 922(a)(4)). Disclosure of this information by the applicant is mandatory if the applicant wishes to transport in interstate or foreign commerce any destructive device, machinegun, short-barreled shotgun, or short-barreled rifle.

2. PURPOSE. To determine whether the proposed transaction of the listed items is reasonably necessary and consistent with the public safety and applicable State and local law.

3. ROUTINE USES. This information will be used by ATF to make the determination set forth in paragraph 2. No information obtained from an application, registration, or records required to be submitted by a natural person in order to comply with the provisions of the National Firearms Act or regulations issued thereunder, shall, except in connection with prosecution or other action for furnishing false information be used, directly or indirectly, as evidence against that person in any criminal proceeding with the filing of the application.

4. EFFECTS OF NOT SUPPLYING INFORMATION REQUESTED. Failure to supply complete information will delay processing and may cause denial of the application.

PAPERWORK REDUCTION ACT NOTICE

This form is in accordance with the Paperwork Reduction Act of 1995. Its purpose is to obtain the information necessary to provide authorization to a person who is not a qualified firearms licensee who wishes to transport interstate or engage in foreign commerce temporarily, any destructive device, machine gun, short-barreled shotgun or short-barreled rifle. The information will be used to identify the registrant, the firearms to be transported and the destination of the firearms. The furnishing of this information is mandatory (18 USC 922a).

The estimated average burden associated with this collection of information is 30 minutes per respondent or recordkeeper, depending on individual circumstances. Comments concerning the accuracy of this burden estimate and suggestions for reducing this burden should be addressed to Reports Management Officer, Document Services Branch, Bureau of Alcohol, Tobacco and Firearms, Washington, D.C. 20226.

An agency may not conduct or sponsor, and a person is not required to respond to, a collection of information unless it displays a currently valid OMB control number.

ATF F 5320.20 (9-84)

OMB No. 1512-0022 (01-31-00)

DEPARTMENT OF THE TREASURY — BUREAU OF ALCOHOL, TOBACCO AND FIREARMS
APPLICATION TO TRANSPORT INTERSTATE OR TO TEMPORARILY EXPORT CERTAIN NATIONAL FIREARMS ACT (NFA) FIREARMS
(See Reverse for Instructions and Privacy Act Information)

FOR ATF USE ONLY
NFA CONTROL NO.

PART I – APPLICATION (Submit in Duplicate) (Print or Type all Entries)

1. NAME AND ADDRESS OF REGISTERED OWNER *(Full Name, Number, Street, City, State, and ZIP Code)*

2. FIREARMS TO BE RETURNED TO ORIGINAL LOCATION? ☐ YES ☐ NO

3. Dates firearm(s) will be away from original location, if to be returned to that location, (or dates in transit, if to be permanently relocated).

1a. TELEPHONE NUMBER *(Include Area Code)*

FROM *(Month, Day, Year)*   TO *(Month, Day, Year)*

4. FIREARM(S) TO BE TRANSPORTED *(Complete New Forms For Additional Firearms)*

MANUFACTURER	TYPE OF FIREARM (Machine gun, etc.)	SERVICE- ABLE (Yes or No)	CALIBER OR GAUGE	MODEL	BARREL LENGTH	OVER- ALL LENGTH	SERIAL NUMBER

5. REASON FOR TRANSPORTATION OF FIREARMS *(Example: Permanent change of Address)*

6. TRANSPORTING FROM *(Number, Street, City, County, State, and ZIP Code)*

7. TRANSPORTING TO *(Number, Street, City, County, State, and ZIP Code)*

8. MODE OF TRANSPORTATION *(Name and Address of carrier, if by common or contract carrier)*

Items 9 thru 11 shall be completed if firearm(s) is/are being temporarily exported.

9. STATE DEPARTMENT LICENSE NO.   10. PORT OF EXIT   11. PORT OF REENTRY

NOTE: If firearm(s) will not be returned or relocated on or before the date specified, submit a new ATF F 7560.8 *(See Instructions "e" and "f")*.

The undersigned certifies that the information on this form is to the best of my knowledge and belief, true and complete, that the transportation does not involve a transfer of title, that the transportation or possession of the listed firearm(s) is not inconsistent with the laws at the place of destination, that all such laws will be complied with, and that, where applicable, all temporary export license provisions under the Arms Export Control Act of 1976 have been complied with.

12. SIGNATURE OF OWNER   13. DATE

PART II – ACTION BY THE BUREAU OF ALCOHOL, TOBACCO AND FIREARMS

By authority of the Director, application to transport or temporarily export the above-listed firearm(s) to and from the location, and for the time period indicated, is:

14. ☐ APPROVED *(with the following conditions, if any)*:

15. ☐ DISAPPROVED *(for the following reason(s))*:

16. SIGNATURE OF AUTHORIZED ATF OFFICIAL

ATF F 5320.20 (9-84) PREVIOUS EDITIONS ARE OBSOLETE

ATF Form 4587 (5330.4)
Application to Register as an Importer of U.S. Munitions Import List Articles

INSTRUCTIONS

1. Persons engaged in the business of importing articles on the United States Munitions Import List are required to register pursuant to Section 38 of the Arms Export Control Act of 1976.

2. Complete this form in duplicate using a typewriter or ball point pen. The owner, a partner, a corporate officer or corporate general manager must sign all copies of the application in ink. Submit both copies to:

Bureau of Alcohol, Tobacco & Firearms
P.O. Box 73198
Chicago, IL 60673

3. Item 4 shows the fee schedule which is prescribed by 27 CFR Part 47. This registration must be accompanied by a check or money order made payable to the Bureau of Alcohol, Tobacco, and Firearms in the amount which is applicable to the number of years for which registration is requested.

4. Fees paid in advance for whole future years of a multiple year registration will be refunded upon request if the registrant ceases to engage in importing articles on the U.S. Munitions Import List. A request for a refund must be submitted to the Director, Bureau of Alcohol, Tobacco and Firearms, Washington, D.C. 20226, Attention: Firearms and Explosives Imports Branch, prior to the beginning of any year for which a refund is claimed.

5. If the application is approved, the Director will return the original to the applicant and retain a copy.

6. After registration, importation of U.S. Munitions Import List articles must be effected in accordance with the procedures set forth in 27 CFR Parts 47, 178 and 179, which provides for the use of Form 6 Part I (5330.3A), Application and Permit for Importation of Firearms, Ammunition and Implements of War, and Form 6A (5330.3C), Release and Receipt of Imported Firearms, Ammunition and Implements of War.

7. Federal Firearms License (Item 7) - is a license issued by the Bureau of Alcohol, Tobacco and Firearms pursuant to Chapter 44 of Title 18, U.S.C. and 27 CFR Part 178. Any person engaged in the business of importing firearms or ammunition as defined in 18 U.S.C. 921(a) must be licensed under the provisions of 27 CFR Part 178.

8. Special (occupational) tax stamp (Item 8) - is a stamp issued by the Internal Revenue Service pursuant to registration required by the National Firearms Act, Chapter 53, Internal Revenue Code of 1954 and 27 CFR Part 179. Any person engaged in the business of importing firearms which fall within the definition of 26 U.S.C. 5845(a) must also register and pay a special (occupational) tax pursuant to the provisions of 27 CFR Part 179.

PRIVACY ACT INFORMATION

The following information is provided pursuant to Section 3 of the Privacy Act of 1974 (5 U.S.C. §552a(e)(3):

1. AUTHORITY. Solicitation of this information is made pursuant to section 38 of the Arms Export Control Act of 1976, as amended (22 U.S.C. §2778). Disclosure of this information by the applicant is mandatory if the applicant desires to import U.S. Munitions Import List articles.

2. PURPOSE. To collect the appropriate fee and to effect registration as an importer under the Arms Export Control Act.

3. ROUTINE USES. This information is used by ATF to aid in its law enforcement and regulatory activities with respect to the regulation of firearms and ammunition. This information may also be disclosed to other Federal, State, foreign and local law enforcement and regulatory agency personnel to verify the information on the application and to aid in the performance of their duties with respect to the regulation of firearms and ammunition; and to the State Department in connection with its duties and responsibilities in the area of foreign affairs. The information may further be disclosed to the Justice Department, if it appears that the furnishing of false information may constitute a violation of Federal law.

4. EFFECTS OF NOT SUPPLYING INFORMATION REQUESTED. Failure to supply complete information will delay processing and may cause denial of the application.

The following information is provided pursuant to Section 7(b) of the Privacy Act of 1974:

Disclosure of the individual's social security number is voluntary. Solicitation of this information is pursuant to 22 U.S.C. §2778. The number may be used to verify the individual's identity.

PAPERWORK REDUCTION ACT NOTICE

This request is in accordance with the Paperwork Reduction Act of 1980. This information collection is mandatory pursuant to 22 U.S.C. 2778. The purpose of this information collection is to allow ATF (1) to determine if the registrant qualifies to engage in the business of importing a firearm or firearms, ammunition, and the implements of war, and (2) to facilitate the collection of registration fees.

The estimated average burden associated with this collection of information is 30 minutes per respondent or recordkeeper, depending on individual circumstances. Comments concerning the accuracy of this burden estimate and suggestions for reducing this burden should be addressed to Reports Management Officer, Document Services Branch, Bureau of Alcohol, Tobacco and Firearms, Washington, D.C. 20226, and the Office of Management and Budget, Paperwork Reduction Project (1512-0021), Washington, D.C. 20503.

ATF F 4587 (5330.4) (7-91)

Form Approved: OMB No. 1512-0021(09/30/97)

DEPARTMENT OF THE TREASURY
BUREAU OF ALCOHOL, TOBACCO AND FIREARMS
APPLICATION TO REGISTER AS AN IMPORTER OF U.S. MUNITIONS IMPORT LIST ARTICLES
(SECTION 38, ARMS EXPORT CONTROL ACT OF 1976)
(See Instruction on reverse)

FOR ATF USE ONLY

REGISTRATION NUMBER	EXPIRATION DATE

To: Director, Bureau of Alcohol, Tobacco and Firearms, Attention: Firearms and Explosives Imports Branch, Washington, D.C. 20226.

The undersigned hereby makes application to register as an importer of U.S. Munitions Import List articles are required by Section 38, Arms Export Control Act of 1976.

1. NAME AND ADDRESS *(Includes ZIP Code)*	2. TELEPHONE NO. *(Area Code)*	3. CURRENT A.E.C.A. REGISTRATION NO.

4. REQUEST TO REGISTER FOR: *(Check one, enclose check or money order for payment of fee indicated. See Instruction 3.)*

☐ 1 YEAR - FEE IS $250.00 ☐ 2 YEARS - FEE IS $500.00 ☐ 3 YEARS - FEE IS $700.00 ☐ 4 YEARS - FEE IS $850.00 ☐ 5 YEARS - FEE IS $1,000.00

5. APPLICANT IS: *(Check one)*

☐ INDIVIDUAL ☐ PARTNERSHIP ☐ CORPORATION ☐ OTHER *(Specify)* _____

6. DATE AND PLACE OF INCORPORATION OR COMMENCEMENT OF BUSINESS

7. FEDERAL FIREARMS LICENSE *(if any)*			8. SPECIAL (OCCUPATIONAL) TAX STAMP *(If any)*	
LICENSE NUMBER	CLASS OF LICENSE	EXPIRATION DATE	STAMP NUMBER	CLASS

9. LIST BELOW THE INFORMATION REQUIRED FOR EACH INDIVIDUAL OWNER, PARTNER, AND PRINCIPAL CORPORATE OFFICER IN THE APPLICANT BUSINESS. IF A FEMALE, LIST GIVEN NAMES AND MAIDEN, IF MARRIES, e.g., "MARY ALICE (SMITH) JONES, JONES", NOT "MRS. JOHN JONES." (IF ADDITIONAL SPACE IS NEEDED USE A SEPARATE SHEET)

FULL NAME	POSITION AND SOC. SEC. NO.	HOME ADDRESS *(Include ZIP Code)*	PLACE OF BIRTH	DATE OF BIRTH

10. DESCRIBE SPECIFIC ACTIVITY APPLICANT IS ENGAGED IN, OR INTENDS TO ENGAGE IN, WHICH REQUIRES REGISTRATION UNDER THE ARMS EXPORT CONTROL ACT

11. UNITED STATES MUNITIONS IMPORT LIST ARTICLES USUALLY IMPORTED *(Specify categories)*

12. PURPOSE OF IMPORTING MUNITIONS IMPORT LIST ARTICLES	13. WHAT PERCENTAGE IS IMPORTED FOR U.S. GOVERNMENT

I declare under the penalties provided by law that this request for registration as an importer of U.S. Munitions Import List articles, including the documents submitted in support of it, has been examined by me and, to the best of my knowledge and belief, it is true, correct & complete.

14. SIGNATURE *(Sign all copies in ink. See instruction 2)*	15. TITLE	16. DATE

APPROVAL (FOR ATF USE ONLY)

17. SIGNATURE OF DIRECTOR, BUREAU OF ALCOHOL, TOBACCO AND FIREARMS	18. DATE

ATF F 4587(5330.4) (7-91)   PREVIOUS EDITIONS ARE OBSOLETE

ATF Form 5630.7
Special Tax Registration and Return, National Firearms Act

INSTRUCTION SHEET
ATF F 5630.7, SPECIAL TAX REGISTRATION AND RETURN
FIREARMS

GENERAL INSTRUCTIONS

If you are engaged in one or more of the National Firearms Act (NFA) activities listed on this form *(see definition)*, you are required to file this form and pay special occupational tax before beginning business. This form is for NFA taxpayers only. Businesses engaged in alcohol and tobacco related activities subject to special tax should file ATF F 5630.5. You may file one return to cover several locations or several types of activity. However, you must submit a separate return for each tax period. The special occupational tax period runs from July 1 through June 30 and payment is due annually by July 1. If you do not pay on a timely basis interest will be charged and penalties may be incurred.

If you engage in a taxable activity at more than one location, attach to your return a sheet showing your name, trade name, address and employer identification number and the complete street addresses of all additional locations.

As evidence of tax payment, you will be issued a Special Tax Stamp, ATF F 5630.6A, for each location and/or business. You must have a Federal Firearms License (FFL) for the location, appropriate to the type of activity conducted. The type of business *(sole proprietor, partnership, corporation)* must be the same for the taxable activity and the FFL. If a trade name is used, it must be the same on the tax stamp and the FFL.

The special tax rates listed on this form became effective January 1, 1988. If you were engaged in NFA firearms related activity prior to this date and did not pay special occupational tax, please contact the ATF National Revenue Center for assistance.

SECTION I - TAX IDENTIFYING INFORMATION

Complete Section I, Taxpayer Identifying Information, as specified on the form. Enter the tax period covered by the return in the space provided. Your return must contain a valid EMPLOYER IDENTIFICATION NUMBER (EIN). The EIN is a unique number for business entities issued by the Internal Revenue Service (IRS). **You must have an EIN whether you are an individual ownership, partnership, corporation, or agency of the government.** If you do not have an EIN, contact your local IRS office immediately to obtain one. While ATF may assign a temporary identification number *(beginning with XX)* to allow initial processing of a return which lacks an EIN, **a tax stamp will not be issued until you have submitted a valid EIN.** Do not delay submission of your return and payment past the due date pending receipt of your EIN. If you have not received a number by the time you file this return, write *"number applied for"* in the space for the number. Submit your EIN by separate correspondence after receipt from the IRS.

SECTION II - TAX COMPUTATION

To compete Section II, enter the number of locations in Col. (d) on the appropriate line(s) and multiply by the tax rate, Col. (c). Insert the tax due in Col. (e). Compute the taxes due for each class and enter the total amount due in the block *"Total Tax Due"*.

INSTRUCTIONS FOR REDUCED RATE TAXPAYERS

The reduced rates for certain tax classes, indicated with an asterisk (*) in Section II, apply only to those taxpayers whose total gross receipts for your most recent income tax year are less than $500,000 *(not just receipts relating to the activity subject to special occupational tax)*. However, if you are a member of a controlled group as defined in section 5061(e)(3) of the Internal Revenue Code, you are not eligible for this reduced rate unless the total gross receipts for the entire group are less than $500,000. If your business is beginning an activity subject to special tax for the first time, you may qualify for a reduced rate in your initial tax year if gross receipts for the business *(or the entire control group, if a member of a control group)* were under $500,000 the previous year. If you are eligible for the reduced rate, check item 12 in Section III and compute your tax using the reduced rate in Section II.

SECTION III - BUSINESS REGISTRATION

Please complete the ownership information in Section III. Supply the information specified in item 11 for each individual owner, partner or responsible person. For a corporation, partnership or association, a responsible person is anyone with the power to control the management policies or buying or selling practices pertaining to firearms. For a corporation, association or similar organization, it also means any person owning 10 percent or more of the outstanding stock in the business.

CHANGES IN OPERATIONS

For a change of address, location or trade name, an amended ATF F 5630.7 must be filed and approved before the change is made. Return your Special Tax Stamp, ATF F 5630.6A, along with the completed ATF F 5630.7 to: Bureau of ATF, 8002 Federal Office Building, 550 Main Street, Cincinnati, OH 45202-3263 and an amended ATF F 5630.6A will be issued. All taxpayers with such changes must return their FFL to the ATF Firearms and Explosives Licensing Center *(address listed on FFL)* for amendment.

If special taxpayers do not register these changes within the appropriate time frames, additional tax and interest will be charged and penalties may be incurred. For a change in ownership or control of an activity, consult the ATF Firearms and Explosives Licensing Center, at 404-679-5040, before beginning the activity. If the Federal firearms licensee discontinues business and retains NFA firearms, this retention may be in violation of law. The licensee should check with State or local authorities.

DEFINITION

IMPORTERS, MANUFACTURERS, and DEALERS of FIREARMS subject to the National Firearms Act *(tax class codes 61, 62, 63, 71, or 72)* are individuals or business entities who import, manufacture or deal in machineguns, short-barreled shotguns and rifles, destructive devices, etc. See 26 U.S.C. 5845 for additional information on the types of weapons subject to the National Firearms Act. *(NOTE: This tax is not required from those persons or entities who deal only in conventional, sporting type firearms.)*

MISCELLANEOUS INSTRUCTIONS

If you do not intend to pay the special tax for the next year, you must dispose of any machineguns manufactured or imported after May 19, 1986, prior to your special tax status lapsing. Title 18, United States Code, section 922(o) makes it unlawful to possess these machineguns unless you are properly qualified. As provided in Title 27, Code of Federal Regulations, Part 179,105(f), the disposition must be made to a government agency or qualified licensee or the weapon must be destroyed.

This form must be signed by the individual owner, a partner, or, in the case of a corporation, by an individual authorized to sign for the corporation.

Please sign and date the return, make check or money order payable to BUREAU OF ALCOHOL, TOBACCO AND FIREARMS, for the amount in the Total Tax Due block, and <u>MAIL THE FORM ALONG WITH THE PAYMENT TO BUREAU OF ATF, Attention: NFA, P.O. Box 371970, Pittsburgh, PA 15250-7970.</u>

IF YOU NEED FURTHER ASSISTANCE
CONTACT ATF NATIONAL REVENUE CENTER
AT
1-800-937-8864
OR
513-684-2979

OMB No. 1512-0472 (09/30/2002)

DEPARTMENT OF THE TREASURY
BUREAU OF ALCOHOL, TOBACCO AND FIREARMS
SPECIAL TAX REGISTRATION AND RETURN
NATIONAL FIREARMS ACT (NFA)
(Please Read Instructions on Back Carefully Before Completing This Form)

SECTION I - TAXPAYER IDENTIFYING INFORMATION

1. EMPLOYER IDENTIFICATION NUMBER *(Required - see instructions)*
2. BUSINESS TELEPHONE NUMBER ( )

FOR ATF USE ONLY
- T
- FF
- FP
- I
- T

3. NAME *(Last, First, Middle)* or CORPORATION *(If Corporation)*
4. TRADE NAME
5. MAILING ADDRESS *(Street address or P.O. box number)*
6. CITY   STATE   ZIP CODE

ACTUAL LOCATION *(IF DIFFERENT THAN ABOVE)*
7. PHYSICAL ADDRESS OF PRINCIPAL PLACE OF BUSINESS *(Show street address)*
8. CITY   STATE   ZIP CODE

9. TAX PERIOD COVERING *(Only one tax period per form)*
   FROM: _____ *(mm/dd/yy)*
   TO: JUNE 30, _____ *(yy)*

SECTION II - TAX COMPUTATION

(a) TAX CLASS *(For Items Marked*, See Instructions)*	(b) TAX CLASS CODE	(c) TAX RATE ($) *(Annual)*	(d) NUMBER OF LOCATIONS	(e) TAX DUE
CLASS 1 - IMPORTER OF FIREARMS	61	$1,000		
CLASS 1 - IMPORTER OF FIREARMS *(REDUCED)**	71*	500		
CLASS 2 - MANUFACTURER OF FIREARMS	62	1,000		
CLASS 2 - MANUFACTURER OF FIREARMS *(REDUCED)**	72*	500		
CLASS 3 - DEALER IN FIREARMS	63	500		

MAKE YOUR CHECK OR MONEY ORDER PAYABLE TO "BUREAU OF ALCOHOL, TOBACCO AND FIREARMS", WRITE YOUR EMPLOYER IDENTIFICATION NUMBER ON THE CHECK AND SEND IT WITH THE RETURN TO BUREAU OF ATF, ATTENTION NFA, P.O. BOX 371970, PITTSBURGH, PA 15250-7970.   TOTAL TAX DUE

SECTION III - BUSINESS REGISTRATION

10. OWNERSHIP INFORMATION: *(Check One Box Only)*   ☐ INDIVIDUAL OWNER   ☐ PARTNERSHIP   ☐ CORPORATION   ☐ OTHER *(Specify)* _____

11. OWNERSHIP RESPONSIBILITY *(See instructions on back; use a separate sheet of paper if additional space is needed.)*

FULL NAME	ADDRESS	POSITION

12. ☐ GROSS RECEIPTS less than $500,000 *(See instructions on back; use a separate sheet of paper if additional space is needed.)*

13. ☐ NEW BUSINESS   DATE BUSINESS COMMENCED *(mm, dd, yy)*

14. ☐ EXISTING BUSINESS WITH CHANGE IN:
    ☐ (a) NAME/TRADE NAME *(Indicate)*
    ☐ (b) ADDRESS *(Indicate)*
    ☐ (c) OWNERSHIP *(Indicate)*
    ☐ (d) EMPLOYER IDENTIFICATION NUMBER (OLD: _____ NEW: _____)
    ☐ (e) BUSINESS TELEPHONE NUMBER ( )

15. ☐ DISCONTINUED BUSINESS

SECTION IV - TAXPAYER CERTIFICATION

Under penalties of perjury, I declare that the statements in this return/registration are true and correct to the best of my knowledge and belief; that this return/registration applies only to the specified business and location or, where the return/registration is for more than one location, it applies only to the businesses at the locations specified on the attached list. **NOTE:** Violation of Title 26, United States Code 7206, is punishable upon conviction by a fine of not more than $100,000 *($500,000 in the case of a corporation)*, or imprisonment for not more 3 years, or both, together with the costs of prosecution.

16. SIGNATURE   17. TITLE   18. DATE

ATF F 5630.7 (10-99) PREVIOUS EDITIONS ARE OBSOLETE

ATF E-From 5013.3
eForm6 Access Request

Instructions

You must complete this form in order to receive a user ID and password to obtain access to ATF's eForm 6 system. Each user must obtain an individual user ID and password which is not to be shared with anyone. Sharing your user ID and password can result in cancellation of your eForm 6 privileges.

Section A – You must check the appropriate box:

(1) Check "Add User" if you want access to eForm 6 for the first time.

(2) Check "Modify User" if you want to change any of the information you originally supplied in Section B or C. In all cases, supply your User ID (Section A, Item 2) and complete only those items in Section B and C that have changed.

For changes to Section C: (i) You must notify ATF's National Licensing Center in Atlanta, GA of any changes to your company name, address, or Federal firearms license numbers, or the Firearms and Explosives Imports Branch of any changes to your Arms Export Control Act registration information, before making any changes in eForm 6; and (ii) If you are deleting a Federal firearms license or Arms Export Control Act registration number, indicate in Section C, Item 15 which number(s) you want deleted from eForm 6.

(3) Check "Delete User" if you no longer want access to eForm 6 for yourself or another user. Please provide the User ID of the user to be deleted, if known (Section A, Item 2).

(4) Check "Reactivate User" if we cancelled your original User ID due to inactivity and you wish to begin using the eForm 6 system again. You must also complete the remainder of the form as instructed below and include your previous User ID.

Section B – You must enter the required information about the individual requesting access to eForm 6 in items 3-13. Also include your business telephone and FAX numbers. Each Federal firearms licensee or Arms Export Control Act registrant must submit **one** eForm 6 Access Request from a responsible person as indicated on item 14. This person will be able to review the User Profiles of all other users registered under that Federal firearms license or Arms Export Control Act registration number. This individual will also receive a confirmation email for each application submitted to ATF, whether via the eForm 6 or paper submission. A Responsible Person is defined as a sole proprietor, or in the case of a corporation, partnership or association, any individual possessing the power to direct or cause the direction of the management, policies and practices of the corporation, partnership or association as they relate to firearms, and in the case of a corporation, partnership, or association any person holding ten percent or more of the outstanding shares of stock issued by the applicant and the officers of that organization. These persons are listed on the ATF Form 7, Application for Federal Firearms License and ATF Form 4587, Application to Register as an Importer of U.S. Munitions Import List Articles.

Section C – You must enter the required information about the company for which you are requesting to file applications. This information must appear exactly as it does on the Federal Firearms License and/or Arms Export Control Act registration. Be sure to enter the correct number in item 16 (example: 1-23-456-08-5A-98765 or A-12-345-6789). You (the individual requesting access) must sign and date the form in items 17-18. If you are both a Federal firearms licensee and an Arms Export Control Act registrant, you must enter **both** numbers in item 16.

Section D – A person listed as responsible person on the ATF Form 7 or ATF Form 4587, must sign and print his or her name and title, and date the form in items 19-21.

You must send the original of this form to:

> Firearms and Explosives Imports Branch
> Bureau of Alcohol, Tobacco, Firearms and Explosives
> 650 Massachusetts Avenue, NW.
> Washington, DC 20226

Your user ID and password will be sent to you separately for security reasons.

Privacy Act Information

We provide this information to comply with Section 3 of the Privacy Act of 1974 (5 U.S.C. 552a(e)(3)).

We require this information under the authority of 18 U.S.C. 925(d). You must disclose this information so we may identify the company on whose behalf applicant claims to act, to verify the scope of the applicant's authority to act, and to evaluate the applicant's qualifications for access to the system.

We use this informaion to approve, grant and control access to sensitive information systems. In addition, the information may be disclosed to other Federal, State and local law enforcement and regulatory agency personnel to verify information on the application and to aid in the performance of their duties. Disclosure may otherwise be made pursuant to the routine uses most recently published in the Federal Register for ATF's Regulatory Enforcement Records System (Treasury ATF.008).

If you fail to supply complete information then there will be a delay in the processing of your application.

Disclosure of your Social Security Number is voluntary. Solicitation of this information is pursuant to section 925(d), Title 18 U.S. C. The Social Security Number may be used to verify the applicant's identity. If you fail to supply your Social Security Number, there will either be a delay in processing your application or you will not be granted access to the system.

Paperwork Reduction Act Notice

This request is in accordance with the Paperwork Reduction Act of 1995. We use this information to authenticate end users in the program to electronically file ATF Form 6 Part I (5330.3A). The information is used by the Government to verify the identity of the end users prior to issuing them passwords. The information we request is voluntary, however, if the requested information is not submitted, the users will not be granted a password and cannot participate in the electronic program.

The estimated average burden associated with this collection is 18 minutes per respondent or recordkeeper depending on the individual circumstances. Comments concerning the accuracy of this burden estimate and suggestions for reducing this burden should be directed to the Reports Management Officer, Documents Services Branch, Bureau of Alcohol, Tobacco, Firearms and Explosives, Washington, DC 20226.

ATF may not conduct or sponsor, and you are not required to respond to a collection of information unless it displays a currently valid OMB control number.

ATF E-Form 5013.3
Revised February 2004

U.S. Department of Justice
Bureau of Alcohol, Tobacco, Firearms and Explosives

OMB No. 1140-0087 (01/31/2007)

eForm 6 Access Request

Submit this form to the Firearms and Explosives Imports Branch, ATF, Washington, DC 20226 | ATF Tracking Number

A - Action Requested

1. ☐ Add User ☐ Modify User Information ☐ Delete User ☐ Reactivate User

2. If Modifying or Deleting, Provide User ID, *if known*

B - User Information: *Please complete this section with all the required data to establish a user identification record.*

3. First Name	4. Middle Initial	5. Last Name	6. Suffix (*i.e., Jr., Sr., III*)

7. Social Security Number *(last 4 digits)*	8. Date of Birth	9. Mother's Maiden Name

10. Employee Title	11. Business E-mail Address	12. Business Phone Number

13. Business Fax Number	14. ☐ Check Here if User Will Be Responsible Person (*See instructions for definition*)

C - Company Information: *Provide information about the company for which you work*

15a. Name of Company as it Appears on Your Federal Firearms License and/or Arms Export Control Act Registration

15b. Street Address of Company as it Appears on Your Federal Firearms License and/or Arms Export Control Act Registration

15c. City	15d. State	15e. ZIP Code	15f. County

16. Federal Firearms License Number and/or Arms Export Control Act Registration Number

Requester's Certification: I hereby attest that the entries on this form are true and correct and that the unique username and password or digital signature that the Bureau of Alcohol, Tobacco, Firearms and Explosives assigns to me are intended as my original signature and I intend that such submissions be treated as bearing an original signature for all intents and purposes when submitting firearm import applications electronically via the eForm 6 System. I have read and agree to be bound by the terms set out in the eForm 6 Notices and Agreement governing the use of the eForm 6 System.

17. Requester's Signature	18. Date

D - Approval Required: *Signature of responsible person with signature authority required to grant access to eForm 6 System.*

Responsible Person's Certification: I authorize the above-named user to complete and execute, on behalf of the company named in Item 15, firearm import applications via the eForm 6 System. I attest that the company intends to be bound by the entries on any such applications and intends that such applications be treated as bearing an original signature for all intents and purposes. I have read and on behalf of the company agree to be bound by the terms set out in the eForm 6 Notices and Agreement governing the use of the eForm 6 System. I hereby ratify and confirm all that the user shall lawfully do or cause to be done by virtue of this authorization.

19. Company Approval Signature By Responsible Person	20. Print Name and Title of Responsible Person	21. Date

ATF Use Only

User Verification Completed	Date	Comments
System Owner Approval	Date	Comments
ATF Operations Completed	Date	Comments
System Administrator Completed	Date	Comments
User Notification Completed	Date	Comments

ATF E-Form 5013.3
Revised February 2004

APPENDIX D

SAMPLE FORM LETTERS

FORM LETTER OF GOVERNMENT AGENCY PURCHASING IMPORTED FIREARMS

(Note: In this example, the department is purchasing firearms from a licensed dealer. If the order includes NFA firearms, the dealer must also be qualified under the NFA to deal in NFA firearms. The dealer will submit the letter to the importer for attachment to the import application.)
(*Letterhead of the Department*)
(*Date*)

Mr. John Doe
Doe's Police Supplies
(*Address*)

Dear Mr. Doe:

This is an order for (*quantity*) (*description of firearms, including type, manufacturer, model, and caliber*) at the price of (*amount*) each, plus shipping charges, for (*name of department, sheriff's office, or agency*).

The number of sworn full time officers in our (*department, office, or agency*) is (*number of officers*). These officers are authorized by law to make arrests and carry firearms in the performance of their official duties.

This order is being paid for with funds that our (*department, office, or agency*) is authorized to use under law for the acquisition of equipment (*Note: If funds of individual officers are being used to buy departmental firearms for the officers' official use, then add "including funds from individual officers who may be required to pay in whole or in part for their equipment to carry out their official duties."*). These firearms will be the property of our (*department, office, or agency*) and are not being acquired for the purpose of resale or transfer, and they will be used to carry out its official responsibilities and duties.

The telephone contact number for this (*department, office, or agency*) is (telephone number).

(*If a purchase order has been issued by the department for the purchase of the firearms, then add the statement here that "Enclosed is our (department's, office's, or agency's) purchase order for these firearms.*)

Sincerely yours,

(*Name of department, office or agency*)

By: _____
   (*Name and title of signing official*)

FROM IMPORTER
FORM LETTER OF DEALER ORDERING NFA SALES SAMPLE

(Note: In this example, a licensed dealer qualified to deal in NFA firearms is purchasing an NFA sales sample from a licensed importer qualified under the NFA to import such firearms. This letter, together with the letter of the law enforcement agency requesting a demonstration of the firearm, will be attached to the importer's application to import the firearm on ATF Form 6.)

(*Letterhead of the Dealer*)

(*Date*)

Mr. Richard Roe
Roe & Son, Importers
(*Address*)

Dear Mr. Roe:

This is an order for (*describe the firearm by type, manufacturer, model, and caliber*) at the price of (*amount*), plus shipping charges.

The firearm will be used by Doe's Police Supplies in a demonstration of the firearm to the (*name of the government department, office, or agency*). Attached is the letter of (*name of the department, office, or agency*), dated (*date*), requesting the demonstration.

The firearm is particularly suitable for use as a law enforcement weapon (*add here a statement showing why it is suitable for such use and cite examples of its use by other agencies if known*). The firearm is currently in production by (*name and location of foreign manufacturer*), so quantities of the firearm are readily available to fill any subsequent orders for the firearm from (*name of the department, office, or agency asking for the demonstration*).[233]

                                  Sincerely yours,

                                  Doe's Police Supplies

                                  By:_____
                                  (*Name and title of person signing*)

---

[233] If the dealer has no information on the availability of the firearm to fill subsequent orders, the importer should include a statement in its letter transmitting the permit application to ATF showing availability for future sales. Also, if the firearm is not currently in production, other facts must be shown establishing that there are quantities available to fill future orders.

FORM LETTER FOR GOVERNMENT AGENCY TO REQUEST A DEMONSTRATION OF AN NFA FIREARM

(Note: In this example, the department is requesting a licensed dealer to obtain an imported NFA "sales sample" for demonstration to the department. The dealer must be qualified under the NFA to deal in NFA firearms. The dealer will submit the letter to the importer for attachment to the import application.)

(*Letterhead of the Department*)

(*Date*)

Mr. John Doe
Doe's Police Supplies
(*Address*)

Dear Mr. Doe:

The (*name of the department, office, or agency*) would like a demonstration of the (*describe the firearm by type, manufacturer, model and caliber*) for possible future purchase and use of our officers in the performance of their official duties.

The number of sworn full time officers in our (*department, office, or agency*) is (*number of officers*). These officers are authorized by law to make arrests and carry firearms in the performance of their official duties.

The firearm requested for demonstration is particularly suitable for use as a law enforcement weapon. (*add here a statement showing why it is suitable for such use and cite examples of its use by other agencies if known*).

The telephone contact number for this (*department, office, or agency*) is (*telephone number*).

                        Sincerely yours,

                        (*Name of department, office, or agency*)

                        By:_____
                          (*Name and title of signing official*)

Made in the USA
Las Vegas, NV
24 November 2022

60238140R00125